Arthur Schnitzler and Twentieth-Century Criticism

Schnitzler, one of the most prolific Austrian writers of the twentieth century, ruthlessly dissected his society's erotic posturing and phobias about sex and death. His most penetrating analyses include *Lieutenant Gustl*, the first stream-of-consciousness novella in German; *Reigen*, a devastating cycle of one-acts mapping the social limits of a sexual daisy-chain; and *Der Weg ins Freie*, a novel that combines a love story with a discussion of the roadblocks facing Austria's Jews. Today, his popularity is reflected by new editions and translations and by adaptations for theater, television, and film by artists such as Tom Stoppard and Stanley Kubrick. This book examines Schnitzler reception up to 2000, beginning with the journalistic reception of the early plays. Before being suspended by a decade of Nazism, criticism in the 1920s and 1930s emphasized Schnitzler's determinism and decadence. Not until the early sixties was humanist scholarship able to challenge this verdict by pointing out Schnitzler's ethical indictment of impressionism in the late novellas. During the same period, Schnitzler, whom Freud considered his literary "Doppelgänger," was often subjected to Freudian psychoanalytical criticism; but by the eighties, scholarship was citing his own thoroughgoing objections to such categories. Since the seventies, Schnitzler's remonstrance toward the Austrian establishment has been examined by social historians and feminist critics alike, and the recently completed ten-volume edition of Schnitzler's diary has met with vibrant interest.

Andrew C. Wisely is associate professor of German at Baylor University.

Studies in German Literature, Linguistics, and Culture:
Literary Criticism in Perspective

Edited by James Walker

About *Literary Criticism in Perspective*

Books in the series *Literary Criticism in Perspective* trace literary scholarship and criticism on major and neglected writers alike, or on a single major work, a group of writers, a literary school or movement. In so doing the authors — authorities on the topic in question who are also well-versed in the principles and history of literary criticism — address a readership consisting of scholars, students of literature at the graduate and undergraduate level, and the general reader. One of the primary purposes of the series is to illuminate the nature of literary criticism itself, to gauge the influence of social and historic currents on aesthetic judgments once thought objective and normative.

Arthur Schnitzler and Twentieth-Century Criticism

Andrew C. Wisely

CAMDEN HOUSE

First published 2004
by Camden House

Camden House is an imprint of Boydell & Brewer Inc.
668 Mt. Hope Avenue, Rochester, NY 14620, USA
and of Boydell & Brewer Limited
PO Box 9, Woodbridge, Suffolk IP12 3DF, UK

ISBN: 1–57113–088–8

Library of Congress Cataloging-in-Publication Data

Wisely, Andrew C., 1963–
    Arthur Schnitzler and twentieth-century criticism / Andrew C. Wisely.
    p. cm. — (Studies in German Literature, Linguistics, and Culture.
Literary Criticism in Perspective)
    Includes bibliographical references and index.
    ISBN 1–57113–088–8 (alk. paper)
    1. Schnitzler, Arthur, 1862–1931 — Criticism and interpretation.
I. Title.   II. Series: Studies in German literature, linguistics, and
culture (Unnumbered). Literary criticism in perspective

PT2638.N5 Z965 2003
833'.8—dc22
                                                      2003020554

A catalogue record for this title is available from the British Library.

This publication is printed on acid-free paper.
Printed in the United States of America.

Contents

Preface

A S WITH OTHER BOOKS in the series *Literary Criticism in Perspective,* the bibliography ("Works Consulted") is arranged chronologically, not alphabetically. A few explanations are in order concerning dates and sources of materials. When introducing Schnitzler's plays, I do not use the date when the work was considered complete or when it was published commercially. Instead, I cite the year of the premiere. The exception is *Anatol,* a play cycle whose one-acts were printed separately as early as 1889, printed together in 1893, with the printings in every case preceding the premiere. When introducing Schnitzler's narrative works, I cite the first date of publication, usually when the work appeared in newspapers or journals before being printed separately.

My references to Schnitzler's works are from Arthur Schnitzler, *Gesammelte Werke in Einzelausgaben: Das erzählerische Werk* (7 vols.) and *Das dramatische Werk* (8 vols.) (Frankfurt am Main: Fischer Taschenbuch Verlag, 1977–78), based on Fischer Verlag's *Gesammelte Werke: Das erzählerische Werk* (2 vols., 1961) and *Das dramatische Werk* (2 vols., 1962). Abbreviations are "*EW*" and "*DW*" respectively. My references to Schnitzler's philosophical writings, especially his views of criticism, are taken from Arthur Schnitzler, *Über Kunst und Kritik,* vol. 3 of *Aphorismen und Betrachtungen,* (Fischer Taschenbuch, 1993), a reprint of the original volume of 1967, which was published as vol. 5 of *Gesammelte Werke.* On the basis of writings unpublished during his lifetime, Schnitzler's autobiography was published in 1967 with the title *Jugend in Wien: Eine Autobiographie* (Vienna: Molden Verlag); my paperback version is the Fischer reprint of 1981. Due to frequency of citation, I cite it in the text simply as *J,* followed by the page number.

Diary entries will be cited according to the day to which they are attributed, not according to the page number on which they appear in the ten-volume *Tagebuch 1879–1931* (Vienna: Verlag der Österreichischen Akademie der Wissenschaften, 1981–2000). My chapter "The Task of Memory" addresses Werner Welzig's introductions and epilogues to the diary project. Because of the enormity of the project and Welzig's involvement in it, I list his essays separately here. Following an introduction to the project: "Zur Herausgabe von Schnitzlers Tagebuch," vol. 1

(1909–1912): 9–33, Welzig contributes epilogues: "Nachbemerkung," vol. 2 (1913–1916): 429–32; "Tagebuch und Gesellschaftsspiel," vol. 3 (1917–1919): 419–27; "Der junge Mann und die alten Wörter," vol. 4 (1879–1892): 471–88; "Bicycle-Lektion," vol. 5 (1893–1902): 489–502; "Preisgeschichten," vol. 6 (1903–1908): 471–90; "Glossar einer Ehescheidung," vol. 7 (1920–1922): 489–98; "Der Traum: Ein Text," vol. 8 (1923–1926): 487–96; "Der Anspruch der Toten," vol. 9 (1927–1930): 499–509.

Acknowledgments

THE LIST OF PEOPLE TO THANK has grown considerably over the course of this project. To my wife Lynn, who joined the project at the halfway point, I owe the most gratitude, for her patience and trust that I knew what I was doing. She provided the supportive environment that paid off tangibly in the manuscript's increased readability. My daughter Kendra has also been infinitely patient with me, although I doubt her fondness for me extends to literary criticism. Family and friends have remained affable and unflagging in their support, asking the sorts of questions that encourage, stimulate, and clarify.

My departmental colleagues at Anderson University gave me the space and understanding during my first halting steps on the project, becoming quickly accustomed to seeing the vacant look in my eyes; the administration helped immensely by granting me a year's sabbatical for the 2001–2002 academic year. Similarly, friends and colleagues at Choate Rosemary Hall have been good sounding boards, especially during meals or early morning runs, and the working environment has been stellar.

A. C. W.
July 2003

Abbreviations

DW   Arthur Schnitzler, *Gesammelte Werke in Einzelausgaben: Das dramatische Werk* (8 vols.) (Frankfurt am Main: Fischer Taschenbuch Verlag, 1977–78), based on Fischer Verlag's *Gesammelte Werke: Das dramatische Werk* (2 vols., 1962).

EW   Arthur Schnitzler, *Gesammelte Werke in Einzelausgaben: Das erzählerische Werk* (7 vols.) (Frankfurt am Main: Fischer Taschenbuch Verlag, 1977–78), based on Fischer Verlag's *Gesammelte Werke: Das erzählerische Werk* (2 vols., 1961).

J   (in text) Arthur Schnitzler, *Jugend in Wien: Eine Autobiographie* (Vienna: Molden Verlag, 1968); in the Fischer reprint version of 1981.

Introduction

AMONG THE SITES OF *fin-de-siècle* modernism in Vienna, there is not yet a museum featuring the life of the physician-turned-author Arthur Schnitzler (1862–1931), who lived his entire life there. Museums that offer alternatives to imperial grandeur are plentiful enough: two radically different buildings, the Upper Belvedere and the Secession, both display the work of Gustav Klimt (1862–1918), famous for his Byzantine friezes of Viennese art nouveau. Another monument to modernism is the Freud Museum at 19 Berggasse, where Sigmund Freud (1856–1939) lived and worked. Yet anyone who looks for the house of Schnitzler, whom Freud termed his *Doppelgänger*, will find only a plaque by the front door at 71 Sternwartestraße, because Schnitzler's museum is of a different sort. More likely his name would surface during a stroll past the Burgtheater on Dr-Karl-Lueger-Ring. Here it would not be surprising to see banners advertising his play *Das weite Land* (The Vast Country), which premiered in the imposing classical structure in 1911. Within walking distance from the Burg is Theater in der Josefstadt, a typical venue for one-acts from the *Anatol* cycle (1888–91). Somewhere near the university, a bookstore of the First District might be displaying the ten volumes of Schnitzler's diary next to eight volumes of his *Ausgewählte Werke* (Selected Works, 1999), or new paperback editions emblazoned with prints by Klimt. The biography section might feature *Arthur Schnitzler: Ein Leben in Wien (1862–1931)* by Giuseppe Farese (1999); the history section might offer the Fischer Verlag translation — "Das Zeitalter des Doktor Arthur Schnitzler: Innenansichten des 19. Jahrhunderts" — of Peter Gay's *Schnitzler's Century: The Making of Middle-Class Culture 1815–1914* (2001); drama in translation might feature a copy of David Hare's *The Blue Room* (1998), the Broadway play based on Schnitzler's *Reigen* (La Ronde, 1900); and finally in the film section one could purchase the Stanley Kubrick/Frederic Raphael screenplay for the 1999 movie *Eyes Wide Shut,* based on Schnitzler's *Traumnovelle* (Dream Novella, 1926). All of these are only the most obvious recent examples at the time of this writing, to say nothing about the dozen or so books on Schnitzler in the criticism section — a number that any decent university library could double or even triple.[1] The level of interest in Schnitzler, evidenced by the continued performance, publication, and filming of his works is, in effect, a powerful museum in its own right.

There is something to this man after all, and it is not sudden popularity that has brought it to the fore. Students of intellectual history remember Schnitzler's role with Freud and other aesthetic modernists in Carl Schorske's *Fin-de-Siècle Vienna: Politics and Culture* (1981), where Freud and Schnitzler were introduced as Jewish sons whose "old morality," inherited from industrious fathers, became explosive when mixed with "new psychology."[2] The term *fin de siècle* in Schorske's title, which my dictionary defines both as "a period relatively free from social and moral traditions or conventions" and as "decadent,"[3] applies in this case only to those sons who were in their prime in 1900, not to their fathers. The response of Freud's and Schnitzler's generation to Victorian values is what makes the books of Schorske and Gay equally intriguing.

Gay, however, does more than explain the central role of privacy in bourgeois life. By using Schnitzler's diary to describe lascivious excess, he leaves readers thinking of Schnitzler solely as "a meticulous chronicler of his sex life," as one reviewer noted shortly before the book's release.[4] Despite prolific scholarship, Gay keeps alive the cliché of Schnitzler the playboy, and the most that Schnitzler admirers can hope for is that the book's perceived authority and Freudian perspective will titillate readers to see whether his fiction lives up to his extra-aesthetic reputation. Anyone who has read a comprehensive sample of Schnitzler's works will find it hard to imagine, for example, that the author of morally incriminating diary entries (less so by the time of his marriage in 1902) also wrote the novella *Casanovas Heimfahrt* (Casanova's Homecoming, 1918) or the novel *Therese. Chronik eines Frauenlebens* (Therese: Chronicle of a Woman's Life, 1928) a decade after that. The first of these indicted adventurism without responsibility; the second documented the effects of bourgeois hypocrisy. Even so, the stereotype of Schnitzler the playboy should not be replaced with the easy antithesis — that he evolved from reprehensible to exemplary — for this too is wishful thinking. Salvaging Schnitzler's reputation to grant him ethical sainthood has been, since the sixties, the danger of the so-called Schnitzler renaissance; something of Schnitzler the satyr must coexist with the satirist.

In the United States, at least, permutations of Schnitzler in Kubrick's film *Eyes Wide Shut,* Hare's play *The Blue Room,* or Tom Stoppard's plays *Dalliance* and *Undiscovered Country* (adapted from *Liebelei* and *Das weite Land*)[5] have contributed more to recognition of his name than have his books. The damage sustained by Austrian cultural goods, worsened by certain stage adaptations and even musicals, has been rectified by

Schnitzler scholarship, and there are occasional productions that attempt to balance his image in the public eye by doing his ideas justice. In New York, for every *Blue Room* or *Circle* there is a *Far and Wide* — Jonathan Bank's adaptation of *Das weite Land,* which he directed at the Mint Theater in February of 2003, and which preserved the complexity of Friedrich Hofreiter's character, no matter how disconcerting the initial effect on the audience.

Here in the introduction, though, I want to furnish a few details about Schnitzler's private sphere and the influences on his life, followed by a sketch of his view of ideal criticism. Thereafter, I will list the reviews and overviews of Schnitzler scholarship that have appeared thus far, and identify my own contribution to the growing layers of criticism. The beginning of Gay's book recounts an anecdote suitable for my own summary. At sixteen, Arthur Schnitzler was forced to read an illustrated treatise on syphilis and skin disease after his father discovered records in his diary of visits to prostitutes.[6] By the time Johann Schnitzler (1835–1893) began discussing hygiene with his son, he was a leading otolaryngologist in Vienna, a far cry from the hungry medical student who had tutored in exchange for room and board. He directed the Allgemeine Wiener Poliklinik (a medical clinic of various specialists), founded and published the medical journal *Internationale Klinische Rundschau,* lectured at the university, made house calls, and still found time to read the *Neue Freie Presse* and attend the plays in the Burgtheater that featured the actors he treated for throat maladies. It was a busy life into which Arthur was born on May 15, 1862, but a comfortable one. The little that Arthur heard about his father's formative years in the Hungarian province of Groß-Kanisza was unembellished, since Johann was keen to reverse the fortunes of his father, a carpenter who spent most of his time drunk. Arthur's one visit as a child to the desolate homestead was enough to discourage later trips. The hard life he saw there held no appeal whatsoever.

Arthur's maternal relatives were within closer reach. His mother, born Louise Markbreiter (1838–1911), was no stranger to medicine when she met his father. Her own father, Dr. Philipp Markbreiter, was a sought-after general practitioner, an expert pianist, who passed on his piano skills to his daughter and grandson. His wife, busy hiding his gambling problem and entertaining, stood out in Arthur's memory for celebrating the major Jewish holidays, a losing battle considering the family's goal of assimilating into Austro-German liberal circles.

Louise Schnitzler managed her husband's professional ambitions and took care of the children, but according to Arthur neither parent could claim much involvement in raising him, his brother Julius (1865–1939), and his sister Gisela (1867–1953).[7] If his father's professional dedication prevented much self-reflection, it at least provided Arthur with a worry-free atmosphere for writing, leaving him unaffected by the stock market crash of 1873 that wiped out his father's savings (J, 49). These savings had been amassed largely during the previous seven years of Austria's *Gründerzeit*, that foundational era of constitutional government that brought expansion in banking, industry, and investment free of governmental intervention. That was the economic modernizing component of liberalism, but liberals wanted to be understood as politically and ideologically astute as well, standing for parliamentary democracy and constitutional rights, the power of the bourgeoisie, freedom of thought and expression, individualism, the nationality principle, education, anticlericalism, and, important in Johann Schnitzler's case, Jewish assimilation.[8] Unfortunately, this bright side of liberalism contradicted its actual route in parliament from 1867 (when the Constitution of the Dual Monarchy took effect) to 1897 (when anti-Semitic Christian Socialism prevailed on the municipal level). The complaint during the last decade especially was that liberal men contented themselves with financial security and their own individual rights, but defaulted to imitating aristocrats instead of securing for women or for other classes, other races, or speakers of other languages the privileges they took for granted.

Accustomed early on to the comfortable dividends of liberalism, Schnitzler's mother balanced her husband's ambitions in science with a genteel musical sensibility. Piano duets formed an intimate bond between mother and son, and throughout Schnitzler's life house concerts did as much to sustain him as did his long afternoon walks. Science and art were apportioned equally in Schnitzler, who credited his father for his logic and blamed his mother for his dilettantism (J, 35). The Dionysian strand held sway whenever he caught himself playing at being a student. Because a personal tutor helped him study his subjects at the Academic Gymnasium in Vienna more efficiently, Schnitzler could dedicate more free time from 1871 onward to theater, concerts, reading, walks, and scribbling ideas for his own storylines. The mark of distinction he received for his oral exit exam on July 8, 1879 was made possible by his exemption from history and physics, and a review of math questions with his tutor left German and classical languages the only subjects really tested (J, 88–89).

More out of duty than conviction, Schnitzler began studying medicine at the University of Vienna in the fall of 1879. As his father's lectures were less impressive to the seventeen-year-old than to the aristocrats in attendance, he welcomed every chance to trade the lecture hall for the billiard hall (*J*, 92). Betting on horses added to his distractions, but he managed somehow to escape significant losses (*J*, 157–60). For his academic specialty, his interest in his own hypochondria made the study of nerve and psychological disorders more alluring than the analysis of cadavers required by internal medicine. The missed lectures did not prevent him from passing all of his exams by the end of May 1885, but his diary of May 7 records his feeling of having made a huge mess of things by studying medicine.[9]

Diary entries make clear the tension between his father's expectations and the writing urge, which Arthur suppressed in the belief that it signaled only a delusion of grandeur (*J*, 189–90). By his eighteenth birthday in 1880, however, Schnitzler counted twenty-three fledgling dramas to his credit and thirteen more in the beginning stages. It was not until 1886 that the Viennese weekly *Deutsche Wochenschrift* published a few of his aphorisms and the satirical short story "Er wartet auf den vazieren-den Gott" (He Waits for the Aimless God). As Schnitzler worked on the stories "Erbschaft" (Inheritance) and "Der Wahnsinn meines Freundes Y" (The Insanity of My Friend Y) in 1887, his father told him that publishing anything else in the papers could endanger his credentials as a young physician. Professional writing more to his father's liking began in January 1887, when he began editing his father's medical journal, *Internationale Klinische Rundschau*. Even then he insisted on having it his own way, concentrating on the works of the forerunners of psychoanalysis. His first contact with Freud came in 1887 when he was reviewing Freud's translations from the French of works by Jean-Martin Charcot (1825–1893) and Hippolyte Bernheim (1837–1919).[10] Schnitzler's own academic treatise appeared in 1889: a compilation of hypnosis experiments performed while he was assisting in his father's otolaryngology division, it was titled "Über funktionelle Aphonie und deren Behandlung durch Hypnose und Suggestion" (On Functional Aphonia and its Treatment through Hypnosis and Suggestion).

Without an underlying sense of vocation, he registered medical achievements as hollow victories. His mandatory military service year saw him consigned in October 1882 to an ambulatory unit that added little to his skills. He preferred using the aura of the uniform to attract women. The sobering aspect of this time was the hazing he experienced from non-Jewish commanding officers, even though ethnic rivalries in German-National reading clubs and dueling fraternities had prepared him somewhat for the liberties taken at his expense (*J*, 155). Hazing during his Gymnasium years would have been more shocking, because hostility toward Jews applied to only a handful of "Judenfresser" (*J*, 77). The racism Schnitzler was subjected to in the early eighties culminated in the infamous Waidhofen Resolution of March 11, 1896, a Pan-German fraternity document inspired by Georg Ritter von Schönerer (1842–1921) that called Jews dishonorable and incapable of demanding or rendering satisfaction through a duel (*J*, 152). Schnitzler, who saw himself as Jewish, Austrian, and German in equal parts, never based his identity on ethnicity, even after political groups began preaching division and difference. The most strident political actor, though not a German nationalist, was Karl Lueger (1844–1910), Vienna's anti-Semitic mayor from 1897–1910, who was notorious for proclaiming himself the arbiter of who was Jewish: "Wer Jude ist, bestimme ich." Faced with the beginning of an anti-Semitic crescendo, Schnitzler could do little more than record its inhumanity.

Understandably, many of Schnitzler's fellow Jews tried to compensate for perceived inferiority by becoming excellent fencers and marksmen, knowing that sheer force spoke more loudly than reason in a feudal atmosphere. This was not the course taken by Schnitzler, who did not feel any compulsion to stand up for Jewish honor or the belief of his forefathers. And in his view, a crime worse than dogmatism was a Jew's attempt at assimilation through Christian baptism (*J*, 93). When his daughter Lili expressed interest in Catholicism, Schnitzler talked her out of it by reminding her that they were Jewish.[11] Not that he himself cared: at eighteen he was honest enough to call himself a dilettante lacking the tact to make the battle against religion his own (*J*, 95). Aside from family and friends, anything staking a claim on his allegiance had to originate with him.

Schnitzler's suspicion of heroic and sentimental rhetoric regarding the honor of women, vocation, country, race, or belief (*J*, 151) became a favorite target for critics, as we will see. But if he lacked the audacity to risk his life for women, he was cavalier enough to charm them incessantly.[12] The details of his romantic interests stem from a diary more sardonic than confessional, as in his account of encouraging his first prostitutes to try their luck in different careers. A certain Venus invited Schnitzler into her apartment, not knowing she would later be reclining nude and listening to him lecture from a book (*J*, 161–62). These first sexual forays were Schnitzler's way of getting attention without responsibility. In the Jewish middle class that demanded most of his time, flirting rarely led to anything more without the promise of marriage. For Schnitzler, though, fear of commitment sabotaged his chances for what he considered an upstanding relationship (*J*, 172–73).

Olga Waissnix (1862–1897), whom Schnitzler considered his life's adventure, seemed to change things. In the four years following their first meeting in 1886, this wife of a resort owner from Reichenau boosted Schnitzler's confidence and encouraged him to shrug off the deterrents to fame. Her friendship came with a moral vigilance Schnitzler did not share, but when in 1890 domestic unhappiness made her desperate to win his heart by any means, Schnitzler had moved on. There were always overlapping interests: in 1887, family gossip centered on Minnie Benedikt (1871–1928), daughter of Moriz Benedikt (1849–1920), the famous editor of Vienna's liberal newspaper *Neue Freie Presse*. Minnie taught Schnitzler tennis and represented a significant dowry — as did Helene Herz (1865–1960) in 1889 — but nothing could keep Schnitzler from recoiling at the thought of marriage.

To worry his family in a different way, Schnitzler turned privately to *süße Mädel*, the sweet girls made famous in the one-act cycle *Anatol* and in his first critically and popularly acclaimed play *Liebelei* (Dalliance, 1895). The most enduring of these relationships with cheerful, uncomplicated women from the Viennese suburbs was with the embroiderer Jeanette Heeger (1865-?). She became his mistress in 1887 and remained with him during his medical training and assistantship, coming to live in the apartment provided for her and pleading entry to his social circle. Schnitzler was not above plaguing her with jealousy and double standards, but sheer habit kept the relationship limping along through 1889.[13]

Schnitzler may with impunity be called a satyr for the years between 1885 and 1900. Two Mizis — Mizi Glümer (1873–1925) and Marie "Mizi" Reinhard (1871–1899) — competed for his favors, finding this practice encouraged by his irresoluteness. Daughter of a government official, Mizi Glümer was sixteen when she met Schnitzler in 1889, but two previous lovers counted against her honor and made her open season for men of Schnitzler's class, even more so as she was an actress. Mizi endured Schnitzler's jealous and belligerent mood swings in the vain hope of hearing a marriage proposal, but Schnitzler's hope of finding a virgin his social equal served as a convenient excuse for him to extend his bachelorhood. News of her infidelity during an acting stint crushed him, enough so that he forgot his own habit of leaving her alone for months at a time while pursuing his adventures. Schnitzler's attempt to cast Mizi as Anna Riedel in *Freiwild* (Wild Game, 1896) in Vienna's Carltheater in 1898 failed because the casting directors assumed few theatergoers would believe a role portraying her as sexually inexperienced.[14]

Women were not the only ones with a claim on Schnitzler's time. In the spring of 1890, Schnitzler could be found in Vienna's famous Café

Griensteidl, discussing projects and ideas with an informal group consisting mainly of budding writers and critics. The group became known as Young Vienna, and included, among others, Richard Beer-Hofmann (1866–1945), Hugo von Hofmannsthal (1874–1929), Felix Salten (1869–1947), Hermann Bahr (1863–1934), Karl Kraus (1874–1936), Peter Altenberg (1859–1919), and Alfred Polgar (1873–1955). Less a literary movement than an assembly of great minds, in less than two years the group began to wear on Schnitzler's nerves. For the most part, it had polarized into coolly distant friends and those whose reviews Schnitzler would find unfair and vindictive. When he took stock of his friends in 1895, Schnitzler noted as most important Salten, Beer-Hofmann, Hofmannsthal, Gustav Schwarzkopf (1853–1939), and Leo Van-Jung (1866–1939), a music teacher and the sole non-writer in the group. Later friends would include the philosopher Arthur Kaufmann (1872–1939), praised in Schnitzler's diary; Heinrich Mann (1871–1950), whom Schnitzler visited whenever in Munich; Georg Brandes (1842–1927), the Danish literary scholar more his father's age, but a faithful correspondent and exponent of liberalism; and of course the Berlin critic and theater director Otto Brahm (1856–1912), who had Schnitzler's utmost respect from the start. When describing friends in his diary, Schnitzler mixed praise with his misgivings, ever insisting on consistency of character. Hofmannsthal's snobbery bothered him, for example, and despite his undeniable talent many a colleague developed an antipathy toward Schnitzler, something he attributed to their envy of his fame.

Erotic pursuits and literary conversation were welcome diversions from the professional life of assisting at the polyclinic, but after his father's death on May 2, 1893, Schnitzler scaled down his own practice to a few office hours per week. The increased attention to writing paid off in stage success. If it was a shame that *Liebelei* came too late for his father to appreciate, Schnitzler also knew that vindicating himself through writing was only possible once he had freed himself from his father's shadow. Freedom from his father's gaze also meant bolder moves in love: half a year after his father's death, Schnitzler met a woman who scoffed at the middle-class propriety represented by the older generation. Adele Sandrock (1864–1937), star of the Burgtheater stage, came to Schnitzler after an affair with Burgtheater director Max Burckhard (1854–1912), but it was clear early on that she would never form a lasting attachment to Schnitzler either. By the fall of 1894, passion had given way to mutual stubbornness, and Schnitzler was relieved to bequeath her early in 1895 to the author and critic Felix Salten.

Sandrock faded from view more quickly than Mizi Glümer, whom Schnitzler was seeing again in 1895 when he began spending time with Mizi Reinhard, or "Mizi II" as his diary called her. The news of this Mizi's pregnancy in January 1897 made him agree to marriage after she gave birth, a step that would have cramped his predilection for two-timing. The stillbirth of a baby boy on September 24, 1898 filled him with as much relief as it did sorrow, but the shock that followed on March 18, 1899 did not fail to penetrate his conscience: Mizi II died of sepsis from a ruptured kidney.[15] This left Schnitzler still single at century's end, but feeling suddenly old.

The woman Schnitzler eventually married, Olga Gussmann (1882–1970), whom he met in 1899, came from the Jewish middle class, offering him not much dowry, but friendship and understanding. It was still a monumental task for Schnitzler to consent to marriage, even after their son Heinrich (1902–1982) was born on August 9, 1902, but his change in thinking was complete by his wedding on August 26, 1903. Heinrich's sister Lili (1909–1928) was born on September 13, 1909, and a year later the family had a place to call their own, when Schnitzler borrowed money from his brother and the bank to buy the house on Sternwartestraße. Despite her friendship and remarkable insight into his works, however, Olga was plagued by frustrated aspirations in acting and singing. Readily influenced by comments from others, she tended to blame the mediocrity of her singing career on factors outside herself, especially her husband. In truth, she lacked the patience, nerves, and volume for a concert hall. For years, Olga's gift for understanding Schnitzler and her love for the children smoothed over the bitter times, but neither could prevent her growing impatience with the role of spouse and mother. In 1918, the equivocating and skirmishing escalated, and in early 1921 Schnitzler gave Olga the ultimatum to stay or leave, insisting that if she left, she spoiled any chance for return. She left; the divorce was finalized June 26 in Munich; and Schnitzler stood the next decade anguished but resolute against her constant pleas to return. Her good qualities could never compensate for the pain involved in opening old wounds.

Heinrich and Lili developed in different directions. Average in school, Heinrich was gifted enough musically to consider pursuing the piano as a career, but a hand inflammation made him opt for acting instead, and his nearly ideal training in this respect took him far. One of his several acclaimed roles on Berlin stages during the twenties was that of Theodor Kaiser in a production of his own father's *Liebelei* at the Schillertheater in 1925. He expanded his range beyond acting alone and was soon directing the premiere of *Anatols Größenwahn* (Anatol's Delusions of Grandeur) in 1932.[16] His sister Lili, meanwhile, compensated for below-average grades with an imagination that delighted her father, but worried him with the lethargic streak at her core. In June of 1927, Lili married Arnoldo Cappellini (1889-?), a poor Italian fascist officer of more than twice her eighteen years. Stationed in Venice, he was clearly devoted to her well-being and liked by the whole family.

The worst news of Schnitzler's life came when his son-in-law telephoned in July of 1928 to report that Lili had bled to death after shooting herself following a minor marital quarrel. It is difficult to appreciate the devastating effect of the news on Schnitzler, who attributed Lili's moodiness to the labile nature of his mother's side of the family. Even this shock was not enough to bring reconciliation with Olga, with whom Schnitzler was happier to correspond than to be near for very long.[17]

Schnitzler never wanted for female attention even in the decade following his divorce, although more than one woman disapproved of the way he and his ex-wife spent time together with their children. The widow Clara Pollaczek (born Loeb, 1875–1951), not content in the role of Schnitzler's mistress, faced sizeable competition from Olga, Vilma Lichtenstern (1885–1927), the Dutch actress Berthe Brevée (1883–1963), the much younger and ebullient confidante Hedwig (Hedy) Kempny (1895–1986), the Swedish massage therapist Ruth Lindberg (1888–1985), and Suzanne Clauser (1898–1981). Clara was herself a gifted writer and translator: for example, she translated Schnitzler's monologue novella *Fräulein Else* (Miss Else, 1924) into French. Remarkable is that the relationship lasted eight years (1923–1931), and that Schnitzler died on October 21, 1931 in the arms of a woman whose desperate love remained unrequited. He had wanted her close, but not so close as to curtail plans or comment on houseguests. As one can expect of one suffering from high blood pressure and advanced otosclerosis, Schnitzler was difficult to live with in his final years. The eight years of resentment Clara and Olga harbored for each other made him grateful for the affection of Suzanne Clauser in the final two years of his life; she understood his moods and translated several of his works into French.

Without question, the women who loved Schnitzler thought of him as more than a satyr, but it is easy to understand why Renate Wagner, a Schnitzler biographer, cautions against assuming the frivolous bachelor matured into a benevolent man. According to Wagner, Schnitzler was anything but gracious, except when loving his children and showing occasional sympathy for his fellow creatures. Egoism and a pronounced sense of justice made him inexorable.[18] It may appear unfair to leave this impression of a harsh, unforgiving writer who felt lonely and forgotten at the time of his death, just as it is certainly unfair to cloak the biography of Schnitzler exclusively in the story of his erotic interests. My intention has been to present a quick picture of Schnitzler's private sphere while saving public history for the chapters to come. Schnitzler's writing ability emerges in this summary as the defining component of his identity. His ruthless honesty about sex has left him fair game for voyeuristic posterity, but is better understood as his bait for being taken seriously as a writer.[19]

With his family accounted for, then, it is safe to say that a fraction of the tenderness Schnitzler felt for his children rubbed off on his literary creations. Releasing a work to the public, he thought, was a little like watching one's own child leave the nest. The object of care, nurture, and labor could be fawned over or preyed upon by directors, publishers, and critics, some of whom had the power to convince thousands of readers to laugh or yawn over it.[20] In his case, the comparison of works to children is not overblown. In 1908, for example, Schnitzler felt a longing for his novel *Der Weg ins Freie* (The Road into the Open, 1908) whenever he stopped working on it for very long.[21] It became such a part of him that he never forgave Hofmannsthal for leaving a complimentary copy on the train.[22] Indecision by directors as to whether to produce his plays was in his view tantamount to treason.

At the age of seventeen, well before finding himself the object of reviews, Schnitzler was already thinking about the qualities of the ideal critic. An author could entrust a novel that was part of him only to a critic able to apprehend its whole and parts in such a way as to render an autonomous verdict.[23] That is, a critic would judge a work impartially if and only if its reputation were ignored, leaving it open to consideration of its aesthetic merit alone. Without the din of reception, the work's themes would allow it to be appreciated whenever and by whomever it was experienced. After realizing just how idealistic this vision of autonomous subjects and objects was, Schnitzler was moved to enumerate the boundaries necessary for criticism. The ideal critic would limit his remarks to the text in front of him, comparing it neither to works of the same author nor to those of other authors. His judgment of aesthetic value would not be put off by an occasional misrepresentation on stage. He would refrain from moralistic remarks, steer clear of commenting on an author's personal life, and discourage an autobiographical connection. Furthermore, the critic would not overlook the obvious or project the imagined onto a work.[24]

Critics insisted on retelling plots ironically and quoting out of context to appear clever. Impressionistic criticism muffled the function of judge, promoter, and educator. Still, if the alternative to subjectivism was an appeal to a higher political or confessional power, Schnitzler chose the former. He refused the judgments of moral codes that bore no resemblance to those that underlay his works. No political exegesis of his works had ever amounted to anything more than *ad hominem* propaganda.

As we shall see, any talk of a standard such as featuring a heroic protagonist points to categories of normative criticism. The aesthetic standard Schnitzler wanted applied to his works had to do with genre, not with demands for a rousing, manly hero. He agreed that novelistic dramas or dramatic novellas would not contribute to success, but he countermanded any moral premise of making literature edifying for the reader. An obvious problem for normative criticism arose with his *erlebte Rede,* a narrative form that allowed Schnitzler to depict external events while revealing a character's state of mind in the third person — for example, in the early story *Die Toten schweigen* (The Dead Keep Silent, 1897). Even harder to address was the stream-of-consciousness monologue in the novella *Leutnant Gustl* (Lieutenant Gustl, 1900), because no omniscient author was busy sanctioning or censoring Gustl's thoughts, or helping the reader to do so. This was a case of modernism pushing beyond the inherited critical norms that would evaluate it.

The ideals of a seventeen-year-old thus turned, with time and experience, into bitter complaints about critical excess. Marcel Reich-Ranicki (1920–), critic for the *Frankfurter Allgemeine Zeitung,* relates an event that is shocking even to readers accustomed to the ebb and flow of an author's fortunes: in 1926, the Prussian Culture Minister ordered that a section for writers be added to the Academy of Arts in Berlin, and asked twenty-thousand readers of the magazine *Literarische Welt* whom they would elect to this honorary section. Twenty-seven authors, including several Austrians, received over a hundred votes apiece — yet one looks in vain for the name of Arthur Schnitzler.[25] Nevertheless, Reich-Ranicki begins his book *Sieben Wegbereiter: Schriftsteller des zwanzigsten Jahrhunderts* (Seven Forerunners: Writers of the Twentieth Century, 2002) with an enthusiastic essay on Schnitzler, for whose melancholic skepticism he finds more sympathy than for Hauptmann's dull intuition or Bertolt Brecht's didacticism. To Reich-Ranicki, Schnitzler is less concerned with ideology than with the concerns of modernity, and this has helped him weather the storms of changing tastes to assume a stronghold in the canon and in the secondary literature.[26]

It may well be the case that when an artwork has heeded the demands of its own genre and style, this "inner necessity" guarantees safe passage through unfavorable reception into belated success. Even a work such as the play *Freiwild* (Fair Game, 1896), which Schnitzler and contemporary critics judged more tendentious than inspired, can outlast authorial and critical misgivings, although this may have more to do with critical focus shifting from genre and style to historical concerns, making study of the text more fruitful than judgment of its performance. No doubt the author's interpretation of his own words changes over time just as much as that of the reader.

Schnitzler's late plays provide another example of the changing fortunes wrought by critical attention. In a virtual one-man crusade during the 1990s, the English professor C. J. Weinberger translated Schnitzler's post-1914 plays into English and supplied each with a critical study. His focus on the plays defied scholarship that had long ranked the late plays inferior to Schnitzler's late prose — beginning with the "perceived obsolescence" cited in reviews of their first performances in the 1920s.[27]

A century of criticism is proof that complete critical autonomy is impossible, whether a critic broadcasts an agenda or not. Singling out an author for study is itself an assumption about relevance. Even if the study is called a quest for discovering the essence or truth of the object, with a little probing a certain vantage point and modus operandi of the critical reconstruction comes to light. My task as metacritic, or historian of critical texts, is to identify a critic's presuppositions about the function of art, and to identify specific questions the critic is raising for the work to answer. To be sure, a primary text itself dictates the questions to which it will supply the answer, but one cannot forego questions that are perhaps not "intuitively" obvious.[28] Which questions advance scholarship and which leave it shortsighted is for posterity to decide. The heavier focus on formalism, philology, and historicism in Schnitzler scholarship does not disqualify him for poststructural readings, however. It is just that either few cultural critics have noticed Schnitzler inviting the questions they deem important, or they have had publishers balking at the prospect of pounding square pegs into round holes. Literary criticism abuses no less than any other institution.[29]

Through the lens of reception theory, Schnitzler's historicity is best viewed as an unfolding event.[30] It is now considered heavy-handed positivism to insist on pinning empirical meaning on a work once and for all. Rather, a work stays open to be constantly rewritten by "interpretive communities," to use Stanley Fish's term; these share interpretive strategies that "exist prior to the act of reading and therefore determine the shape of what is to be read rather than, as is usually assumed, the other way around."[31] Each community, risking being called "reductive" or "superficial" by some other community, successfully writes the text or texts demanded by its own interpretive strategy.[32] For the most part, this observation is understood as an established fact in the metacritical goal of this book's series, *Literary Criticism in Perspective*, which promises "to illuminate the nature of literary criticism itself, to gauge the influence of social and historic currents on aesthetic judgments once thought objective and authoritative." The key difference is that my historiography cannot stop with granting all interpretive communities equal authority, but must also plot their diachronic progression through the twentieth century. To follow Schorske, this means taking notice of two threads: the diachronic, which examines continuity and change within one genre or system of thought — in my case, criticism — and the synchronic, which examines the text in its relationship with concurrent aspects of culture.[33]

On the level of the individual, it is clear that worldview affects aesthetic judgments, but methodologies of academics and journalistic reviewers alike are affected by the geopolitical climate, which often prescribes the aesthetic objects worthy of study. Polarizing concepts such as "nation," "patriotism," "Cold War," "New World Order"; events such as war and its aftermath, administration changes, congressional power shifts, economic recessions and upswings: these concepts and events shape what is expedient or fashionable in literary studies. One obvious example is from the fifties: a fear of sounding too patriotic affected *Germanistik* in postwar Germany, while a fear of appearing even faintly leftist was evident in the United States.

The longer one studies Schnitzler, the wider the critical landscape appears. The most prominent reception studies by country are the following: Margot Elfving Vogel's *Schnitzler in Schweden: Zur Rezeption seiner Werke* (1979); Elisabeth Heresch's *Schnitzler und Rußland: Aufnahme, Wirkung, Kritik* (1982); Elizabeth Lebensaft's "Schnitzler aus tschechischer Sicht: Zur Rezeption in der CSSR," *MAL* 16/1 (1983): 17–22; Françoise Derré's "Schnitzler in Frankreich," *MAL* 19/1 (1986): 27–48; Hans Roelofs's *"Man weiss eigentlich wenig von einander": Arthur Schnitzler und die Niederlande 1895–1940* (1989); Donald Daviau's "The Reception of Arthur Schnitzler in the United States," in *The Fortunes of German Writers in America: Studies in Literary Reception* (1992); and Yukio Ozawa's *Japanisches bei Arthur Schnitzler: Japanische Einflüsse auf Schnitzler und die Rezeption Schnitzlers in Japan* (1995).[34] Richard Allen's 1964 dissertation, "Arthur Schnitzler's Works and their Reception: An Annotated Bibliography," contains a long second chapter,

"The Critical Reception of Schnitzler's Works," which comments on Schnitzler criticism through 1964.[35] Herbert Seidler's "Die Forschung zu Arthur Schnitzler seit 1945" (1976) takes to task all levels of scholarship since 1945: bibliographies and research reviews, primary editions, general studies, analyses of Schnitzler's life, particular themes, dramatic works, and narrative works.[36] Giuseppe Farese's "Arthur Schnitzler alla luce della critica recente (1966–1970)" continues the work of Allen, but in the form of a critical research review — with an index of what is lacking in Allen's work: namely, projects from Farese's own Italy, the German Democratic Republic, and the Soviet Union.[37]

Published in 1982, the fiftieth anniversary of Schnitzler's death, Donald Daviau's "Arthur Schnitzler im Spiegel der Kritik — Fünfzig Jahre nach seinem Tod" delivers less an essay on literary criticism than an image of Schnitzler that illuminates the most important turning points leading to his popularity. Daviau presents critical assumptions that in his estimation require no proof or documentation.[38] Michaela Perlmann's *Arthur Schnitzler* (1987), a commented bibliography and research review, sums up the research on Schnitzler's unpublished works, text editions, diaries, letters, bibliographies, research reviews, commentaries, reception histories, and periodicals; next she comments on comprehensive monographs about Schnitzler and finally she sorts by genre the scholarship on individual works and the particular themes and motifs favored by Schnitzler scholars.[39]

Horst Thomé's "Sozialgeschichtliche Perspektiven der neueren Schnitzler-Forschung" (1988) reviews seven monographs published between 1980 and 1988, commenting additionally on one installment of Schnitzler's diary. Thomé examines in sequence theoretical explanations, explication of the texts, and social functionality of textual meaning; Thomé explains that Schnitzler's texts are not intended as a direct conduit to the historical context to enable detailed descriptions of social institutions, but rather as commentary on the societal components of the "impressionistic syndrome." Schnitzler's texts are "true" to the extent that they convey the typology of impressionism. Matters of production, distribution, and reception round out Thomé's study.[40] Of all the overview authors, Thomé is the most forthcoming about his biases, which are neopositivist in nature.

Several books have examined criticism of specific works, genres, and critics of Schnitzler. Some of the more helpful ones that make an appearance here are the following: *Berlin — Theater der Jahrhundertwende: Bühnengeschichte der Reichshauptstadt im Spiegel der Kritik (1889–1914)* (1986) by Norbert Jaron, Renate Möhrmann, and Hedwig Müller, important for examining the reception of Schnitzler in Berlin, where most of his plays debuted under Otto Brahm. A work that examines the critical connection between Vienna and Berlin is Peter Sprengel and Gregor Streim's *Berliner und Wiener Moderne: Vermittlungen und Abgrenzungen in Literatur, Theater, Publizistik* (1998). Jens Rieckmann's excellent study is the indispensable starting point for understanding literary modernism in Vienna: *Aufbruch in die Moderne: Die Anfänge des Jungen Wien: Österreichische Literatur und Kritik im Fin de Siècle* (1985). Ellen Butzko's *Arthur Schnitzler und die zeitgenössische Theaterkritik* (1991) shows how theater criticism and the views of recognized theater critics were incorporated into Schnitzler's aphorisms, letters, and diary entries, and how he sought revenge for unfair reviews by featuring these critics unmistakably in his fiction. Andrea Willi's *Arthur Schnitzlers Roman* Der Weg ins Freie: *Eine Untersuchung zur Tageskritik und ihren zeitgenössischen Bezugen* (1989) analyzes the journalistic reception during Schnitzler's lifetime of his beleaguered and misunderstood novel of 1908. Finally, Konstanze Fliedl's *Arthur Schnitzler: Poetik der Erinnerung* (1997) interprets Schnitzler's texts as literary reactions to the nineteenth-century crisis of memory, from which, among other things, literary criticism suffered.[41]

These metacritical studies, then, work more comprehensively within a narrower time span, work, or genre, and are not concerned with mapping criticism of Schnitzler's entire oeuvre over time. I want to describe the criticism and examine the reasons behind its judgments, as these studies do. Like Thomé, I can see the merit of featuring sociohistorical investigations for the years 1975–1985, as shown by my chapter that addresses sociohistorical approaches to emancipation in Schnitzler's work. Unlike someone as painstakingly inclusive as Seidler, I am more interested in the currents and constellations of the research; therefore I concentrate on relatively few watershed monographs and essays in the research over a greater period of time. As mentioned, I concentrate on the image of literary criticism that emerges from the critical voices themselves. As Peter Uwe Hohendahl points out, literary criticism is not the history of some philosophical essence evolving toward perfection.[42] It evolves in response to the present, and it falls to the historiographer to "demonstrate literary-critical communication *itself* to be a social phenomenon."[43] Within this communication are voices that resonate loudly or remain ignored or fall silent at certain times, and my interest concerns their critical half-life.

The beginning of Schnitzler criticism arose in a climate of modernism encompassing both naturalism (associated with Berlin and Otto

Brahm) and the notion of "overcoming" it by shifting the focus from terse descriptions of working-class conditions, for example, to minute descriptions of the inner workings of the soul (associated with Vienna and Hermann Bahr). This metropolitan dynamic meant the creation of stereotypes, for which Schnitzler was well-suited: Berlin, on the one hand, rejected Schnitzler's Viennese decadence as polluting either the stream of aesthetic tradition or the progressive stream of solving modern problems; Vienna, on the other hand, disapproved of Schnitzler's modernity out of fear of another Ibsen infiltrating the Burgtheater. He was by turns too modern or not modern enough.

Schnitzler's call for critical boundaries was lost in the transition from journalistic reception to book-length literary "science." The route of literary criticism is evident in the Schnitzler monographs of Freud student Theodor Reik and German literary scholars Josef Körner and Bernhard Blume,[44] but these men would appear superior by far next to the mummified Nazi criticism of the thirties; examined in isolation, though, their ideological moorings become transparent enough.

Truly critical interest (what Weinberger has called "uprooting clichés[45]) in Schnitzler's stories and plays came about haltingly in the fifties, gathered organizational support during the sixties, and had built up relentless momentum by the early seventies. Interest in Schnitzler in the United States was strong enough that by 1962, the centennial of his birth, the major interpretive community of the International Arthur Schnitzler Research Association (IASRA) came into being. It counted many among its ranks who, during the war years, shared the plight of Schnitzler's exiled son Heinrich, but stayed in the United States, whereas he returned to Vienna in the fifties. Philological work in text editions, correspondence, and autobiography resulted in increased evidence for Schnitzler's intentions, and more attention was paid to his mature works of the twenties. Making Schnitzler respectable were scholars such as Ernst Offermanns in Germany, William Rey in the United States, and Martin Swales in Great Britain, all of whom paid tribute to Schnitzler the ethicist and master of far-ranging themes about the human condition, insisting that this version replace the image of Schnitzler the impressionist fixated on love, death, and fate.[46] Schnitzler the modernist was resuscitated by humanist approaches stressing philological, biographical, historicist, and occasionally psychoanalytical approaches. The IASRA was not yet willing, however, to share Schnitzler with someone like Manfred Diersch in the German Democratic Republic, finding that a Marxist approach focused the wrong kind of attention on bourgeois Vienna.[47]

Another wave of critical activity surrounded the fiftieth anniversary of Schnitzler's death in 1981, and showed increased interest in Schnitzler's political views, which could be explained by a combination of intellectual and ethnic inheritance, personal disposition, and historical moment, particularly the experience of anti-Semitism on the one hand and world war on the other. Critical Theory applied the language of emancipation dialectically to the legacy of the Enlightenment. How was Schnitzler himself situated to write about liberation for class, race, and gender? Scholars working in feminism, sociology, and intellectual history, for example, have raised and this question and responded to it through studies such as Hartmut Scheible's *Arthur Schnitzler und die Aufklärung* (1977), Norbert Abels's *Sicherheit ist nirgends: Judentum und Aufklärung bei Arthur Schnitzler* (1982), Rolf-Peter Janz and Klaus Laermann's *Arthur Schnitzler: Zur Diagnose des Wiener Bürgertums im Fin de Siècle* (1977), and Barbara Gutt's *Emanzipation bei Arthur Schnitzler* (1978).

Clearly, any talk of emancipation must also include the psychoanalytical scholarship that rides the popularity of the Schnitzler-Freud connection. If the fifties and sixties saw the rise of Freudian approaches, the 1980s saw the final severance of Schnitzler's literature from Freud's psychoanalysis: Michaela Perlmann's *Der Traum in der literarischen Moderne: Zum Werk Arthur Schnitzlers* (1987) and Michael Worbs's long chapter on Schnitzler and Freud in *Nervenkunst: Literatur und Psychoanalyse im Wien der Jahrhundertwende* (1988) were important instruments to this end, taking care to explicate the differences between the two men, especially with regard to acquiring and assessing psychological knowledge.[48]

Schnitzler scholarship has exhibited an "aging process" in line with that of Schnitzler himself. For one thing, scholarship has turned, over time, to Schnitzler's mature works, especially his prose, and most recently to the late plays. For another thing, as if obsessed with records and memory, scholarship especially of the eighties and nineties has taken on the concerns dear to Schnitzler himself late in life: Schnitzler's diary has come under scrutiny for its own sake, not just to serve as a proof text for the primary texts. This has been facilitated by the recently completed twenty-year undertaking of the Austrian Academy of Sciences to publish fifty-two years of Schnitzler's diary in ten volumes. It is a subtle yet perceptible step from biographical criticism to a New Historicism curious about what it will find in the discourse of the epoch in which Schnitzler's fiction arose, without allowing fiction to monopolize center stage. With Schnitzler holding his own on seminar reading lists, questions of canon-worthiness have been replaced by curiosity about the process of his canonization. The reception of *Reigen* alone has become the focus of major investigations.[49]

Dissolving the barrier between text and context removes the literary work from center stage long enough to permit notice of other types of textual discourse. The diary project appears on the surface to be another resource contributing to the context for Schnitzler's texts, and no doubt the collection will continue to serve as evidence of Schnitzler's intentions in his plays and stories. But scholars involved directly in the project have been content to learn about the age and about Schnitzler without immediately turning that knowledge into interpretation. In other words, the definition and purpose of literature has become fluid, and the background has become foreground along with the text. "Thick description" and synchrony have replaced the metanarratives of "heavy thought."

All this is reason to reflect on Schnitzler's place in the twenty-first century, with some recognition of what scholarship is significant enough to address. It is impossible to engage all pertinent studies with similar precision or depth, due to the sheer volume of the material. An apology for any victims of my neglect must be offered here at the start. At the minimum, I hope to draw from Schnitzler scholarship the best representative examples for understanding the route it took in the twentieth century. At the same time, I hope to reflect on the nature of literary criticism, and encourage the reader to do likewise.

Notes

[1] References made are to Arthur Schnitzler, *Ausgewählte Werke in acht Bänden,* ed. Heinz Ludwig Arnold (Frankfurt am Main: Fischer, 2001); Giuseppe Farese, *Arthur Schnitzler: Ein Leben in Wien,* trans. Karin Krieger (Munich: Beck, 1999); *Eyes Wide Shut,* dir. Stanley Kubrick, screenplay Frederic Raphael, perf. Nicole Kidman and Tom Cruise, WB, 1999; David Hare, *The Blue Room: A Play in Ten Intimate Acts* (New York: Grove Press, 1998); Peter Gay, *Schnitzler's Century: The Making of Middle-Class Culture 1815–1914* (New York: Norton, 2001). *Eyes Wide Shut* (translated into German by Frank Schaff) and *Traumnovelle* were published together by Fischer Taschenbuch Verlag in 1999.

[2] Carl E. Schorske, introduction, *Fin-de-Siècle Vienna: Politics and Culture* (New York: Vintage Books, 1981), xxv.

[3] *The Random House Dictionary of the English Language,* 1st ed., s. v. "fin de siècle."

[4] See Dinitia Smith, "Dissecting the Era of Virgins and Satyrs," *New York Times,* 10 November 2001, sec. A13, A17.

[5] Tom Stoppard, *Dalliance: Undiscovered Country,* adapted from Arthur Schnitzler (London and Boston: Faber and Faber, 1986).

[6] Peter Gay, *Schnitzler's Century: The Making of Middle-Class Culture 1815–1914* (New York: Norton, 2001), xxviii.

[7] Arthur Schnitzler, *Jugend in Wien: Eine Autobiographie,* ed. Therese Nickl and Heinrich Schnitzler (Vienna: Molden, 1968, citations according to Frankfurt am Main: Fischer, 1981), 44–45. Subsequent citations appear in the text in parentheses as *"J"* followed by the page reference.

[8] See Karlheinz Rossbacher, *Literatur und Liberalismus: Zur Kultur der Ringstraßenzeit in Wien* (Vienna: J&V Verlag, 1992), 44–47.

[9] Diary entry of 1 May 1886.

[10] Farese, *Leben in Wien* (1999), 35.

[11] Farese, *Leben in Wien* (1999), 229.

[12] Renate Wagner's *Frauen um Arthur Schnitzler* (Frankfurt am Main: Fischer, 1983) is one investigation that examines the history of the women important in Schnitzler's life. The correspondence between Olga Waissnix and Schnitzler, in the volume *Liebe, die starb vor der Zeit: ein Briefwechsel,* ed. Therese Nickl and Heinrich Schnitzler (Vienna: Molden, 1970), is another document of sociohistorical interest.

[13] Renate Wagner, *Frauen* (1983), 59.

[14] Renate Wagner, *Frauen* (1983), 80.

[15] Farese, *Leben in Wien* (1999), 78.

[16] For a list of his accomplishments, see Reinhard Urbach, "Heinrich Schnitzler — 75 Jahre," *MAL* 10/3–4 (1977): 1–18.

[17] Olga outlived Schnitzler by 39 years and died on January 13, 1970. Shortly before his death she returned to Vienna from Berlin; in 1939 she emigrated to England, then to the United States (Berkeley), returning to Vienna in the fifties and finally going to Italy in the sixties. In honor of Schnitzler's hundredth birthday, she wrote *Spiegelbild der Freundschaft* (Salzburg: Residenz Verlag, 1962), which Renate Wagner considers somewhat misconstrued because Olga had repressed the stormy battles of marriage to focus on the honor of her increasingly famous husband and his circle of friends (Wagner [1983], 126).

[18] Renate Wagner, *Frauen* (1983), 132.

[19] Schnitzler was thinking about the future when writing for the present — this self-cultivation is evident not only in his diary, but also in his autobiography (which nonetheless stops at 1889).

[20] Arthur Schnitzler, *Über Kunst und Kritik,* vol. 3 of *Aphorismen und Betrachtungen,* ed. Robert O. Weiss (Frankfurt am Main: Fischer Taschenbuch Verlag, 1993), 37.

[21] See his diary entry of 2 June 1908.

[22] Hofmannsthal to Schnitzler, 24 July 1908, *Hugo von Hofmannsthal — Arthur Schnitzler: Briefwechsel,* ed. Therese Nickl and Heinrich Schnitzler (Frankfurt am Main: Fischer, 1964), 238.

[23] Schnitzler, *Kunst und Kritik* (1993), 37.

[24] Schnitzler, *Kunst und Kritik* (1993), 57, 62.

[25] Marcel Reich-Ranicki, "Auch das Grausame kann diskret sein," in *Sieben Wegbereiter: Schriftsteller des zwanzigsten Jahrhunderts* (Stuttgart and Munich: Deutsche Verlags-Anstalt, 2002), 16–17. The essay originally appeared 4 February 1984 in the *Frankfurter Allgemeine Zeitung*.

[26] Reich-Ranicki, *Sieben Wegbereiter*, 18.

[27] C. J. Weinberger, *Arthur Schnitzler's Late Plays: A Critical Study* (New York: Lang, 1997).

[28] For further thoughts in this regard, see Richard Macksey, foreword to *The Johns Hopkins Guide to Literary Theory & Criticism*, ed. Michael Groden and Martin Kreiswirth (Baltimore: Johns Hopkins UP, 1994), vii.

[29] Vincent Leitch, *Cultural Criticism, Literary Theory, Poststructuralism* (New York: Columbia UP, 1992), 128–29.

[30] Hans Robert Jauß, "Literaturgeschichte als Provokation der Literaturwissenschaft," *Rezeptionsästhetik: Theorie und Praxis*, ed. Rainer Warning (Munich: Fink, 1988), 126–62, here 128.

[31] Stanley Fish, *Is There a Text in This Class? The Authority of Interpretive Communities* (Cambridge, MA: Harvard UP, 1980), 171.

[32] Fish, *Interpretive Communities* (1980), 171.

[33] See Schorske, *Fin de Siècle* (1981), xxii.

[34] See "Works Consulted" for full bibliographical information.

[35] Richard Allen, "Arthur Schnitzler's Works and their Reception: An Annotated Bibliography," (Diss., U of Michigan, 1964). His book of two years later, *An Annotated Arthur Schnitzler Bibliography: Editions and Criticism in German, French, and English 1879–1965* (Chapel Hill: U of North Carolina P, 1966), is not as helpful, because although it lists publications of primary editions, translations, selected criticism, and general Schnitzler scholarship, it does not contain the chapter of commentary. Hence any references here to Allen will be to the dissertation, unless otherwise specified.

[36] Herbert Seidler, "Die Forschung zu Arthur Schnitzler seit 1945," *Zeitschrift für Deutsche Philologie* 95 (1976): 567–95, here 569.

[37] Giuseppe Farese, "Arthur Schnitzler alla luce della critica recente (1966–1970)," *Studi Germanici* 9/1–2 (1971): 234–68.

[38] Donald Daviau, "Arthur Schnitzler im Spiegel der Kritik — Fünfzig Jahre nach seinem Tod," *Text & Kontext* 10/2 (1982): 411–26; Daviau lists his critical objectives on pages 412–13.

[39] Michaela Perlmann, *Arthur Schnitzler* (Stuttgart: Metzler, 1987).

[40] Horst Thomé, "Sozialgeschichtliche Perspektiven der neueren Schnitzler-Forschung," *Internationales Archiv für Sozialgeschichte der deutschen Literatur* 13 (1988): 158–87.

[41] Norbert Jaron, Renate Möhrmann, and Hedwig Müller, *Berlin — Theater der Jahrhundertwende: Bühnengeschichte der Reichshauptstadt im Spiegel der Kritik (1889–1914)* (Tübingen: Max Niemeyer, 1986); Peter Sprengel and Gregor Streim, *Berliner und Wiener Moderne: Vermittlungen und Abgrenzungen in Literatur, Thea-*

ter, Publizistik (Vienna: Böhlau, 1998); Jens Rieckmann, *Aufbruch in die Moderne: Die Anfänge des Jungen Wien: Österreichische Literatur und Kritik im Fin de Siècle* (Tübingen: Athenäum, 1985); Ellen Butzko, *Arthur Schnitzler und die zeitgenössische Theaterkritik* (Frankfurt am Main: Lang, 1991); Andrea Willi, *Arthur Schnitzlers Roman* Der Weg ins Freie: *Eine Untersuchung zur Tageskritik und ihren zeitgenössischen Bezugen* (Heidelberg: Carl Winter Universitätsverlag, 1989); Konstanze Fliedl, *Arthur Schnitzler: Poetik der Erinnerung* (Vienna: Böhlau, 1997).

[42] Peter Uwe Hohendahl, introduction to *A History of German Literary Criticism, 1730–1980,* ed. Hohendahl (Lincoln: U of Nebraska P, 1988), 10–11.

[43] Hohendahl, *Literary Criticism* (1988), 4.

[44] Theodor Reik, *Arthur Schnitzler als Psycholog* (Minden: Bruns, 1913), Josef Körner, *Arthur Schnitzler: Gestalten und Probleme* (Zurich: Almathea, 1921), Bernard Blume, *Das nihilistische Weltbild Arthur Schnitzlers* (Stuttgart: Knöller, 1936).

[45] Weinberger, *Late Plays* (1997), 3.

[46] William Rey, *Arthur Schnitzler: Die späte Prosa als Gipfel seines Schaffens* (Berlin: E. Schmidt, 1968); Ernst L. Offermanns, *Das Komödienwerk als Kritik des Impressionismus* (Munich: Fink, 1973); Martin Swales, *Arthur Schnitzler: A Critical Study* (Oxford: Clarendon Press, 1971).

[47] Manfred Diersch, *Empiriokritizismus und Impressionismus: Über Beziehungen zwischen Philosophie, Ästhetik und Literatur um 1900 in Wien* (Berlin: Rütten & Loening, 1973).

[48] Michaela Perlmann, *Der Traum in der literarischen Moderne: Zum Werk Arthur Schnitzlers* (Munich: Fink, 1987); Michael Worbs, *Nervenkunst: Literatur und Psychoanalyse im Wien der Jahrhundertwende* (Frankfurt am Main: Athenäum, 1988).

[49] One of these, a two-volume set by Viennese scholars, is proof of how Austria remembers and memorializes Schnitzler in its national and critical memory: Albert Pfoser, Kristina Pfoser-Schewig, Gerhard Renner, *Schnitzler's* Reigen: *Zehn Dialoge und ihre Skandalgeschichte: Analysen und Dokumente* (Frankfurt am Main: Fischer Taschenbuch Verlag, 1993).

1: Journalistic Criticism during Schnitzler's Lifetime

Der Anatol und die Liebelei —
Nichts als sentimentale Plauderei.
Die Frau des Weisen und andere Novellen
Ich sagt' es seit jeher: Nur Bagatellen!
Beatrice? gar Verse! nun hat er vertan —
Der Weg ins Freie? ein Judenroman.
Der Kakadu? bestenfalls Variété —
Das Zwischenspiel? wieder nur Liebesweh.
Der einsame Weg und das weite Land?
Psychologie aus zweiter Hand.
Der Reigen — wir wissen ja — Schweinereien,
Marionetten? aha, jetzt gesteht er es ein.
Der Ruf des Lebens? bum, Spekulation.
Medardus — ? Ausstattungssensation.
Bernhardi, pfui Teufel, ein Thesenstück
Und ohne Weiber, er geht zurück.
Komödie der Worte — die schreibt er ja immer
Nur freilich wird's mit den Jahren schlimmer. —
Was bin ich für einen Mann ihm gegenüber!
Was er auch schreiben mag, ich schreibe drüber.[1]

[Anatol and Liebelei —
Nothing but sentimental chitchat.
Die Frau des Weisen and other novellas
I've always maintained: just bagatelles!
Beatrice? nothing but verses. Now he's really slipped —
Der Weg ins Freie? A novel for and about Jews.
Der Kakadu? a variety show at the most —
Das Zwischenspiel? once again, just the pains of love.
Der einsame Weg and Das weite Land?
Second-hand psychology.
Der Reigen — yes, we know — full of filth.

Marionetten? Aha, now he admits it.
Der Ruf des Lebens? you got it: speculation.
Medardus — ? Theatrical spectacle.
Bernhardi, disgusting, that's a problem-play
That's bound to flop without women.
Komödie der Worte — he's always writing about that
Except that it's gotten worse over the years. —
Who am I measured up against him!
Whatever he comes up with, I'm sure to comment on it.]

A T THE TIME OF SCHNITZLER'S FIRST breakthroughs in the early 1890s with the one-act cycle *Anatol* and the play *Liebelei,* two major strands of criticism dominated the literary scene in Germany and Austria. According to Peter Uwe Hohendahl, these strands were the result of a split in critical self-understanding around the year 1870. The critic as *raisonneur,* an enlightened mediator between the work of art and its intended public, had previously been at home in both newspaper and cultural journal, but was now affected by the commercialization of the press and the rise of scientific discourse in the university. The growing importance of the feuilleton section of the newspaper shaped the strand of criticism identified with an associative imagination, while scientific discourse shaped the strand that used argumentative reason in the cultural journal. Roughly, as a mainstay of a commercialized press, feuilletons were aimed at a heterogeneous public sphere unconcerned with the rules of aesthetics, while cultural journals assumed a readership acquainted with literary conventions.[2]

The background and contradictions of this critical divide form the backdrop for the reception of Schnitzler's dramas from 1890 to 1912. For this beginning phase of Schnitzler's production, Berlin was every bit as important as Vienna. In the 1890s, Berlin was associated with modernist naturalism (also referred to as "Die neue Richtung"), and Vienna was known for modernist impressionism; whether this convenient polarization was warranted or not, it became a convenient template for evaluating fiction in the literary industry of the time.[3] With Berlin one might associate the articulate naturalist spokesman Otto Brahm, director of the Deutsches Theater and Lessing-Theater; the naturalist playwright Gerhart Hauptmann (1862–1946); the cultural journals *Die Gesellschaft* and *Die Neue Rundschau;* and the publisher Samuel Fischer (1859–1934). With Vienna one might associate impressionism or symbolism; staunch conservative opponents of that modernism; Hermann Bahr and his call for "new psychology" to supplant naturalism; newspapers such as the liberal *Neue Freie Presse*, feuilletons; and coffeehouses in which they were read; and above all a readiness for sensation and scandal. To both cities one might attribute a loyalty to Henrik Ibsen and a determination to perform his works, build on his themes, and use him as a critical standard. It is noteworthy that each city's newspapers sent their critics to performances of Schnitzler in the other city, creating an exchange more successful at reinforcing stereotypes than dismantling them. Schnitzler's road to recognition illustrates Hohendahl's notion that literary criticism is an apparatus: judgments rarely reflect a theoretical or aesthetic model alone, but rather the concrete considerations of press, readership, and government.[4] In the case of this Viennese playwright, the victory of the concrete over the abstract is evident in the interplay of production and reception in the two metropolitan capitols and in Schnitzler's contribution to the development of literary modernism.

Berlin Modernism, Viennese Feuilleton: Otto Brahm and Hermann Bahr

In Berlin, modernism in the form of naturalism was promoted by Brahm through the figures of Ibsen, Hauptmann, and finally Schnitzler. Brahm's vital influence in Schnitzler's dramatic career ranged from his directorship of the Deutsches Theater from 1894 to 1904 and of the Lessing-Theater from 1904 until his death in 1912. Except for *Zwischenspiel* (Interlude, 1905), *Marionetten* (Puppet Plays, 1901–4), and *Professor Bernhardi* (1912), Brahm directed all of Schnitzler's plays until 1912 either as premieres or as attempts to improve on earlier productions. Thanks to a close-knit ensemble of actors and an eye for detail, Brahm's success rate was high. Collaboration was possible because Schnitzler met Brahm's criteria, spelled out in the naturalist organization *Verein Durch* and its 1886 publication *Litterarische Volkshefte*, which charged writers to discuss issues of modern life openly. Brahm's exacting directorial standards arose from his experience as a critic working for *Die Nation* and alongside Theodor Fontane (1819–98) for the *Vossische Zeitung*.[5] As a critic, Brahm followed the positivism of his Berlin professor, Wilhelm Scherer (1841–86), whose suggestion that a more empirical model of cause and effect replace speculative criticism had a great deal of influence in the 1870s and 1880s.

Seeking to understand a work by standards not indebted to inherited poetic norms, Brahm was careful in his reviews to include information on its genesis, dramaturgical adaptations, and reception history.[6] As a rule, a review had to distinguish the effect of a play as a text from its effect as a performance, thus separating its essence from any accidental effects.[7] Brahm had little interest in reviewing works that refused to debate current issues. Works that met with his approval, however, received his thorough and sincere endorsement. This was especially the case with Ibsen's *Ghosts*. As a result of performing it in 1889, Brahm brokered his hero to the Berlin audience, preparing it for the themes of syphilis, extramarital sex, and bourgeois hypocrisy that would be addressed henceforth by Hauptmann and Schnitzler.[8]

The obstacle for Brahm was a critical guild still insistent on modern drama's following a traditional plot structure.[9] Brahm argues that a dramatist by definition writes effectively enough to justify repeat performances, and that carrying an idea to fruition is more important than imitating Goethe and Schiller.[10] Whether the message is agreeable or not, a "Tendenzstück," a play that grapples with a single issue, succeeds when it translates the issue it takes up into dramatic terms.[11] He addresses prevailing fallacies as follows: First, criticism should not take a biographical slant that conflates the author with his characters.[12] Second, criticism should avoid postulating a thesis not yet established: there is no sense pronouncing a work satisfactory if the criteria for merit are unclear, for one cannot rely on the watermarks left by earlier plays. Third, criticism should discourage the notion of the purity of the dramatic genre, due to the inevitable overlap of drama and narrative. Lessing, Schiller, Kleist, and Hebbel were all authors whose dramatic style infused their writing in all genres. Friedrich Spielhagen (1829–1911), who called Henrik Ibsen's play *Nora* a novel, showed the need to shift dramatic boundaries to accommodate innovation. Fourth, insisting on a clear division between tragedy and comedy ignores the fact that life itself avoids such divisions — a fact Brahm saw lost on the dramatists and critics.[13] Whether an author's description of reality is tragic or comical, it lies beyond criticism.

Brahm's critical housecleaning was no guarantee that positivism would fare any better than sloppy thought, but it was a necessary part of steering an ailing theater back to its original purpose of raising the consciousness of the audience. In this sense Brahm never forgot Lessing's notion of theater as formation of taste, Goethe's notion of theater as aesthetic education, or Schiller's notion that theater served as a moral institution.[14] Since these literary models did not offer the creative templates necessary for late nineteenth-century drama, though, he put his career on the line by promoting Ibsen's earnest realism above the dramas produced by German epigones and above the French salon comedies of the eighties.[15]

By the time he met Schnitzler in 1894, Brahm had turned his attention from reviewing toward leadership as stage director of the *Freie Bühne für modernes Leben*, a literary club and journal that addressed vital public issues within the censor-free zone of a private theater. As his ample correspondence with Schnitzler shows, the dramaturgical advice he had supplied through reviews was now funneled into advice for production. For Schnitzler, enduring two decades of Brahm's stubborn views was a small price to pay for his consistent support.

In 1894, the *Freie Bühne für modernes Leben* was renamed *Die Neue Rundschau* and became a starting point of literary modernism in the form of Berlin naturalism. Published by Samuel Fischer and overseen by Brahm, the journal contained works by naturalist writers such as Arno Holz, Johannes Schlaf, and Gerhart Hauptmann, and essays by critics such as Georg Brandes, Paul Schlenther, Franz Servaes, Samuel Lublinski, Arthur Eloesser, and Alfred Kerr, all of whom reviewed Schnitzler's plays at one time or another. It also published eight of Schnitzler's stories, a short play, and his novel *Der Weg ins Freie* in six monthly installments in 1908. In 1904, for example, one could read Schnitzler's one-act play *Der tapfere Cassian* (Brave Cassian) in the February issue, which also featured Alfred Kerr's review of *Der einsame Weg* (The Lonely Way).[16]

Brahm also figured in the short segment of Hermann Bahr's career that found Bahr working as a publisher's reader and contributing essays to the *Freie Bühne*. Bahr's role in helping determine or even invent the course of modernism in Berlin and Vienna was enormous, all the more because of his literary presence in both. His critical writings were the major force in the creation of an identity for both cities based on their real and imagined differences. As Austrian proponent of modernism and challenger of Berlin-style naturalism,[17] Bahr was already laying groundwork with his important essay "Die Moderne," which was featured in the first issue of *Moderne Dichtung*, a journal which began publication on the first day of 1890 and was based in Brünn, near Vienna. Like *Die Freie Bühne* in Berlin, *Moderne Dichtung* (renamed *Moderne Rundschau* a year later) advocated a sweeping overhaul of society, and insisted that the most progressive views in biology, psychology, and sociology were necessary for understanding and appreciating contemporary literature.[18] *Moderne Dichtung*'s editor, Eduard Kafka, accepted most submissions that were modern, including Schnitzler's one-acts from the *Anatol* cycle *Die Frage an das Schicksal* and *Anatols Hochzeitsmorgen*. The journal was clearly in alliance with German naturalist journals such as Fritz Hammer's *Die Gesellschaft*.[19] To believe Bahr, Schnitzler and his contemporary decadents had no intention of forming a definable aesthetic program beyond plumbing the depths of the interior life.[20] Nevertheless, the program clearly spelled out in the founding of *Moderne Dichtung* was in fact an eagerness that aimed to integrate itself into existing European currents of naturalism.

From the start, Bahr advertised himself as a prophet in the literary wilderness who was seeking redemption for Austria's epigones.[21] His agreement with the progressive stance of *Moderne Dichtung* was evident in one of his favorite phrases: "Wir haben kein anderes Gesetz als die Wahrheit, wie jeder sie empfindet." This meant that objective truth was made relative to subjective truth via sensation, shifting the focus from the observed object onto the observing subject. According to Bahr, the soul assumed priority over the world of nature and called for trust of sensory information alone.[22] This did not mean that the empirical description touted by naturalism had to disappear — it simply turned inward, and the observing self was now equipped to describe its own moods in detail.

A year before he wrote his essay "Die Überwindung des Naturalismus," Bahr was using "modern" as a dynamic adjective that described naturalism but was not synonymous with it. Reflecting his aesthetic reorientation, Bahr's writing style shifted from Marxist analytical language to feuilletonism, a form Berliners could not help associating with Paris and Vienna.[23] This was exactly the association Bahr intended from his collection of essays *Zur Kritik der Moderne,* also published in 1890, which challenged German literature to mimic France's addition of the fantastic to the objective component of modernism.[24]

It is here that the link between aesthetic form and concrete format requires emphasis. Bahr's associative form was supposed to reproduce the state of the soul so that it could be plumbed by for primary fiction and the criticism that evaluated that fiction. He was really advocating feuilletonism, a mindset that reflected both the worldview of the critic as well as the concrete historical situation of the newspaper press. To understand the phenomenon of the feuilleton — both as an extended review format and as the section featuring such reviews — it is helpful to have an awareness of the state of newspapers and journals at the end of the nineteenth century, especially in Vienna.

A newspaper with international recognition was the *Neue Freie Presse,* founded in 1864 and so successful that it could operate without always having to placate its financiers. After liberal Jewish editor Moriz Benedikt joined the staff in 1872, it doubled its daily circulation to fifty thousand by 1901.[25] Like most liberal newspapers of Schnitzler's and Bahr's class, it united individualism with anticlerical and pro-Jewish persuasions, but remained powerless against the bureaucratic attitudes behind censorship, despite the 1867 constitution's having lifted political and economic restrictions.[26] The *Neue Freie Presse,* being pro-German, opposed the official 1855 concordat in which the state surrendered control of moral and educational matters to the ecclesiastical hierarchy. It opposed the 1867 compromise with Hungary that established the Dual Monarchy, and discouraged Austrian participation in the Franco-Prussian War of 1870. Albeit with reservation, it supported the liberal constitutional party, recognized the social demands of the upward-striving working class, and endorsed election reform that was counter to Prime Minister Taaffe's proposals.[27] Although the government confiscated the paper frequently from 1879 to 1893, editor-in-chief Benedikt's editorial attacks against Taaffe's proposed reforms were so influential that they eventually forced Taaffe out of office.

Strong competition came from the pro-French and anti-German *Neue Wiener Tagblatt,* which made its profits from massive advertising.[28] In addition, the *Wiener Allgemeine Zeitung,* established in 1880, opposed both German and Slav nationalism; the anti-German, anti-Slav, and stock-market-centered *Wiener Sonn- und Montag Zeitung* employed one of Schnitzler's most acerbic critics, Alfred Polgar (1873–1955). The *Arbeiter Zeitung,* a Social Democratic organ founded by Viktor Adler (1852–1918) and Friedrich Austerlitz (1862–1931) also developed into a powerful paper with a daily readership of 100,000 plus, and unlike the *Neue Freie Presse* fought for social justice at home and a European peace based on the solidarity of the international labor movement. On the opposite side of the spectrum from the *Neue Freie Presse* were such mouthpieces as the clerical *Reichswehr* and the anti-Semitic *Deutsches Volksblatt.* Taken as a whole, the Viennese press at the turn of the century offered clear proof of what Schorske calls "politics in a new key."[29] According to Stefan Zweig, a centrifugal political tone underlay the reporting of most newspapers, although not that of the *Neue Freie Presse,* in this era of postrational solutions.[30]

The feuilleton found its niche at the liberal conversational end of the spectrum. Introduced in Paris at the beginning of the nineteenth century by the drama critic Julien-Louis Geoffroy (1743–1814), the feuilleton denoted the lower portion of newspaper's front page under a solid line.[31] This lower space, which in France at the time often featured a serial novel, today denotes the separate section of European newspapers dedicated to cultural discussions, a fact that illustrates the intervening separation of politics and art. Viennese papers usually filled the space "unter dem Strich" either with commentary on the lead news article or with an extended review of a performance or book. Making no claim to be essay or treatise, the feuilleton served to link, in an informal, chatty style, all conceivable topics that came to a writer's mind.[32] Alfred Polgar called it an easily digestible form that left readers hungry while charming them with something like the whoosh of a playground slide: "Man ist unten und könnte nicht sagen, wie man hinunter kam."[33]

Like Karl Kraus, who on principle refused offers to write and edit feuilletons, Schnitzler believed the attitude behind the genre affected news reporting and shortened attention spans, producing further negative consequences for memory. In his view, the reason a feuilletonist wrote so quickly was to escape the voice of conscience.[34] To be sure, there is just cause for Schnitzler's consternation. One journalist finished reviewing Schnitzler's novel *Der Weg ins Freie* before half of the six newspaper installments had appeared.[35] Still, Schnitzler's sensitivity to critique was strong enough to influence his view of all feuilletons. True, feuilletons were not likely to pay attention to the details of a plot, but this hardly disqualifies them from holding educational value for readers of the time, and sociohistorical value for readers now. Failing at its ostensible function as a review, feuilletons could nonetheless succeed as a highly readable satire on liberalism, Austrian etiquette, and the press itself.[36]

After reading feuilletons in the *Neue Freie Presse* for sixty years, the pacifist philosopher and inventor Josef Popper-Lynkeus (1838–1921) came to view them as a kind of "Volksuniversität."[37] Indeed, the *Neue Freie Presse* employed gifted journalists and critics who became household names: music critic Eduard Hanslick (1825–1904), Daniel Spitzer (1835–1893) with his eagerly-awaited weekly feuilleton "Wiener Spaziergänge" (which politicians recycled occasionally as parliamentary speeches), long-time fixture Ludwig Speidel (1830–1906), who regularly reviewed Schnitzler's plays, and Hugo Wittmann (1839–1923). In Schnitzler's own generation one could peruse the columns especially of Theodor Herzl (1860–1904), Stefan Zweig (1881–1942), Raoul Auernheimer (1876–1948), and Felix Salten (1869–1947).

Vignette writer Peter Altenberg, who reviewed Schnitzler's plays of the late 1890s, provides an example of the charismatic tone of feuilletonism. Having attended the Burg premiere of *Die Gefährtin* (The Companion) on March 1, 1899, Altenberg wrote that his remarks were not intended to criticize, but to discreetly display the originality of the reviewer.[38] More bluntly than most, Altenberg confirms that his motive for writing this review, aside from it's providing desperately needed income, is to leave an entertaining impression about the play, not to convey any real information about it. His extreme individualism exemplifies the apolitical personality encouraged by the economically liberal press.

It should thus be clear that the feuilleton reflected the sociohistorical reality of the organ in which it appeared — the increase in circulation, but also competition, in the newspaper industry — at the same time that its format commented on the ideology of the theater-going class with the time to be amused by it. This reality helps clarify Bahr's role in the development of autonomous criticism, particularly at the juncture of his disagreements with Brahm.

The overarching difference, as Sprengel and Streim have remarked, was between Brahm's institutional naturalist criticism and Bahr's autonomous criticism: for Bahr, criticism as a genre of modernity could no longer be considered subservient to drama, prose, and poetry.[39] While co-editor of the *Freie Bühne*, Bahr used the French form of *causerie* to submit anonymous musings under the rubrics "Von neuer Kunst" and "Suggestionen." Consciously modeled after French critic Jules Lemaitre's impressionistic, associative style, these sketches signaled a switch from evaluative to lyrical criticism, from a focus on the object of criticism to one on the critic.[40] The erstwhile Marxist Bahr put the description of spiritual states above that of objects.[41] An inverse relationship developed between Bahr's demands of modernist authors and his own critical self-conception: while telling Schnitzler to disappear behind objective self-description, Bahr himself increasingly filled the role of expositor, especially of his own ideas.

Not surprisingly, then, the feuilleton provided the best fit for Bahr's epistemology. In his last contribution to the *Freie Bühne*, Bahr defines the feuilleton as a genre affecting the nerves by dissolving the object world into mere stimulations from the senses. This epistemology of modernity at the level of the nerves can only be pessimistic, due to the nature of truth as inconstant, associative, and untrustworthy. Those who experience this "feuilletonistische Anschauung" are members of the fin de siècle.[42] Bahr's feuilletonistic style, his negation of naturalism, and his resounding French decadence were not consistent with Brahm's vision for the journal, and he resigned in July of 1890 when Brahm complained to Samuel Fischer (publisher of the *Freie Bühne*) about the "parfümirten Ekel" (rank repulsiveness) of Bahr's pseudonymous "Suggestionen."[43]

Bahr's 1887 essay on Ibsen in *Deutschen Worten*, written before he had "overcome" naturalism, called for criticism to bypass the provincialism responsible for the dismal Viennese reception of Ibsen's *Nora* in 1881, when the play was pulled after only three performances because of a suffocating pedanticism out of keeping with an audience that expected to be entertained.[44] Instead, the critic's job was to comprehend artists and art works in the context of their development and in relationship to their environment of ideas. Ibsen's themes, supported to a fault by Young Vienna, became the gold standard for Viennese modernism. Clearly Ibsen was the stumbling block of establishment criticism, making understandable Hofmannsthal's talk at seventeen of toppling all the newspaper patriarchs hostile to modern literature.[45] Bahr was promoting Viennese writers as a separate regional school with a trademark symbolist style, but Young Vienna already existed informally, with writers such as Schnitzler, Hofmannsthal, and Beer-Hofmann pursuing projects of their own. The most formal contact they had was to seek out each other's advice and support, frequently by reading each other their drafts and sending complimentary copies to each other.

As of September 1892, Bahr was feuilleton editor and theater critic for Vienna's *Deutsche Zeitung*. By 1894 he was feuilleton editor for *Die Zeit*, a Viennese liberal and pacifist weekly, modeled after the American paper *The Nation*, that offered notes on politics and business, with discussions of theater performances and original prose.[46] Bahr left the paper in 1899 to work for the *Neue Wiener Tagblatt*,[47] and it was largely because of his propaganda that Berlin readers formed their image of a symbolist literary modernity in Vienna. The adjectives "wienerisch" and "norddeutsch" postulated theater techniques, acting styles, and sub-genres — a Viennese play, a Viennese novel — as products of regionalism.[48]

Schnitzler had occasion to be grateful for Bahr's interventions on his behalf, some of which were crucial. A letter from Bahr resulted in the offer of Samuel Fischer Verlag to cover half the printing cost of *Anatol;* Bahr stepped in for Schnitzler when the Burgtheater stopped performing Schnitzler's one-act *Der grüne Kakadu* (The Green Cockatoo) in 1898; he was part of the protest against Paul Schlenther's failure to perform the Renaissance drama *Der Schleier der Beatrice* (The Veil of Beatrice) as promised for the Burg in 1900; and he intervened during the misapprehensions surrounding the Wiener Verlag's printing of *Reigen* in 1903. According to Donald Daviau, these endorsements were partly out of Bahr's concern for Schnitzler, and partly for the sake of advancing the cause of Austrian literature. As much as Bahr's malleable convictions sound like the rhetorical exercise of arguing both sides of an issue, Daviau explains, they are really evidence of his effort to raise cultural awareness.[49] All in all, Bahr stacked the cards in favor of Vienna's moderns over Germany's. As a conduit to Fischer, as a connection to the Burgtheater, and as an editor who published the work of his protégées in *Die Zeit*,

Bahr documented the "new psychology" of Young Vienna and assured it of a wider audience for its disparate ideas.

The Cultivation of Feuilletonism: Hermann Bahr and Alfred Kerr

"Was er bringt, ist nichtig. Aber wie er es bringt, darf gelten" (What he expresses is paltry, but how he expresses it is significant).[50] This appraisal by Bahr in 1893 of the importance of style over content in Schnitzler's *Anatol* cycle began thirteen years of interaction with Schnitzler's plays, from *Anatol* to *Zwischenspiel* (1906). In this instance, Bahr was describing the *Anatol* cycle as proof of Schnitzler's virtuosity in shaping a single feeling to perfection: Schnitzler's Parisian style holds more promise than the Parisian theme of salesgirls, cocottes, and debauchees, of which Anatol is the humbler Austrian version. Bahr's prophecy is that Schnitzler cannot hope for any profound effects on emotions given the secular themes and subjects he has skimmed from the surface of the times.[51] Convinced in his reviews that Schnitzler's charm prevails over depth, Bahr's call for Schnitzler to storm the stages of the monarchy sounds hollow.

Bahr's reviews show evidence of a feuilletonistic style seeking effect through short phrases and ironic turns. A more questionable ethical aspect surfaced with Bahr's review of *Liebelei* in 1895, however. In a conversation with Schnitzler, he confessed to having written two feuilletons for *Liebelei:* one in the event of its failure, in which he would praise it beyond measure, and one in the event of its success, where he would take it to task.[52] Because the play was a smash, Bahr opted for the latter, criticizing Fritz, Theodor, Christine, and Mizzi for echoing the resigned and listless types in *Anatol* and *Märchen*. If Schnitzler neglects to give a moral to the story, Bahr will deliver it instead: "Seid selber etwas! . . . Lebt, statt euch bloß leben zu lassen!" (Make something of yourselves! . . . Live, instead of just drifting!).[53] Drama, according to Bahr, is the art of bringing individuals into situations of conflict that force them, so to speak, to find their own colors — but at such drama Schnitzler fails regularly.[54]

It takes little time to realize how seriously Bahr takes his paternal role, which is evident again in his review of the one-act *Der Puppenspieler* (The Puppeteer, 1904), which premiered in Vienna's Carl-Theater on December 12, 1904. Comparing the perceived demise of Austria-Hungary to the fateful last night in *Der Schleier der Beatrice,* when the world is falling apart in Cesare Borgia's hands, Bahr preaches action and passion even in the face of death: "Ich glaube nicht mehr, Arthur, daß

Entsagung Reife ist. Ich glaube, sie ist nur innere Schwäche. . . . Ich glaube nur noch an die große Kraft ungestüm verlangender Leidenschaft" (448: Arthur, I no longer believe that resignation is maturity. I believe it is only inner weakness). It is no wonder that Bahr's criticism advocates strength and action. In late January of 1903, he had nearly died following an operation for appendicitis performed by Schnitzler's brother, Julius. The experience had sobered him enough to cause his return to his Catholic roots, which he kept on display from that point onward.[55] This accounts for the personal, experiential component in his criticism that overwhelms the aesthetic merit that can be deciphered in a close-reading of the play. Calling for Schnitzler to be more proactive, Bahr appears to retain nothing from his devotion to decadence except the pathos, as his review of *Der Puppenspieler* shows: "Wenn das Leben mir nicht gemäß ist, wer sagt dir denn, daß ich darum mich ändern muß, statt es? . . . mich verlangt nach kühneren [Gedanken], die die Kraft hätten, die Fäuste zu ballen und ins Leben zu strecken und es nicht zu lassen, bis es uns segnen wird" (If life doesn't suit me, who's to say that I have to change, instead of it? . . . I'm after more audacious [thoughts] with the strength to keep their fists up until life finally agrees to bless us).[56]

Bahr also shows a conservative streak in his 1899 dedication page for *Wiener Theater (1892–1898),* which contains his reviews on Viennese theater written originally for the *Deutsche Zeitung* and *Zeit.* Here, Bahr thanks Ludwig Speidel, feuilleton icon of *Neue Freie Presse,* for helping him progress from demands for a "recht vagen Schönheit" to a pure view of drama and the essence of theater that has put a stop to his moodiness. Speidel has taught him that the duty of criticism is to lend support to the writer of the work in question.[57] This is more than momentary sycophantism, for Bahr has in fact relinquished his modernism to become more conservative and normative by the end of the nineties. What will always ring true for Bahr in Schnitzler's work is what he himself has experienced, as is evident from his review of *Zwischenspiel:* "Dieses: man lebt mit einer Frau, hat sie gern und weiß doch eigentlich nichts von ihr, sie kann morgen eine andere sein, über Nacht. . . . Und dieses: wir glauben unser Schicksal zu regieren, aber es spielt mit uns und unser eigenes Leben lebt über uns hinweg" (This: you live with a woman, like her and know actually nothing about her, she can change completely overnight. . . . And this: we think we control our destiny, but it plays with us and our own life passes us by).[58] It is at least obvious that Schnitzler was more grateful for Bahr's patronage than for his advice.

Like Bahr, Berlin's Alfred Kerr (i.e. Alfred Kempner, 1867–1948), was at home in the realm of mood and nerves, but was more driven by verbal dexterity than by pathos. His customary exhibition of apathy toward an author under review surfaced rarely with respect to Schnitzler.[59] In an attempt to provide respectability for criticism within modernism, Kerr provided feuilletons for the monthly *Neue Deutsche Rundschau*, which grew out of Brahm's journal *Freie Bühne* in 1894 (becoming the *Neue Rundschau* in 1903). His 1896 review of *Anatol* and *Liebelei* reports his having devoured the one-act *Frage an das Schicksal* from *Anatol*.[60] According to Kerr, Schnitzler has the grace to take from symbolism only what he needs, inject it with realism, and depict atmospheres wafted through by "zartem Leichtsinn," shrouded in "schwermütigem Zweifel," swirled about by "holdem Betrug," full of "süßesten Elends," "stummen Schluchzens," "verschollener Thränen" and "toter Seligkeit." This relieves the pressure of naturalism's obsession with milieu: "Er verzichtet auf die Vollständigkeit — hosiannah! — und setzt die Andeutung an die Stelle des Quatschens. Endlich wieder!" (He avoids exhaustive description — hosanna! — and replaces chatter with nuance. Finally!)[61] As a decadent more pampered than degenerate, Anatol remains a refreshing alternative to his French counterparts and makes up for a few over-polished phrases of Schnitzler's.[62] *Liebelei*, on the other hand, carries an unnecessarily tragic conclusion. Kerr regrets that Schnitzler has Christine begin to evaluate the injustice done her by Fritz, instead of surrendering to pain, for bringing consciousness to bear on the tragedy spells the end of its effect.[63]

Kerr's review of *Der einsame Weg* in the *Neue Rundschau* is typical of his style and worldview. Referring to Paul Bourget's novel *Cosmopolis,* Kerr explains that he prefers cosmopolitan urban poets to earthy rural poets because a pale knowledge of the human soul satisfies longer than rosy-cheeked vulgarity.[64] The charms of the play make Schnitzler's readers long to trade places with his characters: after all, who doesn't want a life free of concerns and commitments, filled with women and the adoration of an eighteen-year-old? Who doesn't enjoy an occasional foray into melancholy (Kerr, 1904, 505–6)? The twilight turns the hedonist's allures into sadness, not because Schnitzler finds the pursuit of pleasure inherently wrong, but because it had to end sometime (506).

Stephan von Sala, for example, twenty-seven years Johanna's senior, derives a sick sense of charm from her suicide, which makes Sala's own decision for suicide a terrible thing indeed (506). The breath of sweet sadness from Schnitzler is less a "Weltbild" (view of the world) than a "Weltmannsbild" (view of a man of the world) (507) and later generations will have trouble understanding it. For this reason, Kerr advises Schnitzler to train himself, like Ibsen, in the clarity for which the Latin races are known; at the same time, he charges critics to avoid all manner of confusion and ambiguity, which are signs of impotence and swindling (508). Such concreteness, a trademark of the rural poet disdained by Kerr, nonetheless needs to be subsumed by city poets, in order for them to illuminate the workings of the human soul (508). Such concreteness, a trademark of the "Landdichter" Kerr discussed earlier, needs to be achieved for "heilige Großstadtpoesie" to illuminate the workings of the human soul (508). This view resembles Bahr's call for a precise readout of the soul's condition.

Unlike such writers as Thomas Mann and Hofmannsthal, Schnitzler rarely explained his works' intentions, which no doubt contributed to misunderstanding in the press.[65] Responding to Kerr's review privately, though, Schnitzler appeared most bothered that Kerr should take issue with Sala's behavior, even though it fit the character. More liberated than most critics, Kerr became slightly dogmatic whenever praising elements that corresponded to his worldview. The third act of *Der Ruf des Lebens* (The Call of Life, 1898), for example, considered by far the worst by Schnitzler, is the act Kerr finds the best, because what the physician says corresponds to Kerr's worldview: namely, that life goes on.[66] Schnitzler mentions nothing about Kerr's criticism of the second act: that the female protagonist Marie treads over two corpses to reach her cursed lover, making it a bit extreme that she can still want to sleep with a lieutenant (whom she has seen once before) after poisoning her father and witnessing a murder.[67] Kerr also questions the likelihood of Marie's poisoning her father instead of giving him a sleeping potion. It is going too far to excuse the murder because of its cleansing effect on a domestic atmosphere (497). But Kerr is willing to forget the second act for the sake of the third, in which he is gripped by Schnitzler's affirmation of life, no matter how terrible the experiences of the previous night have been for the characters: "Wenn man nur dann lebt! wenn man nur atmen darf! alles andere bleibt hiergegen wurst!" (497–98: To live! To be allowed breath! All else pales by comparison!). Kerr can call it true because it rhymes with his own recent thoughts about the call of life. Really, his conclusion supports Schnitzler's views more than Schnitzler himself has been willing to admit. Kerr's simple statement "Das Natürlichste ist, am Leben bleiben zu wollen" (The most natural thing is to want to stay alive) accords with Schnitzler's view that morality begins by admitting that a fear of death is natural. Kerr becomes Schnitzler's ally by recognizing that a work is progressive by virtue of helping to dismantle the notion of the hero (498). To both men, then, fear is less reprehensible than it is understandable.

Kerr's call for clarity commits him neither to encouraging artistic production nor to proffering it, like Brahm, to the literary public. Instead, as his own success grows, he touts criticism as a genre qualified to join the classical triad of epic, lyric, and drama. Fittingly, the title editors gave in 1982 to a compilation of Kerr's reviews, *Mit Schleuder und Harfe* (With Slingshot and Harp) points to his self-fashioning as part feuilletonist, part polemicist in the struggle against established literature. His words oscillate between a singing harp and a snapping slingshot, and he answers to no one. This lyrical belligerence, according to Russell Berman, flaunts Kerr's "unresolved antithesis" of life and art, in which the elite critical personality must transcend all discussions of art in the public sphere.[68]

Although we have concentrated on Kerr's earlier feuilletons on Schnitzler, it is interesting to note the role of the critic by the twenties: the social tensions and chaos of the Weimar Republic provide the critic with a blank check for a countermanding rationality.[69] Kerr considers himself among the intellectuals, providing the throng with electricity to light its way in a dark hall and prevent it from being trampled to death. Still shy of representing the public, Kerr seeks to educate it with "a reason that it is the task of the intelligentsia to proclaim as revelation."[70] Kerr peppers his prophetic work of demystification with occasional forays into politics. It is hard to imagine a platform with which Bertolt Brecht, in his mission to represent criticism for the masses, would disagree more. For Brecht, the notion of specialists bringing enlightenment to passive recipients is irreconcilable with the need to transform readers into critics.[71]

Normative Modernist Criticism: Paul Goldmann

Both Bahr and Kerr positioned themselves as charismatic personalities, hoping to win for themselves the audience they were ostensibly attempting to win for the author under review. Paul Goldmann (1865-?), on the other hand, who reviewed theater in Berlin for the *Neue Freie Presse*, was not in the business of wit. He furnishes examples of what might be labeled, somewhat paradoxically, modernist normative criticism. In other words, his tone mimicked the scolding tone of longstanding critics such as Karl Frenzel (whose essays on Berlin theater appeared in Berlin's *Neue Deutsche Rundschau*), but was concerned less about Schnitzler's perceived ignorance of traditional dramatical rules than about his forsaking of modern themes. Goldmann published three volumes of Berlin reviews, all of them introduced by explanations of his disappointment with modern drama in Germany. *Die "neue Richtung"* (The "New Direction") appeared in 1903, followed in 1905 by *Aus dem dramatischen Irrgarten* (From the Dramatic Labyrinth) and in 1908 by *Vom Rückgang der deutschen Bühne* (On the Decline of the German Stage).[72]

Goldmann's review of the Renaissance drama *Der Schleier der Beatrice* shows his moralistic concern that Schnitzler's characters are not tragic enough "als daß sie ein Recht hätten, sich so zu erdolchen und zu vergiften" (to have the right to be stabbed or poisoned).[73] Outfitting the characters of a Renaissance drama with the moods of a spoiled Anatol undercuts effective tragedy and invites failure. After all, drama must justify the action on stage. It is bad enough that Beatrice shares Anatol's inconstancy, which Goldmann grants her because she is a woman — "und darum ist sie so ganz besonders wandelbar" (115: which is why she is particularly fickle). The inexcusable fact, though, is that the play's two male heroes share Beatrice's fickleness. Filippo sets the audience muttering by taking seriously Beatrice's dream that she has become the duke's bride. Can a serious drama suggest a dream is sufficient cause for Filippo's abrupt dismissal of Beatrice (118)? And for the duke to insist on the propriety of marriage is uncharacteristic behavior, since most high-ranking Renaissance men would think nothing of having their way with Beatrice (122–23). At one time or another, both men shut out Beatrice for inconsequential reasons (124). Goldmann questions whether death has to be the immediate and sole solution to unsuccessful love, as though lovers had no will to make each other happy by staying alive. Jealousy is not a credible motivation for the suicide Filippo and Beatrice have planned, leaving only an aftertaste of moods reminiscent of Anatol (120). Despite the play's shortcomings, Goldmann considers Schnitzler among the few writers serious about German drama, a writer whose greatness is impeded only by his lingering Anatol-melancholy (124).

Goldmann agrees with Kerr that in both *Der einsame Weg* and *Der Schleier der Beatrice,* Schnitzler's suicides are short on tragic necessity (189). Johanna's drowning even causes some in the audience to laugh: no one should be laughing at a play superior to Hauptmann's *Rose Bernd,* but one can demand that an author sufficiently motivate an effect so crass as suicide and begin to see how unsuitable it is to have tragic necessity supplanted by mood (191). Still, Goldmann believes that the real fault with the play resides in the coldhearted womanizers Fichtner and Sala, whose egoism hints at no alternative. They are wired to destroy the women they seduce (193–94). That Schnitzler punishes them with loneliness in old age is not a moral enough punishment, because confession without regret falls short (195).

Goldmann can tell, judging by the hissing at the Berlin premiere of *Der Ruf des Lebens* at the Lessingtheater in 1906, that Schnitzler's dramas suffer not only from insufficient motivation for tragedy, but also from characters so morally despicable as to be unbelievable. Marie's father delights in refusing to grant his daughter any vacation from caring for him. Max cavorts with Marie minutes after his mistress is shot in cold blood by her husband, the colonel, whose revenge will not be satisfied until the entire regiment dies for her adultery.[74] As always, Goldmann criticizes the use of death as a cheap dramatic vehicle, especially because there is no sense of death's grandeur either in how characters die or in how death is discussed (170–71).

Like death, love forfeits its intended grand effect and sinks to the level of erotic mood, but Goldmann dismisses abnormal sex drives that masquerade as a "call of life" (168). For Marie to kill her sick and autocratic father to satisfy an erotic mood (Goldmann is interpreting rather strictly here) is less tragic than it is repulsive (169). Strong theatrical effects cannot paper over a plot and characters that lack credibility (172). Thus it behooves Goldmann, as Schnitzler's honest friend (as fell to Bahr before him), to warn him relentlessly of failures springing from plots taken from a narrow sector of erotic experiences from which no guiding principles can be derived (172–73). Anatol-eroticism will restrict his writing: he must search for the path "zum echten, großen Leben" (173: to the authentic, great life).

This taste of Goldmann's criticism poses the question of whether his misgivings about Schnitzler are influenced by his aesthetics or due to interpretation alone. A *Neue Freie Presse* correspondent needs to base observations on more than impressions, and indeed a look at the introductory essays to Goldmann's collected reviews reveals a modernist impulse that has been softened and even negated by a normative aesthetic. The principle of benevolent criticism, attributable to Otto Brahm, does not in Goldmann's view diminish the necessity to purge poor art to create the space for authentic art to develop (1903, 16). During the time that Ibsen's standard for modern drama has held sway in Germany, Ibsen himself has been the only high point. Hauptmann's *Die Weber* has been a happy surprise, but fellow dramatists Otto Erich Hartleben and Georg Hirschfeld have become stuck following the outdated naturalist milieu standards of Zola and the Goncourts instead of Maupassant (Goldmann

1903, 8–10). "Weil ein Dichter ein Naturalist sein kann, so folgt daraus noch lange nicht, daß ein Naturalist ein Dichter ist" (11: While a writer may well be a naturalist, this is no guarantee that a naturalist is a writer).

According to Goldmann, instead of pointing the way, the moderns have gotten in the way. Germany's only equivalent to a Tolstoy, Ibsen, or Wilde is the composer Richard Wagner, who would capture the heart of the *Volk* if he dropped composition for writing (1905, 8–9). Confused about their mission, German writers have mistaken "modern" for "naturalistic," and Brahm's decade of tenacious leadership of Berlin's Deutsches Theater, which promised a new direction, has settled instead for a monotonous repertoire built largely around Hauptmann (1905, 13). Presenting stark and ugly facts does not yield a convincing image of reality. Busy producing mediocrity, naturalists have neglected the cultivation of personality that might lead to real greatness. It is a wonder that such "kleinen Geister" (small minds) are considered by definition to be better than journalists (1905, 25–27). Due to the competitiveness of Berlin theaters, "modern" becomes a tag for selling dramas, and one can always count on perversion and vulgarity to compensate for an author's lack of creativity and strength (1905, 30–31).

As Goldmann sees it, the Tolstoys and Ibsens of the 1880s, unconstrained by philistine morality or technical limitations, had expanded both the topical repertoire and the ability to depict those topics through drama (1908, 10). Such issues included, among others, the clerical debate, the plight of the individual under capitalism, the effect of scientific progress on metaphysical needs, the liberation of women, and the homesickness for nature (1908, 12–13). Goldmann hears the clarion sounding for young German writers, calling them to achieve greatness by learning their trade from the French and then to address an urgent problem of their generation without resorting to a naturalistic milieu depiction. The savior of German drama will be recognized by stormy approval from the theatergoing audience and by profound disapproval by the literary guild (1908, 43). Unable to escape this disapproval himself, Goldmann justifies his withdrawal from public debate with the notion that freedom from answering his opponents gives him the space to proclaim the failure of modern art, whereby he can trust that history, even as he writes, is vindicating his opinions (1908, 14).

The motivation for the plot of Goldmann's own criticism becomes transparent in his review of Schnitzler's one-act cycle *Lebendige Stunden* in *Neue Freie Presse* (January 22, 1902).[75] In the third one-act, *Die letzten Masken,* Karl Rademacher is a dying journalist who plans to assuage his feelings of inferiority toward Alexander Weihgast, now a successful dramatist, by revealing that Weihgast's wife had a two-year affair with him. But Goldmann's plot description exceeds mere interpretation to reveal an uncommonly bitter envy toward Schnitzler. Ostensibly, though a mere journalist, Rademacher is more of a writer than Weihgast, because his profession has taught him to experience more deeply. The thousands of articles that have arisen and vanished with the day depict a personality still unrecognized by the public, because the public has been duped into recognizing only the formula "literarisch" while assuming journalism's separation from literature (1902, 4). Weihgast has not had to write for a newspaper, since his skill has consisted of anticipating audience tastes and finding a literary form to match what Goldmann considers impoverished thoughts and a simplistic worldview (4).

By the time of Weihgast's arrival, Rademacher has already vented his venom in a practice run on his hospital roommate. In real life, however, Goldmann/Rademacher clearly vents his feelings of inferiority in full view of the *Neue Freie Presse* readership. Schnitzler, more recognized and successful in the public eye than Goldmann ever would be, comes across as the more mean-spirited of the two. Goldmann calls for him to put aside the one-act and express the spirit of the times in a drama of grand style (1902, 4). What is more, Schnitzler owes the public a strong and mature work based on something besides the love affairs that set the tenor of his one-acts: "Denn die Liebe, obwohl sie eine nicht unwichtige Angelegenheit des Daseins bildet, ist doch immer nur eine Episode im Leben, während in Arthur Schnitzlers Schriften umgekehrt das Leben oft als eine Episode in der Liebe erscheint" (4: Even though sex makes up a significant aspect of existence, it is still but an episode within life, whereas in Arthur Schnitzler's writings life appears frequently as an episode within sex).

Schnitzler traced most of Goldmann's complaints to jealousy, but also to a fickle commitment to modernism. Before working for the *Neue Freie Presse,* Goldmann had been employed by the *Frankfurter Zeitung,* for which his uncle Fedor Mamroth wrote theater reviews. In the late eighties and early nineties, he and Mamroth co-edited and published a journal of modern literature, *An der schönen blauen Donau,* in which three of Schnitzler's stories (*Amerika, Mein Freund Ypsilon, Der Andere*) and two short plays (*Alkandis Lied, Episode*) appeared. What is more, he had introduced Schnitzler to Richard Beer-Hofmann and Hugo von Hofmannsthal, and with Kerr had gotten to know Schnitzler during a two-week hiking trek through the Swiss Alps.

Goldmann's advice against the modern one-act form therefore indicated a shift from modern to academicist thinking, a shift Schnitzler attributed more to circumstances than to any particular conviction. Any gratitude Schnitzler showed for being published in Goldmann's journal was returned as jealousy, since it was clear that by 1896 Goldmann was standing in his protégé's shadow. In that year, while covering the trial of the Jew Alfred Dreyfus (1859–1935) in Paris for the *Frankfurter Zeitung*, Goldmann fought a duel to defend his written opinion that Dreyfus's indictment was based on a judicial error. Schnitzler reminded Goldmann that *Freiwild* had been written against compulsory dueling and its myth that standing behind a conviction with one's life somehow legitimized the conviction. According to Ellen Butzkow, Schnitzler writes Goldmann into his journalistic comedy *Fink und Fliederbusch* (1917) as Abendstern, the malleable critic of the democratic paper *Die Gegenwart*, which like the *Neue Freie Presse* avoids confrontation with other papers by always insisting on smoothing out differences. Schnitzler's issue is with critics being paid to write opinions parroting the official stance of the newspaper, and Abendstern/Goldmann is one who stifles his own opinion in order to stay employed.[76] Struggling to survive as a journalist, Goldmann made it clear that he would be producing masterpieces on the scale Schnitzler did, if he only had a physician's practice and a father's money on which he could rely: this warrants reading the above criticism of *Die letzten Masken* allegorically.

Goldmann's reviews are rough on Schnitzler, but not so acerbic as those of Alfred Polgar, Karl Kraus, Heinrich Hart, Julius Bab, or Paul Lerch, to name but a few. He acknowledges that Schnitzler is doing more for modernity than most of the writers championed by Brahm. Schnitzler still needs guidance from a well-meaning friend concerning some shortcomings: Goldman finds that the plays use material better suited for a novella, have a lack of compelling motivation for tragic events (i.e. overuse death as a cheap dramatic vehicle), contain too much reflection and not enough action ("Anatol-Stimmungen" rather than great feelings) and have predictable themes, and that Schnitzler lacks the ambition to attempt a *Lustspiel* or something greater than a one-act play. Goldmann's envy for the fame of a successful author, meanwhile, is unmistakable.

From the foregoing, it is clear that *Literaturkritik* at the turn of the century reflected bias and personal impressions rather than the science advocated by Bahr and Scherer.[77] Feuilletonists often cultivated a personal style at the expense of thoroughgoing analysis of the text, hence the text, through no fault of its own, became a means to the critic's end. Schnitzler insisted on focusing on the negative reviews, regardless of his relatively fair reception by the liberal press. In his oversensitive estimation, literati withheld praise because they were jealous of his success.[78] Unwilling to take criticism lying down, Schnitzler leveled at his critics their own accusations of repetitiveness and lack of imagination, adding for good measure that they reflected the breakdown of the liberal values of integrity and fairness. To Schnitzler, the loss of critical autonomy was as much a question of responsibility as of social causes. A journalist's inconsistent convictions signaled moral corruption.[79] In his aphorisms on art and criticism, Schnitzler repeatedly presents Goethe as a model for consistency, and turns the tables on accusations of moral corruption by exposing the "written prostitution" of his critics — Georg Lukács's term for how feuilletonism allows surface freedom but no departure from a deeper party line.[80]

At their worst, Schnitzler's reviewers produced a form of kitsch designed for quick consumption.[81] At their best, critics could transcend the fake essence of feuilletonism that made it as shallow as his characters were accused of being. Critics such as Albert Kerr had made the case for criticism as the "fourth genre," but serious criticism had to wait for the beginnings of *Literaturwissenschaft,* where the attempt was not to usurp the object of study or push across one's own agenda, but rather to bring the reader toward a fuller, well-reasoned understanding of an author's works. Whether there is such a thing as "literary science" is debatable, especially when one bears in mind that a few feuilletonists displayed a talent far greater than so-called objective academic criticism.

Notes

[1] Arthur Schnitzler, "Mein Kritiker," quoted in Lore B. Foltin, "The Meaning of Death in Schnitzler's Work," in *Studies in Arthur Schnitzler: Centennial Commemorative Volume,* ed. Herbert W. Reichert and Hermann Salinger (New York: AMS Press, 1966), 35–44, here 37.

[2] Peter Uwe Hohendahl, "The Epoch of Liberalism, 1820–1870," trans. Jeffrey S. Librett, in *A History of German Literary Criticism,* ed. Hohendahl (1988), 179–276, here 275–76.

[3] Peter Sprengel and Gregor Streim, *Berliner und Wiener Moderne: Vermittlungen und Abgrenzungen in Literatur, Theater, Publizistik* (Vienna: Böhlau, 1998), 45.

[4] See Hohendahl, "The Epoch of Liberalism, 1820–1870," 181.

[5] Oskar Seidlin, introduction to *Der Briefwechsel Arthur Schnitzler — Otto Brahm,* ed. Oskar Seidlin (Tübingen: Max Niemeyer Verlag, 1975), xvi–xvii.

[6] Russell Berman, "From Empire to Dictatorship, 1870–1933," Hohendahl (1988a): 277–357, here 301–2.

[7] Maxim Newmark, *Otto Brahm: The Man and the Critic* (Menasha, WI: George Banta Publ. Co., 1938), 134.

[8] Newmark, *The Man and the Critic* (1938), 136.

[9] Otto Brahm, *Über Drama und Theater*, vol. 1 of *Kritische Schriften*, ed. Paul Schlenther (Berlin: Fischer, 1915), 378.

[10] Brahm, *Kritische Schriften* (1915), 378.

[11] Newmark, *The Man and the Critic* (1938), 118.

[12] These fallacies are discussed in Newmark, *The Man and the Critic* (1938), 119–27.

[13] Brahm, *Kritische Schriften* (1915), 323.

[14] Newmark, *The Man and the Critic* (1938), 133.

[15] Seidlin, *Briefwechsel* (1975), xv.

[16] Alfred Kerr, "Der einsame Weg," *Neue Rundschau* 15/4 (April 1904).

[17] Reinhard Urbach, in his book *Schnitzler-Kommentar zu den erzählenden Schriften und dramatischen Werken* (Munich: Winkler, 1974) captures Bahr's role aptly with the image of a Griensteidl ventilator fanning the warm wind of French impressionism and the storm of Berlin naturalism (22). However, Bahr was far less interested in the latter.

[18] Eduard Michael Kafka, "Gesellschaftliche Zusammenhänge," *Moderne Rundschau* 3/1 (April 1, 1891), 2, quoted in Gotthart Wunberg, introduction to *Die Wiener Moderne: Literatur, Kunst und Musik zwischen 1890 und 1910,* ed. Wunberg (Stuttgart: Reclam, 1981), 23.

[19] Sprengel and Streim, *Berliner und Wiener Moderne* (1998), 83.

[20] Bahr, "Die Décadence," in Bahr, *Studien zur Kritik der Moderne* (Frankfurt am Main: Rütten & Loening, 1894), 26–32, reprinted in Wunberg, *Wiener Moderne* (1981), 225–32, here 225.

[21] Wunberg, *Wiener Moderne* (1981), 31.

[22] Wunberg, *Wiener Moderne* (1981), 33.

[23] Sprengel and Streim, *Berliner und Wiener Moderne* (1998), 50.

[24] Bahr was also following Ola Hansson's criticism of naturalism: see Sprengel and Streim, *Berliner und Wiener Moderne* (1998), 52–53.

[25] Kurt Paupié, *Handbuch der österreichischen Pressegeschichte 1848–1959,* vol. 1: *Wien* (Vienna: Wilhelm Braumüller, 1960), 144–45.

[26] Richard Grunberger, "Jews in Austrian Journalism," in *The Jews of Austria: Essays on Their Life, History, and Destruction,* ed. Josef Fraenkel (London: Vallentine, 1967), 83–95, here 83–84. See also Karlheinz Rossbacher, *Literatur und Liberalismus: Zur Kultur der Ringstrassenzeit in Wien* (Vienna: J&V, 1992), 88.

[27] Paupié, *Pressegeschichte* (1960), 148.

[28] Fritz Schlawe, *Literarische Zeitschriften 1885–1910* (Stuttgart: Metzler, 1965), 91–92.

[29] See Carl Schorske, *Fin-de-Siècle Vienna: Politics and Culture* (New York: Vintage Books, 1981), 116–80.

[30] Stefan Zweig, *Die Welt von gestern: Erinnerungen eines Europäers* (Frankfurt am Main: Fischer, 1970), 58 (reprint of the original edition, Stockholm: Bermann-Fischer, 1946).

[31] William Johnston, *The Austrian Mind: An Intellectual and Social History 1848–1938* (Berkeley: U of California P, 1972), 120–21.

[32] L. H. Bailey, "Ferdinand Kürnberger, Friedrich Schlögl, and the Feuilleton in Gründerzeit Vienna," in *Austrian Life and Literature 1780–1938*, ed. Peter Branscombe (Edinburgh: Scottish Academic Press, 1978), 59–71, here 59.

[33] Alfred Polgar, "Der Wiener Feuilleton" (1906), reprinted in Polgar, *Sperrsitz*, ed. Ulrich Weinzierl (Vienna: Löcker Verlag, 1980), 33–37, here 33–34.

[34] Andrea Willi, *Arthur Schnitzlers Roman* Der Weg ins Freie: *Eine Untersuchung zur Tageskritik und ihren zeitgenössischen Bezugen* (Heidelberg: Carl Winter Universitätsverlag, 1989), 121–22.

[35] Ellen Butzko, *Arthur Schnitzler und die zeitgenössische Theaterkritik* (Frankfurt am Main: Peter Lang, 1991), 22–23, 29.

[36] Rossbacher, *Ringstrassenzeit* (1992), 83–84.

[37] Raoul Auernheimer, *Das Wirtshaus zur verlorenen Zeit: Erlebnisse und Bekenntnisse* (Vienna: Ullstein Verlag, 1948), 87.

[38] Peter Altenberg, review of *Die Gefährtin*, by Arthur Schnitzler, *Extrapost* (6 March 1899), 5, reprinted in Robert Werba, "Ein Außenseiter der Theaterkritik: Peter Altenberg und das Wiener Theaterjahr 1898/99," *Maske und Kothurn* 20/2 (1974): 163–90, here 177.

[39] Sprengel and Streim, *Berliner und Wiener Moderne* (1998), 57.

[40] Sprengel and Streim, *Berliner und Wiener Moderne* (1998), 59.

[41] Jens Rieckmann, *Aufbruch in die Moderne: Die Anfänge des Jungen Wien: Österreichische Literatur und Kritik im Fin de Siècle* (Tübingen: Athenäum, 1985), 25–27.

[42] Sprengel and Streim, *Berliner und Wiener Moderne* (1998), 63–64.

[43] Sprengel and Streim, *Berliner und Wiener Moderne* (1998), 65.

[44] Rieckmann, *Aufbruch* (1985), 16.

[45] Rieckmann, *Aufbruch* (1985), 78.

[46] Rieckmann, *Aufbruch* (1985), 85.

[47] Wunberg, *Wiener Moderne* (1981), 49.

[48] Sprengel and Streim, *Berliner und Wiener Moderne* (1998), 90, 95.

[49] Donald Daviau, introduction to *The Letters of Arthur Schnitzler to Hermann Bahr*, by Arthur Schnitzler (Chapel Hill: U of North Carolina P, 1978), 21.

[50] Hermann Bahr (1893), "Das junge Österreich," *Deutsche Zeitung*, 20 September 1893 (1–2); 27 September (1–3); 7 October (1–3), morning ed. Abridged and reprinted, in Wunberg, Wiener Moderne (1981), 297.

[51] Bahr, "Das junge Österreich" (1893), in Wunberg, Wiener Moderne (1981), 298.

[52] Diary entry of 21 January 1896.

[53] Hermann Bahr, *Das Wiener Theater (1892–1898)* (Berlin: Fischer, 1899), 83–84.

[54] Bahr, *Wiener Theater* (1899), 86.

[55] Daviau, *Letters* (1978), 28.

[56] Bahr, Hermann, Review of *Der Puppenspieler*, by Arthur Schnitzler, Carl-Theater, 12 December 1904, in Bahr, *Glossen zum Wiener Theater (1903–1906)* (Berlin: Fischer, 1907), 440–49, here 447.

[57] Hermann Bahr, dedication to Ludwig Speidel, *Wiener Theater* (1899).

[58] Hermann Bahr, review of *Zwischenspiel*, by Arthur Schnitzler, in Bahr, *Glossen* (1907): 91–92.

[59] Butzko, *Zeitgenössische Theaterkritik* (1991), 23.

[60] Alfred Kerr, Arthur Schnitzler, reviews of *Anatol* and *Liebelei*, by Arthur Schnitzler, *Neue Deutsche Rundschau* 7/3 (March 1896): 287–92, here 288.

[61] Kerr, *Anatol and Liebelei* (1896), 289.

[62] Kerr, *Anatol and Liebelei* (1896), 287–90.

[63] Kerr, *Anatol and Liebelei* (1896), 291.

[64] Alfred Kerr, review of *Der einsame Weg*, by Arthur Schnitzler, *Neue Rundschau* 15/4 (April 1904): 504–8, here 504–5.

[65] See Urbach, *Schnitzler-Kommentar* (1974), 29.

[66] Schnitzler, "Bemerkungen zu Alfred Kerrs Schriften," Schnitzler (1993), 137. Schnitzler finds Kerr's objection as banal as Kerr's wish that Hofreiter in *Das weite Land* was not such a good tennis player.

[67] Alfred Kerr, "Oedipus und der Ruf des Lebens," review of *Der Ruf des Lebens*, by Arthur Schnitzler, *Neue Rundschau* 17/5 (May 1906): 492–98, here 496.

[68] Berman, "Empire to Dictatorship" (1988), 305–6.

[69] Berman, "Empire to Dictatorship" (1988), 310.

[70] Berman, "Empire to Dictatorship" (1988), 311.

[71] In this respect, Berman likens the later Kerr to the Hungarian Marxist critic Georg Lukács (1885–1971), whom he also counts among the elite. See Berman (1988), 326–28.

[72] Paul Goldmann, *Die neue Richtung: Polemische Aufsätze über Berliner Theateraufführungen* (Vienna: C. W. Stern, 1903); *Aus dem dramatischen Irrgarten: Polemische Aufsätze über Berliner Theateraufführungen* (Frankfurt am Main: Literarische Anstalt Rütten & Loening, 1905); *Vom Rückgang der deutschen Bühne: Polemische Aufsätze über Berliner Theateraufführungen* (Frankfurt am Main: Literarische Anstalt Rütten & Loening, 1908).

[73] Paul Goldmann, review of *Der Schleier der Beatrice*, by Arthur Schnitzler, Deutsches Theater, in Goldmann (1905), 109–24, here 110. Subsequent references appear in parentheses in the text.

[74] Paul Goldmann, review of *Der Ruf des Lebens*, by Arthur Schnitzler, in Goldmann (1908), 164–73, here 169–70.

[75] Goldmann, "Feuilleton. Berliner Theater: *Lebendige Stunden* von Arthur Schnitzler," *Neue Freie Presse*, morning ed. (22 January 1902): 1–4.

[76] Butzko, *Zeitgenössische Theaterkritik* (1991), 108–9.

[77] Richard Hamann and Jost Hermand, *Deutsche Kunst und Kultur von der Gründerzeit bis zum Expressionismus*, vol. 3, *Impressionismus*, 2nd ed. (Berlin: Akademie-Verlag, 1966), 113–15, 233.

[78] Butzko, *Zeitgenössische Theaterkritik* (1991), 36.

[79] Schnitzler, *Bemerkungen* (1993), 19.

[80] Georg Lukács, *Writer & Critic, and other Essays* (New York: Grosset, 1970).

[81] Matei Calinescu, *Five Faces of Modernity: Modernism, Avant-Garde, Decadence, Kitsch, Postmodernism*, 2nd. ed. (Durham, NC: Duke UP, 1987), 229.

2: The First Critical Monographs

ON MAY 12, 1933, the newspaper *Neuköllner Tageblatt* reported that students had burned books the previous night, stoking a blaze as a Nazi band beat out march music. One student, for example, flinging books of Heinrich Mann, Ernst Glaeser and Erich Kästner into the flames, shouted his incantation against moral decadence: "Gegen Dekadenz und moralischen Verfall! Für Zucht und Sitte in Familie und Staat!"[1] This fiery ritual not only pronounced the literal loss of free speech, but also the style of criticism under National Socialism, which was in fact no criticism at all, but evidence of hegemonic power scattering the opposition to clear the way for one oppressive ideal. The cremation of intellectual property was also the inevitable outcome of decadence rhetoric during Schnitzler's lifetime, no matter how innocent its critical intentions early on.

This escalating suffocation of criticism is documented in Rolf Geissler's account of the Nazi dichotomy of decadence and heroism. Geissler argues that to survive, criticism must recognize historical truth in retrospect, because it cannot rely on pure assertions. A judgment about art becomes criticism only when it corresponds to internal properties of the work that are independently verifiable. Openness to the historical nature of truth runs counter to the polemics of authoritarianism, of course; criticism becomes superfluous when all opposing interpretations have been defamed or their authors convinced to conform.[2]

In Nazi criticism Schnitzler was remembered as little more than the decadent author of *Reigen,* an author whose works such as *Der Weg ins Freie* (1908) or *Professor Bernhardi* (1912) were variations on the theme of *Entartung* (degeneration). Even while his works were being labeled decadent, though, serious scholarship of his works began to take shape in the final two decades of Schnitzler's life, and three of these major works are featured here: Theodor Reik's *Arthur Schnitzler als Psycholog* (1913), Josef Körner's *Arthur Schnitzlers Gestalten und Probleme* (1921), and Bernhard Blume's dissertation *Das nihilistische Weltbild Arthur Schnitzlers* (1936). Of these, only Reik's book appeared early enough to ignore the growing rhetoric of *völkisch* — soon to be Nazi — criticism.

Psychoanalysis as Theme: Theodor Reik, *Arthur Schnitzler als Psycholog* (1913)

Reik, a thoughtful and zealous follower of Freud, who was one of his close colleagues, published the first scientific and highly disputed investigation. Reading Reik's book during a close scrutiny of psychoanalytical methods, Schnitzler found Reik's critique of his works thorough and mostly accurate. A section of the book even records a collaborative effort by Reik and Schnitzler to interpret the dreams of Georg von Wergenthin, the protagonist in Schnitzler's novel *Der Weg ins Freie.*[3] Reik's book is perhaps best introduced by Konstanze Fliedl's appraisal that it is both psychoanalysis and detective novel, because Reik makes Schnitzler into a patient suspected of archetypal crimes.[4] According to his own account, Reik has chosen to study crime because of a vicarious interest in it. Like most detectives, he has been motivated by the guilt of his own repressed murderous instincts, but unlike most, he is aware of the motivation. As a psychoanalyst interested in literature, he finds it natural to examine Schnitzler's psyche indirectly via his characters, so as to bring to light any incriminating evidence against Schnitzler. Patricide and incest are two of the main crimes whose clues lie in the texts or in the author himself.[5] As Fliedl observes, Schnitzler's memory takes on the status of a confession he is forced to sign.[6]

Reik finds his first clues for patricide in Oedipal triangles, whereby sons attempt to vanquish their fathers or surrogate fathers in love and work. In the example of *Der Ruf des Lebens* (1905), the officer Max tries to steal the wife of his father-figure colonel. Really, the Oedipal triangle expands to encapsulate any level of generational conflict. In *Der Weg ins Freie,* Georg von Wergenthin is not only haunted by his deceased father, but must listen to paternal advice from Dr. Stauber about his responsibility toward Anna, and this message is echoed by his older brother Felician. Dr. Stauber and his son also reproduce Schnitzler's career conflict with his father concerning the choice between medicine and writing. Moreover, Reik cannot help noticing that Schnitzler was preoccupied enough by memories of his father to feature him in *Professor Bernhardi* (1912) (146–47).

The crime of incest is central to the plot of *Frau Beate und ihr Sohn* (1913), a work that is really a variation on the theme of lovers who are maternal. Many Schnitzler figures seek lovers who appeal to their need for mother surrogates and are thus incapable of providing more than temporary satisfaction (133). Beyond those archetypal crimes, several other Freudian concepts emerge in Reik's analysis of Schnitzler. The most basic of these — the benefit of cathartic therapy — is evident in *Die Toten schweigen* (The Dead Keep Silent, 1897), where Emma believes peace will come from divulging to her husband the news of her infidelity and Franz's death (92). There is the voyeurism and exhibitionism in *Fräulein Else* (1924), attributed in terms of infantile sexuality to abnormal childhood activity. Then there is Freud's theory of "secondary defenses," by which motifs of jealousy are marks of penance and prevention (91). In *Die Hirtenflöte* (The Shepherd's Pipe, 1911), for example, Erasmus's wisdom masks a jealousy that is a classic "Affektverschiebung": Erasmus denies his own denial. Men who promise to be a refuge for their returning wives fool themselves, because they are at least a step removed from self-knowledge. Schnitzler's male figures are also frequently jealous as a result of their own impulse to infidelity, which they project onto their partners (101). Underneath jealousy are hidden homosexual proclivities as well: a woman becomes irresistible to the degree another man has had a claim on her. Rivals fan the flame of libido — Reik draws here on Wilhelm Stekel's 1912 essay "Masken der Homosexualität" — so that one can interpret Fedor's hatred of Fanny's first lover in *Märchen* as an unconscious desire (117). Similarly, dormant childhood sexuality becomes latent through feelings of sympathy in the story *Der Andere* (The Other Man, 1889), where the protagonist's heart goes out to his own wife's lover, whom he notices at her grave (122).

The concept of a defense mechanism is apparent in *Der Weg ins Freie*, where Heinrich Bermann describes "Verstehen" as a genteel sport having little to do with feelings or actions, and unable to protect from suffering. This view of "Verstehen" is itself a protection mechanism that keeps Heinrich from facing his own jealousy (96). The sadistic trait of jealousy is close to masochism. Those who have been wronged derive pleasure from the pain they are in no hurry to see leave — and they cannot forgive wrong, either. Reik quotes Friedrich Schleiermacher's saying: "Eifersucht ist eine Leidenschaft, die mit Eifer sucht, was Leiden schafft" (104: Jealousy is a passion that fervently seeks suffering).

Dreams, too, reveal crimes, and in the dreams of his characters Schnitzler provides Reik with protocols that demand exposition. Even though they are fictional constructs, their dictated status is proof to Reik of a form that approximates real sleeping dreams. He interprets the dreams of Beatrice in *Der Schleier der Beatrice* and of Berta in *Frau Berta Garlan* before turning to Georg's dreams in *Der Weg ins Freie*, where Schnitzler aids him. Reik's thoughts on the first of the dreams must here suffice to show his method. Using Freudian economic terms, he categorizes the dream as one that has arisen because the day residue has provided an entrepreneur that has turned for support to the capitalist of the unconscious (175).

The catalyst for the dream is traceable to the occasion when the duke has marveled at Beatrice's beauty, paying no attention to her older sister Rosina, who is heartsick for his return. Beatrice is satisfied the duke has paid attention to her at the expense of her sister (175). The dream itself is an outlet for revenge against her often abusive sister. Instead of the unconscious wishes present in most dreams, one notices here subconscious and unresolved wishes. Beatrice's wish that she, a poor shopkeeper's daughter, might become the lover of a duke is answered and suppressed by a reference to the fidelity she owes Filippo Loschi. But the triumph over her sister flatters her ego. Fearing her sister, she flees to her room to change clothes for Filippo — but really for the duke.

The dream fulfills her ambition and desire for revenge, at the same time furthering her erotic attraction to the duke and her narcissism, which is an infantile leftover that delivers the necessary impetus to the subconscious to spark the dream. Beatrice's attitude toward her sister reflects the usual ambivalence between siblings. Rosina, a veteran of love, demands Beatrice's obedience through harsh words and slaps. She has taken over the maternal role, which Beatrice now imitates: she too is disloyal to her lover (Filippo) in order to offer herself to a higher man. Her identification with the mother is manifested in the dream. Filippo, who bows his knee in the dream, is like all the others, while the duke replaces him as lover.

A second determining factor for the dream goes directly against the strong maternal identification to focus on the duke as the father surrogate. Beatrice thus jettisons the mother in order to become her father's wife, fulfilling the law that children fixate on the parent of opposite gender. The small element of the dream reinforcing this interpretation is that the father of Beatrice and Rosina has experienced time as frozen since his wife's infidelity. He treats his children as though they were still young, playing with them and telling them fairy tales. This delusion hastens the surfacing of incestuous leanings; Beatrice also is always referred to as a child (176–78). Her childlike nature makes for a dream more easily interpretable than most adult dreams, while showing a clearer wish fulfillment. After finishing his interpretation of this and the subsequent dreams, Reik makes it clear that their function is to fulfill the wishes that were incompatible with the moral consciousness of the characters, allowing an outlet for affects either impermissible or impossible to achieve in waking life (205).

Reik's rigid psychoanalytic categories and practice of psychoanalyz-ing both Schnitzler and his characters are apparent in a "Freudian slip" to which Fliedl draws attention from her careful reading. Due to a mis-placed comma, the sentence he intends — "Die Art Schnitzlers, Gefühle zu zergliedern und ihren verborgenen Zusammenhängen nachzufor-schen, ist die psychoanalytische" (Schnitzler's way of analyzing emotions and their hidden connections is psychoanalytical) — actually reads "Die Art, Schnitzlers Gefühle zu zergliedern und ihren verborgenen Zusammen-hängen nachzuforschen, ist die psychoanalytische" (the way to analyze Schnitzler's emotions and their hidden connections is psychoanalytical).[7] Reik has received his permission from a fictional source for dissecting Schnitzler's feelings: Friedrich Hofreiter in *Das weite Land* (1908) calls poets born criminals lacking the courage for bold deeds.[8]

Schnitzler himself appreciated Reik's examination of non-erotic rela-tionships between siblings and between friends, because it noticed what professional critics ignored.[9] Any praise, though, was tempered by his reservation expressed in a letter to Reik on December 31, 1913:

> Wo Sie innerhalb des Bewußten bleiben, gehe ich oft mit Ihnen. Über mein Unbewußtes, mein halb Bewußtes wollen wir lieber sagen — weiß ich aber nozch immer mehr als Sie, und nach dem Dunkel der Seele gehen mehr Wege, ich fühle es immer stärker, als die Psychoanalytiker sich träumen (und traumdeuten) lassen. Und gar oft führt ein Pfad noch mitten durch die erhellte Innenwelt, wo sie — und Sie — all-zufrüh ins Schattenreich abbiegen zu müssen glauben.[10]
>
> [Whenever you stay inside the conscious realm, I can follow you. About my unconscious, or shall we say subconscious, I still know more than you, and there are more roads to the dimness of the soul than psycho-analysts could ever dream (and claim to interpret). The point where a path crosses straight through an illumined interior world: that is where they — and you — believe it necessary to make a turn into the realm of shadows.]

In his 1963 book *The Need to be Loved*, Reik closes a short discussion of the erotomania in Schnitzler's *Tagebuch der Redegonda* by sharing a memory of walks he took with Schnitzler on the Sommerheidenweg near Vienna: "I vividly remember that our conversations moved from general topics to personal things, and that he sometimes revealed suspicious thoughts and paranoiac tendencies."[11] It is perhaps the feeling of being the constant object of analysis that fed Schnitzler's ambivalence toward Reik, and this surfaced in a dream that preceded the appearance of Reik's 1913 book. Reik irritates Schnitzler by joking with him too intimately, but Schnitzler regrets becoming short with him. Schnitzler predicts that the one who succeeds in showing psychoanalysis its limits will be great, and Reik agrees. He interprets Reik's intimacy as the relentless search for the most intimate clues of one's life, which makes his own irritated response understandable.[12]

Expressionism as Standard: Josef Körner, *Arthur Schnitzlers Gestalten und Probleme* (1921)

In a review of Reik's book, Josef Körner (1888–1950), who taught German literary history in Prague from 1913 to 1928, dismissed the scientific value of psychoanalysis, citing the skepticism of natural scientists toward Freud's departure from inherited models.[13] Reik's preface had, after all, provided the disclaimer against viewing his book as anything other than a scientific exploration. If Reik's analysis of characters was suspicious enough, his analysis of a still-living Schnitzler was inexcusable.[14] Körner's main objections concerned Reik's appeal to Freud's notorious sexual symbolism and his theory of infantile sexuality. In his attempt to turn up unconscious causes for Schnitzler's determinism, Reik's "Maulwurfarbeit" missed the obvious point that Schnitzler is fully aware of his themes, as the one-act parody of his themes, *Zum großen Wurstel* (1900), shows.[15] Psychoanalysis functions on the heuristic level with erotic authors, Körner concedes, but shifting from art to biographical details leaves little hope of progressing toward a truly literary science.[16] To understand an author is to understand the means by which he transforms experience into art.

Körner published *Arthur Schnitzlers Gestalten und Probleme* (Arthur Schnitzler's Figures and Problems, 1921) and the essay "Arthur Schnitzlers Spätwerk" (1927)[17] to demonstrate that a careful reading of the text in its final form was adequate for understanding its significance for the author's entire corpus (11). This approach avoids the shortcomings of biography, philology, sociology, and psychoanalysis, claims Körner. Biography breaks down into gossip about the author's life; philology spends too much time analyzing a work's development; sociology scrutinizes class, epoch, place, and occupation too closely; and psychoanalysis, as he showed already, reads sex into a work instead of letting a work reveal its true message (10). No matter what critical approach is in fashion, anything other than a close reading distorts the true message of the work and disrespects genial privacy. Körner's apparent concern for protecting the author is, however, a ploy to preserve the specimen for his dissection alone. To read Körner is to notice that what advertises itself as impartial judgment actually consists of strict standards for love, a disdain for positivism, a partiality to the fairy-tale form, and an unwavering support for expressionism.

Early in his book, Körner attributes Schnitzler's positivistic assessment of his figures to his medical training (20). In other words, the clinical habit of examining problems from various perspectives seals his failure to write convincing problem-plays. *Märchen* (1893), *Freiwild* (1896), and *Vermächtnis* (1897) all could have benefited from the single-issue argumentation developed and fine-tuned by Ibsen. Positivism also informs the objectionable behavior of Schnitzler's characters, who reflect his immanent worldview in three stages: first, the *Anatol* period corresponds to Schnitzler's naturalism of the nineties and features love without concern for consequences; second, the *Zwischenspiel* period of roughly 1897–1913 puzzles over marital questions and human determinism; third, the *Casanova* period since 1913 has been interested in the theme of aging. As Schnitzler has developed into an older and wiser physician, his description of love and its consequences has changed, but his reluctance to prescribe changes in behavior has not.

In every stage, Schnitzler's egoistic rentiers cause indignation, committed as they are to the erotic above any convictions or career aspirations (20–21). Any sign of impending attachment and responsibility sounds their warning alarms. Although he is a figure who does pursue a career, Friedrich Hofreiter, the main figure in *Das weite Land,* insists on coming and going freely without attachments (26). Schnitzler turns a blind eye toward the lechery of such figures because he finds seduction less reprehensible than opportunism and hypocrisy — and occasionally more eloquent (26). But Körner wants Schnitzler to map the moral of his story more distinctly. Anatol, or Fritz Lobheimer (from *Liebelei*), feast on life without having to pay (27). Cowardly and arrogant in equal measure, they expect worship from their conquests, and if not already two-timing, are longing for the next relationship (31). Even Professor Bernhardi, a rare exception to the erotic theme, is not immune from self-righteous egoism. Because his medical training reflects liberal individualism, he rejects the expectations of the Zionists to make him their political hero, claiming that his affair is purely personal. Party affiliation, like any committed relationship, would restrict his options (26).

The women do not improve the prospects of commitment either, at least in the early works. Despite social inclinations, they are more interesting to Schnitzler as "das Rätselwesen Weib," puzzling creatures vulnerable to every erotic advance (34). In *Der Schleier der Beatrice,* for example, Beatrice is motivated by her compulsive female nature alone, just as all Schnitzler's females are closer than men to the most basic of elements (60). This determined puzzlement about females Körner reads as Schnitzler's degrading projection of his own problems. Interestingly, Sol Liptzin, in the first English monograph on Schnitzler, published a decade later in 1932, would call female instinct less puzzling than healthy and natural: "While woman has retained her capacity to respond naturally, naively, instinctively, man has been handicapped by an over-abundance of rationalization. Schnitzler's women want love. Schnitzler's men offer understanding."[18]

Such a distinction is too subtle for Körner, who nevertheless makes no effort to set the record straight on anti-Semitic literary scholar Adolf Bartels's reduction of Vienna's *süße Mädeln* (sweet girls) to a whoredom (102). Instead, Körner is more concerned to register every instance of this sentimental legacy — Katherina in *Dr. Gräsler, Badearzt* (Dr. Gräsler, Spa Physician) and in *Der Ruf des Lebens,* Elise in *Der Mörder* (The Murderer, 1911), and Amy and Anna in *Der Weg ins Freie* (103) — and posits it as an entrenched social type between lady and prostitute that offers the warmth lacking in these two, for the sweet girl loves unhesitatingly and with a clean conscience (104). Unlike Frank Wede-kind (1864–1918), whose naturalism focuses on the consequences of sexual promiscuity, Schnitzler prefers to focus on the sweet sorrows of love (37). That his women are prostitutes more by nature than by career suggests that this trait is in every decent woman: "Denn in ro-mantisch-hohem Sinne ist ihm jedes Weib eine Dirne, das nicht in reiner Liebesleidenschaft sich ergibt oder genommen wird" (104–5: For in a high romantic sense he views every woman a whore whose passion in surrendering or being taken is anything less than pure).

Without a doubt, Schnitzler conceives of love in terms less idealistic than existential. Love is a selfish passion that stifles reason and leaves characters ready to commit atrocities, neglect duties, and betray coun-tries. Whether based on nerves, needs, self-deception posing as nobility, or something else, love is the force that drives one person into the arms of another to experience life's sweetest intoxication (52), making every pursuit worth the effort. As Christine Weiring's father in *Liebelei* realizes, his code of honor had shielded his sister from love's dangers, but also love's bliss. The nadirs and zeniths of such experience write Schnitzler's definition of love, not the other way around.

Körner notices three noteworthy messages: first, love ought to mean being there for someone else. This is Sala's remark in the play *Der einsa-me Weg* (1904), in which Irene becomes faithful to Julian only after losing him through her frivolity (65–67). Second, the urge to return is the essence of fidelity: this is Henri's viewpoint in *Der grüne Kakadu* (1899). Third, marital love cannot tolerate casual commitments. As Cäcilie and Amadeus illustrate in the play *Zwischenspiel* (1906), marriage based on either sex or friendship alone will fail, and *Die Hirtenflöte* (1911) illustrates that a tolerant husband, more than an unfaithful one, is in grave danger of seeing his marriage dissolve. A better model is depicted in the one-act *Bacchusfest* (Bacchus Party, 1915), where the husband uses eloquence to win back his wife from a rival. Naturally, unbridled sexual freedom and unlimited tolerance are uncalled for, but the heart's unpredictability in fidelity rightly factors in forgiveness for the occasional misstep. In all of Schnitzler's discourse on love, however, Körner finds "Liebe" too elevated a term for describing "erotische Emp-findungen so gemäßigter Temperatur" (193: erotic sensations of such moderate temperature). Similarly, he considers Schnitzler's use of the word "Abenteuer" excessive (38).

The second half of Körner's book explores the themes of death, illusion, and determinism, with an additional chapter devoted to the disappointing treatment of social issues in the novel *Der Weg ins Freie*. He argues that the call of life is more pressing even than love, particularly in Schnitzler's early novella *Sterben* (Dying, 1894) and the dramas *Der Schleier der Beatrice* and *Der Ruf des Lebens*. Quite simply, Schnitzler is as skeptical about bravery in the face of death as he is about fidelity in the face of temptation. As is demonstrated by Marie in *Sterben* and Beatrice in *Schleier der Beatrice*, suicide pacts are the pacts most easily broken (135). The fear of death and love of life are heightened existentially by the desperate orgies preceding fateful battles (137–39). *Der Ruf des Lebens*, Schnitzler's most decisive turn from naturalism and Körner's favorite of Schnitzler's plays, explores all the permutations of the death motif and the incomprehensibility of non-being (144).

At the start of his book, Körner had suggested that Schnitzler's interest in sex was exaggerated by his Jewishness. Is it any wonder, Körner asks, that the expulsion of Jews from politics into aesthetics produced so many treatises on sex: Schnitzler in literature, Otto Weininger (1880–1903) in philosophy, and Sigmund Freud in biology (14)? But anyone committed to positivism, Jew or not, is already stunted morally by seeing only what is in front of him and considering everything else a farce (159). In *Casanovas Heimfahrt* (1918), positivism is behind Marcolina's refutation of Casanova's philosophy, which she finds as full of rhetoric, meaningless, and obsolete as the aging adventurer himself (159). Marcolina thus expresses Schnitzler's cosmological uncertainty, in which chance reigns sovereign (160). Any time chance and fate are viewed together, the unforeseeable becomes the inescapable. The most notorious example of an unreflected cosmology of passivity is Lieutenant Gustl, who conveniently sidesteps a suicide of honor after learning the baker who insulted him has died; without this stroke of fate he might have shot himself to death, and it would have all been in vain (160–61). The one-acts of the cycle *Marionetten* — *Zum grossen Wurstel* (1901), *Der Puppenspieler* (1903), and *Der tapfere Cassian* (1904) — illustrate the consequence of playing with lives as a means to an end. Still, determinists must argue against the sovereignty of chance. Crushing and incomprehensible, fate is part of Schnitzler's confession of determinism: "Das Naturgesetz ist das Schicksal!" (169: The law of nature is fate!). Instead of finding meaning in fulfilling their duties, as do the characters of Theodor Storm, Schnitzler's figures surrender to an ethical nihilism from which suicide offers the only escape (169).

The premonitions and occultisms sprinkled throughout Schnitzler's otherwise closed universe are his way of having a laugh at the expense of mysticism (178). Comparisons of four mystical novellas in the collection *Dämmerseelen* — *Das Schicksal des Freiherrn von Leisenbohg* (Dozing Souls: The Fate of Baron Leisenbohg, 1903), *Die Fremde* (The Unknown Woman, 1902), *Die Weissagung* (The Prophecy, 1902), *Das Tagebuch der Redegonda* (Redegonda's Diary, 1909) — to the stories of Romantic writer E. T. A. Hoffmann have been erroneous (176): to Körner, the novellas simply illustrate fate's way of thwarting one's best intentions, and Schnitzler's view that we deem ourselves free, when we are really marionettes forced to dance to the tune of the all-powerful puppeteer (181).

Körner's final chapter links Schnitzler's pessimistic worldview with naturalism and pronounces it as falling far short of expressionism in ethical depth. It is not that Schnitzler was ever a convinced naturalist, certainly, but his beginning as a physician explains his predilection for forms such as novellas and one-acts that lend themselves to case studies. Not only are the sudden changes that mark a novella unwelcome in a larger work, but also his scientific worldview leaves him unconcerned about depicting the mood of a scene in detail (222). His novellas do not rival those of his countryman Ferdinand von Saar, whose treatment of similar themes surpasses Schnitzler's in originality and depth (223). After all, Schnitzler's flair for atmosphere, much less his audience's stomach for it, would scarcely endure for much longer than one act (223), since dialectical and conditional approaches to truth bring with them inevitable shortcomings: hence Schnitzler is unable and unwilling to offer an ultimate solution to the problems addressed in his works (221).

Turning from content to style, Körner dissects what is left of his subject. Although Schnitzler's dialogues are beyond reproach, he cannot help noticing that they thrive on virtuosity, not creativity, and that the elegant societal language of his characters is as devoid of individuality and solidity as their actions. Nothing of "aktive, wertsetzende Kraft" (active, morally progressive strength) applies to his virtue of tolerance, either: "Ihn kümmert nur, was gegeben, nicht, was aufgeben ist" (225: Only givens concern him, not tasks). The charm that keeps audiences awake doubles as Schnitzler's Achilles' heel, because it shows humor cavorting with psychology to the detriment of both (224). To label Schnitzler's ever-present irony overwrought is appropriate, because expressionist writers, by contrast, have the integrity to refuse to write for the sake of outward effect (224). Schnitzler has nothing beyond his cleverness to point toward God. More aesthetic than ethical, psychological than cosmic, Schnitzler only confirms his inferiority to expressionism by clinging to the immanent in the face of the transcendent. The skeptical positivist, swearing allegiance to the kingdom of his senses alone, keeps at bay any possibility of metaphysical certitude (225).

This harsh assessment becomes only more intriguing in Körner's follow-up study in 1927, "Arthur Schnitzlers Spätwerk," which addresses five works published since Körner's monograph: the dramas *Komödie der Verführung* (Comedy of Seduction, 1924) and *Der Gang zum Weiher* (The Way to the Pond, 1926), and the novellas *Fräulein Else* (1924), *Die Frau des Richters* (The Judge's Wife, 1925), and *Traumnovelle* (Dream Story, 1926). Körner is determined to argue significance for Schnitzler beyond the eternal topics of love, death, and fate that made him famous before the war (53). Works like *Der Schleier der Beatrice* and *Die Hirtenflöte* (for Körner the queen of the novellas) still hold appeal because their settings are removed from the present, thus preserving the magic and wonder of a world without machines. Now, by returning to myth, Schnitzler effectively disarms his critics of the complaint of anachronism (54).

In his book, Körner had identified a third stage of Schnitzler's production, from *Der einsame Weg* (1904) onward, which featured the punishment of egoism through the aging process. Adventurer figures such as Casanova were paying for their sins with the piercing loneliness of abandonment (27–28). To Körner, the works since *Casanovas Heimfahrt* offer even more reason to disavow Schnitzler's early moral relativism. The impressionist's resigned "So ist das Leben" (Such is life) has become the judge's "So geht es nicht" (This can't go on). Until Schnitzler relinquishes his relativistic position entirely, however, his clarity remains inferior to that of expressionism, effectively ensuring that his writings will remain stunted and at odds with themselves (83).

Körner's long essay still finds Schnitzler balking during the 1920s at a decisive liberation for his female figures. A fixation on female sexuality misses their essence and avoids the what Körner calls the most pressing problems of the day (61). From his perspective, liberation seems to mean the ability to give and receive love while avoiding subordination and the trap of marriage (72). At this, Leonilda in *Der Gang zum Weiher* is more successful than Judith in *Komödie der Verführung*. Without a vision for female autonomy, Schnitzler poses no questions about Leonilda's use of freedom to her own benefit and that of society (61). Indeed, in all his mature works, Schnitzler insists on the slippery slope of moral instability in all women. Still, the dogma of virginity receives too much attention considering it is not tied to a visible moral standard, (62), Körner insists, while the latitude Schnitzler grants his male protagonists remains largely undisturbed (63).

Caught between impressionism and the absolute morality of expressionism, Schnitzler has not reached a decision about free will and fate either (80). Four years before his essay in *Preussische Jahrbücher*, Körner had reviewed, in the same journal, Richard Specht's book *Arthur Schnitzler: Der Dichter und sein Werk* (1922), which he found troublesome both in style and in its mistaken proclamations of Schnitzler's freedom of the will, especially since Schnitzler's entire oeuvre professed determinism.[19] Now, confronted with more evidence of moral responsibility in Schnitzler's works, Körner acknowledges some freedom of agency, but stops short of pronouncing unequivocal self-determination. *Der Gang zum Weiher*, for example, shows the chancellor's belief in free will qualified immediately by the views of his sister Anselma. What counts as responsibility in the play is that the poet Sylvester Thorn, a poet version of composer Georg von Wergenthin from *Der Weg ins Freie*, meets a justice that should have been Georg's. Both men leave their pregnant girlfriends in the lurch; both babies they have fathered die in childbirth by umbilical strangulation. Now, in a work almost two decades later, Sylvester's suicide offers a solution more moral than that of the novel, which has none (75).

In the sparse space he reserves for the three novellas, Körner praises the scarcity of psychological commentary in *Die Frau des Richters*, because it corresponds to expressionism's vision of presenting the workings of the soul via deeds and gestures (155). This is not the usual case study for which Schnitzler is known. The "Hoffmannesque" parts of *Traumnovelle* (the costumier Gibiser, for example) Körner wants to attribute to

Schnitzler's inspiration from expressionism, although he finds them more reminiscent of Hoffmann's character "Dr. Mabuse" than of recent expressionist examples (161–62). In *Die Frau des Richters*, the phrase *coup de foudre* from love-philosopher Stendhal's *De l'amour* helps explain the sudden desire that overwhelms the judge's wife (157). Stendhal's psychosexual rule that women are quicker than men to forgive infidelity (67) also helps Körner explain Fridolin's reluctance to forgive Albertine's dreams in *Traumnovelle* (159). Stendhal is more Körner's authority than Freud, as Körner shows in a footnote explaining his deferral of the sexual interpretation of the dream to the "in so saftigen Dingen erfahreneren Psychoanalytikern" (158: psychoanalysts who are more experienced in such juicy things). As mentioned already, Körner does not dismiss psychoanalysis outright, but the closest he comes to acknowledging Freud is noting that Schnitzler's insights into the complicated soul overlap with the findings of contemporary psychology concerning the mutability of the ego.[20]

Since his positivist and impressionist beginnings have remained with him, the elderly Schnitzler cannot match the idealistic energy of expressionists, according to Körner, but at least his works contain a measure of wisdom (162). Psychological fresh air has been Schnitzler's answer to stifling naturalism (this recalls Alfred Kerr's praise) but Körner rests his defense there. Schnitzler, ever stubborn and shallow, cannot rival the compelling depth of metaphysical literature, because even with the ethical shift in his late works, a life of immanence remains the highest value and death the absolute devaluation: "Diese Dichtung ist ohne Wort Gottes" (162: This writing is lacking any divine inspiration).

The essay thus concludes with startling vengefulness. Körner had been advocating Schnitzler halfheartedly, only to become, in the end, a judge whose transcendent standards are fixed temporally by expressionism. By staying in tune with the divine, expressionism has redeemed literature and, by extension, criticism. Schnitzler's "eternal" questions have remained in quotation marks (162). The war has caused a shift in the political, societal, and moral questions of a failed bourgeois era only seemingly secure, and in whose graveyard stillness the only sound that was heard came from the hunt for sexual pleasures (162). Suddenly not Stendhal but Körner is the authority on love, assigning it a suitable place next to all the experiences of equal value in a world spinning out of control. To be sure, Körner has questioned all along Schnitzler's need to debunk the sexual double standard, and admonishes Schnitzler to believe more strongly that love and loyalty are nothing less than "Worte eines Begriffes" (67–68). Schnitzler's dialectic of love must submit to the new moral order after all. True, love and death will themselves never become outdated; it is simply that expressionists depict experience as more profound and resonant:

> Eine Liebe, die Hingabe nicht fordert, sondern ersehnt; eine Liebe, die nicht dem Weib und dem Geschlecht nachgeht, sondern der Gattung und Gott; ein Todesgefühl, das die Angst vor der Vernichtung der Individuation verwandelt in Verlangen nach der Aufhebung des Individuums ins All, weil alle Vereinzelung Sünde ist, Abfall von Gott und nur ihr Durchbruch Erlösung. (163)

> [a love that doesn't demand dedication but longs for it; a love that doesn't pursue women and sex, but conjugal relations and God; a sensation of death that turns the fear of individual annihilation into the longing to dissolve the individual into the cosmos, because all isolation is a sin and a falling away from God, and salvation comes only from breaking through it.]

Enough to cancel anything previously positive about Schnitzler, this assessment, Körner hastens to say, is not intended to debase. Nothing would be more inappropriate than trying to assess a writer's value by a prevailing worldview (163) — nevertheless Körner seems to forget having just criticized Schnitzler's ethics for falling short of expressionist standards. Even if patterned after expressionism, aesthetic mastery is not enough. Körner's prophetic authority on religious matters, stated in the tone of conventional wisdom, sounds eerily oracular when read decades later: "So wird Arthur Schnitzler . . . zu erneutem Glanze aufsteigen, gleich andern großen Poeten, die nach flüchtigen frühen Triumphen durchs Fegefeuer der Befehdung hinüberschritten in das Paradies unbestrittener Anerkennung" (163: So shall Arthur Schnitzler . . . rise up to renewed glory, just as other poets, after initial fleeting triumphs, have stridden through the purgatory of rampant feuds into the paradise of undisputed respect).

It was not enough to judge a work on its own merit after all, as Körner had insisted at the beginning of his book. However, tabulating the sins of Anatol and his successors remains enough to indict Schnitzler without having to go into great biographical detail. Whatever his views of timeless ethical and aesthetic values, in truth the best thing Körner has to say about fellow Jew Schnitzler — and the way he can best help him reach that paradise of undisputed respect — lies in the notion of *Heimat*. Alienation and expulsion from where one feels most at home is not limited to Sylvester Thorn's dilemma in *Der Gang zum Weiher*, but states the anti-Semitic reality of Schnitzler's life at a time when postwar living conditions have produced the hunt for scapegoats. Schnitzler's "niemals verleugnetes Judentum" (never-denied Jewish origins) has become in literary circles an occasion for increasing hostility.

One incident inspires Körner to direct an apology to Schnitzler on behalf of German-speaking Czechs. During a reading tour in Czechoslovakia in late October and early November of 1922, rightist extremists of the club "Die Eiche" created a disturbance during one of his readings. Unlike the anti-Semitic fisticuffs from his student days, when an altruistic organization refused to continue offering stipends to poor medical Jews from the provinces, now the disruptions of the Swastika-clad youths featured rubber billy clubs.[21] Schnitzler's renewed interest in the Jewish problem thus stems from being denied the intellectual and spiritual right to *Heimat* (81).

To the extent that Körner's descriptions of expressionism keep from becoming prescriptive, they parallel the way Otto Brahm championed naturalism as long as it was considered vanguard modernism. But the comparison stops there, because positivism, for Körner, lacks any redeeming qualities. An affinity to an assessment made by Hermann Bahr is also evident: when Schnitzler turned fifty in 1912, Bahr took him to task for his denial of absolute truth, and construed this denial as less a matter of principle than as a product of Schnitzler's close association with a dying culture.[22] Körner regards his denial more in terms of an absence of principle than as a sociological effect.

Nihilism as Explanation: Bernhard Blume, *Das nihilistische Weltbild Arthur Schnitzlers* (1936)

Taking his cue from intellectual history would have been outside Körner's interpretive scope, but this is the starting point for Bernhard Blume's Stuttgart dissertation of 1936: *Das nihilistische Weltbild Arthur Schnitzlers*.[23] No matter how insightful a psychological examination of Schnitzler as Jew, physician, or citizen of Vienna might be, Blume promises not to explain Schnitzler's works by explaining Schnitzler. His aim is rather to expound how Schnitzler's works express the nihilism of moribund liberalism (3). Showing the effects of formidable background reading, Blume's introduction is proof enough of the reason scholars of the next generation called his dissertation the seminal work on Schnitzler.[24]

The difference in approach between Körner and Blume immediately becomes apparent. Although professing an intrinsic approach he considered neutral, through his preferred grid of expressionism Körner attrib-

uted Schnitzler's inability to grasp the higher truths of love to his reluctance to part fully with the positivism left over from medical studies and
naturalist beginnings. Schnitzler's faults were remediable and Körner
meant his rebukes for the best; what Blume calls nihilism Körner would
have translated as positivism and deemed curable. But Blume prefers to
discuss Schnitzler's nihilism — the inability to acknowledge any value as
ultimately binding — as a reflection of his age and the inevitable outcome of Enlightenment thought, placing it beyond the scope of judgment. Immediately Blume lists a few nihilistic themes in Schnitzler, such
as the crippling fear of death, a poisoned sense of pleasure, comfortless
suffering, isolation, and the futility of self-deception and role-playing (3).

Blume's thesis finds support in Nietzsche's *Wille zur Macht* (Will to
Power, 1906), which described how European art was accelerating toward catastrophe because security, the supreme bourgeois value, had
come undone.[25] Buttressed by reason, security became one of the greatest casualties of the First World War, and the money that had guaranteed
it fell victim to inflation immediately thereafter (4). Schnitzler's answer
to the loss of security is no answer at all: it is the turn neither to pious
explanations nor to brave deeds, but to deedless nihilism (5). Blume is
careful to distinguish between nihilism and *Verfall* — that term usually
interpreted as decadence and applied to Jewish art and artists by Nazi
cultural propaganda. Just because Schnitzler continues to write about
decadent *Lebensgefühl* after the war does not mean that art itself is in
decay; one does not, despite Gottfried Benn's suggestion, overcome
nihilism by policing form.[26]

Lost along with security was the reign of reason, which had begun
by promising individual liberation and ended by witnessing mass destruction. This trajectory is nothing new, but it is made interesting by
Blume's footnotes, which make mention of Ernst Jünger's *Arbeiter*
(1932), Otto Gmelin's *Naturgeschichte des Bürgers* (1929), and Moeller
van den Bruck's *Das dritte Reich* (1931) in addition to Gottfried Benn's
Nach dem Nihilismus (1932). Moeller van de Bruck's work describes the
Enlightenment as having transformed thinking individuals into calculat-
ing ones and as having "degenerated" Europe: "Sie hat Europa entar-
tet."[27] Here is reason to read Blume carefully, because any mention of
"Entartung" recalls the title of Max Nordau's *Entartung* (Degeneration)
(1895), as well as the 1939 Munich exhibit of degenerate art, in which
expressionist art, viewed literally in the worst light, was juxtaposed with
healthy, fresh Aryan counterexamples. It is more than a matter of word
association, however. Once the Enlightenment is made culpable for
military losses, it can become the enemy of the dependable, honest *Volk*,

as can the qualities it preached but failed to deliver: freedom of speech, individual liberties, and the rule of law.

Blume is aware of writing at a point where the middle class is being replaced by the reign of the soldier. He cites Max Scheler's prophetic essay "Über Gesinnungs- und Zweckmilitarismus" (On Militarism as Attitude and Purpose) in which Scheler describes the new soldier-ethos of the *Volk* in terms foreign to the bourgeois: honor is above utility, the interest of the whole above privileged interests, struggle and work above comfort, discipline above materialism and hedonism, and the value of sacrifice above what the sacrifice accomplishes.[28] Thus the new ethos of discipline and struggle, attempting to shape fate, is diametrically opposed to the anxious elimination of unpredictability from daily life, a task Werner Sombart identified as the essential bourgeois trademark.[29]

Theater, once a pulpit for disseminating values, has become a puppet theater for effacing them. Schnitzler shows liberal values degenerating into anti-values: *Leutnant Gustl* (1900), for example, depicts an officer's honor as a pitiful residue of convention compared to Major Tellheim's sensitivity in Gotthold Lessing's play *Minna von Barnhelm* (1767). In Schnitzler's *Freiwild*, the clash of military and civilian values ends in a draw: Paul Rönning's determination not to duel, too hesitant to appear convincing, comes off as poorly as Karinski's hotheaded militarism. Nihilism is thus the absence of any unequivocal verdict (6). The sterling example is *Der Weg ins Freie*, which signals the end of the *Bildungsroman:* Georg von Wergenthin already has all the *Bildung* he needs, and is in point of fact crippled by his legacy rather than taking from it a reason for decisive action. Liberation from personal and political attachments brings isolation (6). Because Schnitzler cannot count on the common knowledge Lessing could with *Nathan der Weise*, even *Professor Bernhardi* becomes nothing more than a case study. Bernhardi holds his opinion without trying to convince others of it (6). *Bildung* is clearly no longer the object of middle-class quests. If there is no afterlife, no values are worth fighting or dying for, and even men's duels do not support convictions so much as they do sport and convention.

Long before the First World War brought the ultimate loss of security, nineteenth-century writers such as Heinrich von Kleist (1777–1811), Georg Büchner (1813–37), and Arthur Schopenhauer (1788–1860) had already demonstrated the flaws in Enlightenment arguments attempting to guarantee universal security. Büchner's *Lenz* (1839) even anticipates Robert's schizophrenia in Schnitzler's *Flucht in die Finsternis* (Flight into Darkness, 1931) (12). A brief comparison of *Der grüne Kakadu* with Büchner's *Dantons Tod* (Danton's Death, 1835) shows that Büchner's heroes fail after trying, but Schnitzler's heroes fail from the very start. If anything unites Büchner and Schnitzler, it is the resigned view that elitist inhumanity has stepped aside for mass inhumanity. As for the French Revolution, so for the present: Schnitzler has the wherewithal to notice that decadence has been replaced by barbarism (12).

Against this backdrop of epochal death sketched out in Blume's introduction, Schnitzler's treatment of death takes on vivid contours, because every dying character reenacts the death of reason, duty, freedom, and security. In Schnitzler, nihilism becomes existential, with death becoming the only human certainty besides sex left to discuss, albeit devoid of any comfort or transformation (15). The quintessence of Schnitzler's world is the episode, a flare-up of sexual intensity that sweetens the looming execution (16). Schnitzler only expedites the execution of his characters by recording how they act with only one night or day left until a duel or battle. Since every instinct shuns death, the only meaning characters can give it is rhetorical, whether based on Fatherland, honor, duty, or redemption. In their incessant flight from death, Schnitzler's characters exchange a large bill for many small ones, experiencing the death of happiness in the melancholy of the passing moment and all it contains: "Nichts bleibt, nichts hat Bestand und Dauer, alles vergeht, verwelkt, bröckelt ab, löst sich auf und zerfällt" (23: Nothing remains, nothing has substance and duration, everything comes to an end, wilts, crumbles, dissolves, and vanishes). Truth applies only in the moment, and because Schnitzler's figures distrust its duration, to swear eternal love is only to parrot the language expected of one's role as lover (23–24).

Schnitzler's reluctance to believe in love stems from viewing it as an organism subject to illness and death. Why hold anyone responsible for breaking up something already in demise? Few organic events of love ever receive much cultivation from those whom love momentarily possesses. Instead, fate and passivity determine the attractions and breakups of lovers languishing in sensations. For example, the main figure in the story *Frau Beate und ihr Sohn* (Frau Beate and Her Son, 1913) cannot transcend the longings and fears that cascade over her, leading less a life of her own choosing than one in surrender to a compelling "Es" (26).[30]

Like Körner, Blume identifies the price for compulsive love in the fate of Schnitzler's aging characters from *Der einsame Weg* onward (28). Loneliness, not wisdom, comes from pursuing experiences rather than knowledge in one's youth. Casanova is the best example of one whose personality has remained stunted because sexual episodes have steered his life (29–30). Because the story *Der blinde Geronimo und sein Bruder*

(Blind Geronimo and His Brother, 1900) is not about sex but about two brothers, it remains the sole example of real understanding between two people. In general, though, Schnitzler writes about his own experience: isolation unaware of potentially satisfying companionship (38).

Love is moribund because Schnitzler's characters try so desperately to put distance and time between themselves and the partners who threaten their freedom (33). They avoid commitment, either to keep their options open or to fall back on the comfort of memories (34). Caught between the warmth of community and the cold of isolation, characters often see suicide — thirty-two times in Schnitzler's works — as the only way to free themselves from reality (43): "Immer gibt diesen Menschen die Gegenwart zu wenig" (46: The present always gives these individuals too little).[31] Though they may dream of experiencing more, they are too weak to implement their fantasies (47); if temptation is ever avoided, it is more a sign of weakness than of scruples (49).

Another version of passivity applies to characters who live for gambling. Winning and losing depends less on skill than on chance. With nothing better to do, those unaware of any overarching meaning or binding commitment are always playing at something (55). Playing games of high stakes is as passive as playing roles; Blume points out the many instances of theater terms that accompany the actions in which the characters find no meaning. Self-presentation precludes authenticity, and even feelings have become contrived gestures (56). Frau Ehrenberg's salon in *Weg ins Freie* is not immune from masquerade either. All attempts at composure, banking on the effect one creates, belie the fear of exposing the ego and the ultimate attempt to keep death at bay (57–58). No real emotion or spontaneity escapes these egos: the husband in *Liebelei*, for example, is calm when delivering the duel challenge to Fritz. *Frau Berta Garlan* depicts a woman feigning a higher social rank to entice a star. This make-believe world finds a mask donned as much for one's own sake as for the sake of others (58–59).

Not surprisingly, Blume's discussion of puppeteers is more pessimistic than Körner's. Sex is a brutal enough force, but the true power in a meaningless universe belongs to chance. Not so much withholding truth as offering it dialectically, Schnitzler goes about exposing the poseurs he has set in motion (63). Once illusions in a nihilistic world are destroyed, however, nothing remains (64). The articulate, desperate attempts of his characters to alleviate suspicion of their role-playing only arouse it more (66).

It would appear that one studies Schnitzler in vain for solutions to survive his uncompromising, empty universe. Overcoming his familiar melancholy is possible only by death; all the efforts of his characters reenact the denial of the truth (66). All along, Blume has lacked the moralistic tone of Körner, attributing Schnitzler's pessimism to a consistent and uncompromising worldview borne of experience and observation rather than composed of inferior precepts of naturalism and impressionism. Blume nevertheless finds Schnitzler suggesting a solution to the problem of setting one's foot on ground that is forever shifting: become intentional about art's mission to destroy the illusion of lasting happiness. Such a mission need not suspend beauty, however, and this is where Schnitzler shines (66). Breaking Schnitzler's rule against assuming characters speak his mind, Blume suggests that the poet Heinrich in the one-act *Lebendige Stunden* (Living Hours, 1901) expresses it best. Of his poetry, Heinrich remarks: "Es ist nicht der schlechteste Beruf, solchen Stunden Dauer zu verleihen, über ihre Zeit hinaus" (68: It is not the worst calling to lend such hours a certain staying power). Giving shape to the episodic, Schnitzler at least ensures longevity for his message of dialectical justice: "Wenn es, bei Hebbel, das Wesen der Gerechtigkeit im Drama verlangt, daß alle Recht haben, so macht es die Gerechtigkeit bei Schnitzler aus, daß alle Unrecht haben" (71: Whereas Hebbel sees the essence of dramatic justice demanding that everyone be right, Schnitzler's version of justice is that no one is right).

The irony is that Schnitzler the artist uses physicians to unmask the artists in his plays. Thus his two professions are represented most frequently in his works. In the first half of his literary output, he identified more with the artist advancing aestheticism, talking about himself. The second half has been more about life and attains far-reaching validity — because it is really about death, reported by the physicians whose immediacy to it keeps them objective, sober, and clear (74). Körner had accused Schnitzler the physician of sacrificing absolute truth for a physician's empiricism; Blume finds the physician able to destroy illusions in a world in which liberal values have dissolved into nothing. The best one can hope for is to eradicate false hope.

In conclusion, the last twenty years of Schnitzler's life saw the first noteworthy extended criticism of his works. Reik revered Schnitzler almost as much as he did Freud and subjected both Schnitzler and his characters to analysis, discriminating little between them. While Schnitzler applauded Reik's willingness to tackle topics such as incest and patricide without preformed judgment and to point out the non-erotic relationships in his works, he criticized Reik's appeal to the unconscious as long as empirical answers were forthcoming. Reik's neuroses and death wishes were as compelling as the literature he interpreted. Nevertheless, he is remembered for showing that psychoanalytic interpretation could be done successfully, so long as the recurrent situations and motifs were allowed to determine the Freudian interpretations, and not the other way around.

If Reik's book showed the influence of feuilletonism, Körner shows a talented and sparing style. Reik's hopes for psychoanalysis were matched by Körner's hopes for the literary community, which he hoped could surmount Schnitzler's pessimism concerning love and death. Tragically, the Jew Körner changed his opinion of Schnitzler to the extent that this largely Aryan community of idealism of which he wanted to be a part had no room for him except at Theresienstadt, the Jewish concentration camp in Czechoslovakia to which he was deported in 1944; this was grounds, during and following his internment, for appreciating Schnitzler's pessimism after all.[32] Nevertheless, the substance of his work *Arthur Schnitzlers Gestalten und Gedanken* was anything but favorable for Schnitzler's reputation in posterity.

Bernhard Blume puts nihilism at the center of his study, reminding his readers that Schnitzler, like Georg Büchner, does not announce health appearing on the heels of decadence, but barbarism. As Schnitzler unmasks futile schemes to postpone death, he records the dissolution of liberal values of freedom into desperate bourgeois security. In retrospect, one can see that Blume was reacting to the climate of National Socialism and was under the constraint of his dissertation director Hermann Pongs. In a short newspaper essay in 1956 noting the twenty-fifth anniversary of Schnitzler's death, Blume revised his nihilist image to state more strongly that Schnitzler was not the same as the figures he depicted. He preserved enough distance from his characters to safely qualify as someone more hopeful than nihilistic, but one nevertheless adept at depicting a valueless world. On this world Schnitzler brings to bear a sobriety neither expecting nor receiving any sympathy. Blume writes: "Er ist darin eher dem Forscher im Laboratorium zu vergleichen, der die Insekten, die er untersucht, weder liebt noch haßt, sondern kennt, darstellt, beschreibt" (He is more akin to a lab researcher of insects, who neither loves nor hates them, but rather knows, depicts, and describes them).[33]

Notes

[1] *Neuköllner Tageblatt*, 12 May 1933, quoted in Rolf Geissler, *Dekadenz und Heroismus: Zeitroman und völkisch-nationalsozialistische Literaturkritik* (Stuttgart: Deutsche Verlags-Anstalt, 1964), 22–23.

[2] Geissler, *Dekadenz und Heroismus* (1964), 22–23.

[3] Reik, *Arthur Schnitzler als Psycholog* (Minden: Bruns, 1913), 235.

[4] Konstanze Fliedl, *Arthur Schnitzler: Poetik der Erinnerung* (Vienna: Böhlau, 1997), 454.

[5] Fliedl, *Poetik* (1997), 456.

[6] Fliedl, *Poetik* (1997), 455.

[7] Reik, *Psycholog* (1913), 217.

[8] See Fliedl, *Poetik* (1997), 457–58.

[9] See Schnitzler's letter to Hans Henning of 2 April 1914, quoted in Michael Worbs, *Nervenkunst: Literatur und Psychoanalyse im Wien der Jahrhundertwende* (Frankfurt am Main: Athenäum, 1988), 218.

[10] Schnitzler to Reik, 31 December 1913, in Bernd Urban, "Vier unveröffentlichte Briefe Arthur Schnitzlers an den Psychoanalytiker Theodor Reik," *MAL* 8/3–4 (1975): 236–47; also quoted in Worbs, 218–19.

[11] Theodor Reik, *The Need to Be Loved* (Toronto: Ambassador Books, 1963), 59.

[12] Schnitzler, diary entry of 8 July 1913, quoted in Fliedl, *Poetik* (1997), 449–50.

[13] Josef Körner, "Arthur Schnitzler und Siegmund Freud," review of *Arthur Schnitzler als Psycholog*, by Theodor Reik, *Das literarische Echo* 19 (October 1916–17): col. 802–5.

[14] Körner, *Schnitzler und Freud* (1916–17), 804.

[15] Körner, *Schnitzler und Freud* (1916–17), 804.

[16] Körner, *Schnitzler und Freud* (1916–17), 805.

[17] Josef Körner, *Arthur Schnitzlers Gestalten und Probleme* (Zürich: Amalthea Verlag, 1921); "Arthur Schnitzlers Spätwerk," *Preussische Jahrbücher* 208 (1927): 53–83; 153–63. Page references appear subsequently in the text and apply, unless noted, to whichever of the two works is being discussed.

[18] Sol Liptzin, *Arthur Schnitzler* (New York: Prentice Hall, 1932), 48.

[19] Josef Körner, review of *Arthur Schnitzler: Der Dichter und sein Werk. Eine Studie*, by Richard Specht, *Preussische Jahrbücher* 194 (1923): 202–5, here 204.

[20] Körner, *Gestalten und Probleme* (1921), 66–67.

[21] Guiseppe Farese, *Arthur Schnitzler: Ein Leben in Wien*. Trans. Karin Krieger (Munich: Beck, 1999), 239.

[22] Richard Allen, "Arthur Schnitzler's Works and their Reception: An Annotated Bibliography" (Diss., U of Michigan, 1964), 34.

[23] Bernhard Blume, *Das nihilistische Weltbild Arthur Schnitzlers* (Stuttgart: Buchdruckerei Knöller, 1936). Subsequent page references appear in the text.

[24] Albert Fritzsche, for example, concurs with Ernst Offermanns and William Rey in praise of Blume's dissertation (Fritzsche, *Dekadenz im Werk Arthur Schnitzlers* [Bern: Herbert Lang, 1974], 8).

[25] Friedrich Nietzsche, *Der Wille zur Macht,* quoted in Blume, *Weltbild* (1936), 4.

[26] In a footnote, Blume (4) contends briefly with Gottfried Benn's *Nach dem Nihilismus* (1932).

[27] Moeller van den Bruck, *Das dritte Reich* (1931), 103, quoted in Blume, *Weltbild* (1936), 5.

[28] Max Scheler, "Über Gesinnungs- und Zweckmilitarismus," in *Schriften zur Soziologie und Weltanschauungslehre,* vol 2: *Nation und Weltanschauung* (1923), quoted in Blume, *Weltbild* (1936), 14–15.

[29] This is the conclusion I draw from reading Blume's discussion of Sombart's *Bourgeois* on p. 11. The embrace of risk is also quite different than the image Zweig conveys in *Die Welt von Gestern* of the importance of every kind of security for the bourgeois, particularly his own father's confidence in the ability to fortify his entire life "against every intervention of Fate" (15).

[30] Marianne Kesting states that if Schnitzler's characters are weak, it is not due to moral inadequacy, because, as with Hauptmann and Maeterlinck, the fate which characters suffer is more important than they themselves are: See *Entdeckung und Destruktion: Zur Strukturumwandlung der Künste* (Munich: Fink, 1970), 129.

[31] Horst Thomé has called this spatial-temporal flux or flight from attachments "Kernlosigkeit," perhaps expressed best by the Romantic notion of "shadowlessness" and presented in its extreme as leading to madness, as in Schnitzler's *Flucht in die Finsternis* ("Kernlosigkeit und Pose: Zur Rekonstruktion von Schnitzlers Psychologie," *Text & Kontext* 20 [1984]: 62–87).

[32] See Fliedl, *Poetik* (1997), 478–79.

[33] Berhard Blume, "Arthur Schnitzler" (20 October 1956), in *Aufsätze aus dem Stuttgarter Neuen Tageblatt und der Stuttgarter Zeitung 1933–1966* (Stuttgart: n.p., n.d.) 23–26, here 25–26.

3: Schnitzler as Humanist Institution

FROM BLUME'S 1936 DISSERTATION to the aftermath of National Socialism, very little productivity was evident in Schnitzler scholarship, with no criticism of monograph size matching that of Körner's investigation until Françoise Derré's *L'oeuvre d'Arthur Schnitzler: Imagerie viennoise et problèmes humains* (1966). But the mid-sixties is too late to take up the discussion, because enduring criticism of general nature, though lesser scope, is apparent much earlier, for example in Oskar Seidlin's 1953 edition of the correspondence of Schnitzler and Brahm.[1] For that reason, criticism discussed in this chapter spans the time from the early fifties to the early seventies, beginning with Seidlin's discussion of Schnitzler as an impressionist and ending with Ernst Offermanns's calling Schnitzler a critic of impressionism. If this contrast sounds simplistic — it is taken from Herbert Seidler's 1976 research review[2] — it at least documents the increasing agility of scholarship in reconciling voluntarism, "which regards man as a free agent responsible for his acts," with determinism, "which views man as governed by forces beyond his control."[3] If they are without choice, Schnitzler's characters are slaves to their impressionism in a nihilistic universe; if free will becomes an ingredient in their makeup, however, they can be wary of viewing life as unconnected impressions and nothing more, and such wariness enables the step toward meaning and ethics.

At the same time that Schnitzler's books were being blacklisted in Europe during the thirties and forties, primary Schnitzler scholarship was being produced by refugees who had settled in the United States and by exiles who had returned to Europe after the Second World War. The majority were humanists shaped by the experience of displacement and sensitive to reinstating the reputation of an author similarly maligned. Their close readings of Schnitzler announced a thematic range far surpassing the well-worn clichés of love, death, and play. Retaining Körner's suspicion of positivism, they nevertheless rescued Schnitzler from the blurry charge of agnosticism and boldly explored his connections to Freudian psychology (addressed here in a separate chapter). Lifting Schnitzler out of the gloom of the thirties and forties made it easy to venerate the object of resuscitation, so intent were scholars to focus on the values that overlapped with their own. This critical humanist main-stream nonetheless saw its tolerance tested by any sort of dogmatism — chiefly Marxism — reminiscent of the pseudo-criticism many had already been forced to endure.

In 1951, Frederick Beharriell recorded that immorality, superficiality, and monotony still counted as the main complaints leveled at Schnitzler. He steered away from the preoccupation with *Anatol* and *Liebelei* and toward more promising themes such as the struggle against convention; the interplay of illusion and reality; ethical responsibility; the hollowness of the code of honor; psychiatric insights; moral double standards; patri-otism; and the tragedy of the lonely, uprooted individual.[4] Freed some-what from the erotic rubric, investigations during the fifties began treating Schnitzler as an ethicist intent on exposing both the bourgeois hypocrisy toward the lower classes and the self-deception festering in his impressionistic characters.

Determinism, Freedom, and Renaissance

In 1953, Oskar Seidlin (i.e. Koplowitz, 1911–) edited the correspon-dence of Schnitzler and Brahm seventeen years after having submitted his Basel dissertation "Otto Brahm als Theaterkritiker: mit Berücksichtigung seiner literarhistorischen Arbeiten." Seidlin's introduction presents Schnitzler's texts with a sobriety reminiscent of Blume's dissertation (also of 1936), leaving the impression that Schnitzler's world of characters is devoid of any moral guidance.[5] The epic drama *Der junge Medardus* (Young Medardus, 1910), for example, shows fate at work dashing all human plans. Medardus intends to humiliate Helene Valois and liberate the Austrians from Napoleon, but instead he falls in love with Helene, which diminishes the appeal of killing Napoleon. Unaware of her intent to murder Napoleon, Medardus kills Helene, believing she has become Napoleon's mistress. Ironically, revenge doubles the bereavement and leaves alive the pillager of the fatherland (B, xxix). The final burlesque twist is that when Medardus responds to Napoleon's gratitude by swearing to see him dead, he is promptly executed, buried with military honors, and proclaimed a hero. Nothing, of course, has come of his impulses.

The overriding of individual psychology by fate was in Seidlin's view the subject of *Der Ruf des Lebens* (1905) as well. Here, too, impulses are stronger than the oath the regiment swears to cleanse the thirty-year-old shame on the regiment by fighting its next battle to certain death. The suicide pact is the commander's strategy to punish his wife's seducer, but even he fails to see the culprit in an officer he believes innocent. A world of deception keeps veiled in secrets even those to whom one feels closest (B, xxx–xxxi). What is more, the forgotten past may reassert itself suddenly in the present, as happens in *Spiel im Morgengrauen* (Daybreak, 1926), where Leopoldine Lebus, the object of Lieutenant Willi Kasda's one-night stand long ago, reappears to even the score (B, xxxiv–xxxv).

Although Seidlin's examples are not incontrovertible proof of Schnitzler's nihilism, they indirectly question moral agency. Cosmic fate would at least permit a pure tragic strain in a narrative, but Schnitzler shows his characters at the mercy of vainglory or revenge that poses as fate and explains away a character's own impulsivity. Seen in this way, morality becomes possible only when the rhetoric of fate has been traced to the individual psychology that has given rise to it. Nevertheless, Schnitzler seems to insist that something inexplicable remains that defies any attempt to disenchant and thus control it.

Seidlin was careful to downplay determinism in his second edition (1975) of the Schnitzler-Brahm correspondence. The weight of research was shifting toward viewing Schnitzler as the critic of his epoch instead of its advocate. As early as the thirties, Sol Liptzin had registered Schnitzler's belief in a moral seismograph,[6] while scholars such as Richard Plaut and Frida Ilmer countered Blume's determinist categorization of Schnitzler in much the same way as Blume did in 1956.[7] After the 1962 centennial of Schnitzler's birth, scholars like Robert Weiss steered the discussion toward personal responsibility, noting (like Körner) Schnitzler's rejection from *Der einsame Weg* (1904) onward of his earlier relativism.[8] To Weiss, Schnitzler's unorthodox wonder at an unfathomable universe shines through in his aphorisms, in which proof of God's existence is posited not as an awareness of divinity, but as the capacity to doubt it.[9] This capacity in turn suggests free agency and thus responsibility, with the vocabulary of freedom making it possible to blame tragedy on human choice, not on nameless fate.

The 1962 centennial was the sign of a significant paradigm shift toward freedom and ethics in the criticism. In April 1961 — a year and a month before the one-hundredth anniversary of Schnitzler's birth — a group of scholars meeting at the annual University of Kentucky Foreign Language Conference founded the International Arthur Schnitzler Research Association. It sought "to stimulate interest in, and actively encourage research on, the Austrian author, playwright, and physician Arthur Schnitzler (1862–1931) and his work, and the age in which he lived."[10] The eight papers presented a year later at the same conference, compiled as *Studies in Arthur Schnitzler,* were but one proof of a Schnitzler renaissance; by May 1963 the JIASRA (Journal of the International Arthur Schnitzler Research Association) carried the names of more than a hundred active and associate members. Weiss, president of the association until 1976, made the bold prediction that Schnitzler's work would be considered timeless on intrinsic value alone, a remark that both echoed and superseded Körner's injunction forty years earlier for criticism to concern itself exclusively with the text, not with the author or anything else outside it.[11] Weiss and his colleagues resuscitated author, text, and milieu after years of neglect.

The renewal of interest was fueled chiefly by Fischer Verlag's new four-volume edition in 1961–62 of Schnitzler's narrative and dramatic works, ending decades of relative silence blamed first on Schnitzler's slipping in popularity in Berlin after the First World War, then on his banishment as a decadent playwright from 1933 onward, and finally on the belief that his subtle dramas were inappropriate for a starving postwar public.[12] The new edition of fiction was supplemented in 1967 by the volume *Aphorismen und Betrachtungen* (Aphorisms and Observations, 1967) under Weiss's editorship. The sixth and final volume, *Entworfenes und Verworfenes* (Things Sketched and Discarded, 1977), followed a decade later under Reinhard Urbach's editorship.[13] Urbach based that work on *Der Nachlaß Arthur Schnitzlers,* published in 1969 by Gerhard Neumann and Jutta Müller. In 1974 Urbach had published his volume of *Schnitzler-Kommentar zu den erzählenden Schriften und dramatischen Werken,* a reference work of paramount importance, for which a long life was prophesied.[14] Schnitzler's autobiography appeared in 1968 under the title *Jugend in Wien* (Youth in Vienna, and by 1970 edited volumes of Schnitzler's correspondence with Hofmannsthal, Brahm, Brandes, and Olga Waissnix had appeared. Perhaps the major accomplishment of the decade, however, was Richard Allen's bibliography and review of the seven decades of research in English, German, and French leading up to his study. Such a monumental task would not have been undertaken without the conviction that sound philology was the starting point for overturning stereotypes of hitherto *Tageskritik*-inspired research. All of this is in addition to the monographs of secondary literature of the sixties, to be mentioned shortly.

The renaissance in Schnitzler studies ran parallel to the politicization of the decade. The lead players in the renaissance were interested in individual rights, having been forced to flee regimes disputing the freedom of opinion, but were also aware that the inferno of Europe's twelve-year-long suicide (as Kurt Bergel called it) and its painful re-emergence had created a huge chasm between the present era and those aspects of Schnitzler's world that the older scholars had experienced and could understand.[15] Not surprisingly, it was less the author of *Liebelei* than the political skeptic of 1914 and beyond that resonated with scholars such as Bergel and Weiss, who had been forced to flee Nazi Germany. In other words, the Second World War alerted Schnitzler's advocates to revisit his experience of the First World War.

Four years before compiling and editing *Aphorismen und Betrachtungen* in 1967, Weiss had considered it a heinous oversight that reading lists consistently ignored Schnitzler's mature work, which contained his "infinitely more important" essays and philosophical studies.[16] His inclusion of philosophical pieces in the volume nevertheless led Herbert Seidler to question whether he might not have done better to include more aesthetic pieces reflecting both the strength of the material and scholarly consensus, not just editorial interest.[17] What Seidler means by "scholarly consensus" is not the work of the members of the IASRA and its journal *Modern Austrian Literature*, however. In Seidler's opinion, the journal contains articles "wissenschaftlich wenig oder gar nicht belangvoll" (of little scientific substance), and the centennial commemorative volume *Studies in Arthur Schnitzler* is "leider nicht sehr ergiebig" (unfortunately has little to offer).[18] The scholarship Seidler finds most useful involves textual editions with commentary, work on correspondence, individual interpretations of single works, and encompassing thematic studies. He cannot praise Reinhard Urbach's textual criticism enough (569, 580–81).

The unflagging praise in Weiss's apologia of Schnitzler is evident in his view that "neither praise nor adverse comments could detract him from the path that his artistic evolution, his personal honesty, and his social conscience delineated."[19] According to William Rey's review of the first *Festschrift* of the Schnitzler renaissance, *Studies in Arthur Schnitzler*, the IASRA was to safeguard intrinsic interpretations of its object of admiration; it was time to stop enlisting the aid of Freud, Mach, and Nietzsche, for Schnitzler provided the solution to his own puzzles.[20] What Schnitzler said, went, and any criticism alert to the gaps in the author's vision was dismissed as speculative.

The sheer volume of investigations in the sixties and seventies, evident in any bibliography or in the space devoted to Schnitzler in any university library, makes it necessary to limit the following discussion of impressionism and ethics to four major investigations: in the United States, William H. Rey's *Arthur Schnitzler: Die späte Prosa als Gipfel seines Schaffens* (Arthur Schnitzler: The Late Prose as Pinnacle of his Production, 1968); in Great Britain, Martin Swales's *Arthur Schnitzler: A Critical Study* (1971); in the Federal Republic of Germany, Ernst L. Offermanns's *Arthur Schnitzler: Das Komödienwerk als Kritik des Im-*

pressionismus (Arthur Schnitzler: The Comedies as Criticism of Impressionism, 1973); and in the German Democratic Republic, Manfred Diersch's *Empiriokritizismus und Impressionismus: Über Beziehungen zwischen Philosophie, Ästhetik und Literatur um 1900 in Wien* (Empiriocriticism and Impressionism: On Philosophy, Aesthetics, and Literature Around 1900 in Vienna, 1973).

Structural Humanism: William H. Rey, *Arthur Schnitzler: Die späte Prosa als Gipfel seines Schaffens* (1968)

The thesis of Rey's book *Arthur Schnitzler: Die späte Prosa als Gipfel seines Schaffens* (1968) is that a careful reading of Schnitzler's late prose should be sufficient for overturning stereotypes of decadence and nihilism.[21] His task is to examine the structures in the novellas from *Casanovas Heimfahrt* (1918) to *Flucht in die Finsternis* (1931). Beyond the usual hostile anti-Semitic camps, those who have exercised a negative influence on Schnitzler interpretation are Josef Körner, Bernhard Blume, and Hermann Broch (1886–1951). First, Rey finds Körner's 1927 article problematic because Körner leaves no room for Schnitzler the positivist to reveal any metaphysical interests. Second, Blume's opinion of Schnitzler the nihilist still stands, despite his revision of the thesis that Schnitzler chronicles nihilism and nothing else. Third, Rey considers Broch's thesis that *fin-de-siècle* Vienna was the value-vacuum and kitsch-capital of Europe productive only if one begins to regard the alleged decay of values to be "compost" for incredible intellectual creativity (16). Unconcerned about Schnitzler's place in literary history, Rey wants instead to awaken gratitude for Schnitzler's talent, because journalistic criticism has tended to read the late narratives as entertainment literature and has missed the point that Schnitzler's depth lies hidden on the surface (12–13). Nevertheless, it is obvious that Schnitzler's narrative becomes his crowning achievement after 1918, at the same time that his dramatic production begins to fade in significance (14).

An example of the depth Schnitzler has hidden on the surface applies to his constant treatment of death. Reluctant to think that the positivistic skeptic Schnitzler would equate death with nothingness, Rey enlists the aid of the novellas *Spiel im Morgengrauen* and *Fräulein Else*. In the former, Lieutenant Willi Kasda becomes self-aware only when contemplating the prospect of death, discovering in the free act of suicide a dignity that eluded him in life, thus supplying the ideal counter-example to Lieutenant Gustl's cowardly waffling over the military's honor code. Else also outshines Gustl by electing the peace of death over the fear if its emptiness (Rey 1968, 20). Schnitzler's irony toward Gustl's self-deception has become sincere tragedy in documenting Else's victim status.

Even if traceable to Schnitzler's views, Rey's acceptance of the narrator's account as the definitive reading is open to question. Without addressing the particulars of the three narratives mentioned, one should bear in mind Swales's view that Schnitzler "ruthlessly unmasks the false relationship to death" of his characters and of a society which had, as Broch wrote, many conceptions of dying, but few of death.[22] To be sure, suicide cannot be said to denote freedom from convention, and a more productive question to pose against the grain of tragedy is what Kasda ought to do about his shame. Schnitzler could have Kasda choose to continue living, even if it brings dishonor under one system, for one might well imagine survival a worthwhile activity. In fact, Swales notes that what Schnitzler considers moral — partly because it is difficult — is the business of everyday responsibility that shuns the easy escape. Rey confuses ethics with tragedy, failing to see that death's effectiveness on the level of plot should not crowd out equally valid choices. Careful to endorse Schnitzler at all costs, Rey is in danger of advocating tragedy that is good for the stage but not necessarily instructive for life, unless one examines who is fooling whom.

If one doubts whether tragedy always represents the higher solution in terms of a mode of operation, one can still allow, with Rey, that suicide appears the only escape for some characters. Else's pathos, for example, turns on the interrelationship of choice and desire. She first chooses to honor her mother's request to petition Felix Dorsday for money to rescue her father from financial and legal ruin. The main choice is whether she can honor Dorsday's offer of money for nudity. There is little doubt that desire invades the decision process itself, blurring what is rational and freely chosen; and the line between morality and psychology is never distinct. It would seem that Schnitzler blames Else's predicament on the people around her. Her father's gambling, her mother's request for help, and Dorsday's request for nudity are all more clearly "immoral" than her exhibitionism, as Rey writes, because they derive from irresponsibility that has resorted to dehumanization for the sake of money. Yet Rey's drive to valorize Schnitzler and his figures leads to premature judgments, as Manfred Diersch makes us aware. (See the final section of this chapter)

Rey's structuralist observations concerning *Traumnovelle* reinforce the impression that Schnitzler has mastered all polarities of high and low, good and evil, faithful and unfaithful. In his 1962 article on *Traumno-velle*, he had flatly insisted that the common interests of Schnitzler and Freud were not enough reason to read the poet through the eyes of the psychologist, because psychoanalysis offered no special key for unlocking Schnitzler's work. The unconscious was the region in which Schnitzler cast his questions about the true nature of human beings, making *Traum-novelle* one of the great examples of humanistic German literature.[23]

Six years later, his chapter on *Traumnovelle* still rebuffed psychoana-lytical speculation, convinced as he was that Schnitzler had left dogma behind to follow his own humanistic insights (Rey 1968, 111) and re-state the myth of temptation and redemption through love (99). Mar-riage means understanding one's fundamental polarity with one's spouse, and that each experiences the spiral of erotic temptation, giving in, guilt, and suffering, which leads to mutual trust and confession, sincere com-munication, and finally mutual pardon. The readiness to sacrifice pre-serves marriages from the disintegration of impulsive acts (98).

The polarities between marital partners are matched by polarities in the narrative structure: "Die Nacht steht gegen den Tag, Unterwelt gegen Oberwelt, Chaos gegen Ordnung, Traum gegen Wirklichkeit, Lust und Tod gegen Liebe und Leben" (Rey 1968, 99: Night stands against day, underworld against world above, chaos against order, dream against reality, lust and death against love and life). The typical dichotomous structure in *Traumnovelle* is the bourgeois world of career, security, health, day, and family, poised against the nocturnal world of Fridolin's seedy, piano-playing acquaintance Nachtigall (102). Further, middle-class predictability opposes the extremes and tensions intrinsic to the other world: power and sacrifice, veiling and unveiling, lower and upper class, sacred and demonic, enticement and refusal, morbidity and frivol-ity. Schnitzler has Fridolin examine the world of night from the perspec-tive of day, but also the world of day from the perspective of the irrational. In her dream, Albertine had wanted to let Fridolin perish, but can sit angelically across from him at lunch; upon leaving, he again be-comes conscious that all this order and security was pretense and illusion (107). Therefore the contrast between dream and reality is not stark after all, because the waking world appears dreamlike and unreal (109).

Dreams allow each spouse to shed superego restraints for the sake of libido, which in Albertine's case appears with a sadistic streak (Rey 1968, 109). It is precisely when we compare him with Freud, however, that Schnitzler the humanist is announced most fervently. Freud would fail to comprehend the act of kindness of the prostitute Mizzi, for example, when she foregoes Fridolin as a customer to preserve his health. Her good deed creates an echo that resounds in Fridolin's humanity, proving that "das Hohe auch in der Tiefe zu finden ist" (the upstanding can be found in the depths), for a sexual liaison has attained ethical meaning (110). Similarly, at the aristocratic masked ball, the woman in nun's habit who offers to take Fridolin's punishment is proof of ethics asserting themselves in the most macabre underworld of lust and horror — of goodness and humanity emerging suddenly out of a free-for-all barbarism (111). Prostitute and nun both serve as humanistic saviors.

Ignoring psychoanalysis, then, Rey's humanistic reading brings out the polarities of characters and forces, and he marvels at the speed with which Schnitzler turns his characters' complete abandon into moral reflection. Schnitzler is not about dualism, however, but about echoing Goethe's wisdom that light and dark, good and evil, high and low always appear in tandem (Rey 1968, 112). To Rey, the purpose of the adventurous underworld is to teach Fridolin, otherwise lost in the comfortable bourgeois world of day, the fundamentals of morality. By confessing that his curiosity has led to the death of the atoning nun, Fridolin reaches a higher level of moral maturity, having traveled from deception to discovery (113).

Morality *ex negativo:* Martin Swales, *Arthur Schnitzler: A Critical Study* (1971)

Since Sol Liptzin, no one had published a full-length study on Schnitzler in English until British scholar Martin Swales entered the field with *Arthur Schnitzler: A Critical Study* (1971). In a review, Frederick Beharriell faulted Swales for not acknowledging the already broad research base, for ignoring the importance of depth psychology, and for not including *Fräulein Else* on his list of Schnitzler's best artistic achievements.[24] It was not that Swales was separating morality from psychology, however, especially if by psychology one meant Schnitzler's subtle exposure of self-deception. It is just that Swales's approach is less straightforward and optimistic than that of Rey, because he emphasizes the need to weigh, sift, and even negate the contradictory voices of Schnitzler's ironic "both — and" narration. The ambiguity that Rey misses in his concern with structure is documented by Swales in his chapter "The Ambiguous Narrator," for example, where he examines two stories — *Die griechische Tänzerin* (The Greek Dancer, 1902) and *Der letzte Brief eines Literaten* (The Last Letter of a Litterateur, 1932) — to identify how a narrator's underlying jealousy or animosity resides in predictable patterns of self-righteousness, protests, excuses, appeals to fate, and half-truths. Ambivalence occurs in the gap between the events described and the way the narrator chooses to interpret them (83). Once a reader becomes aware of that gap, the stories the narrator chooses to tell and his manner of telling them become fair game for critique. A moral condemnation of a character, for example, may be the narrator using self-righteousness as a screen for his own insecurities (86). The truth may reside in the opposite of the narrator's claims and skill at fabricating a world of appearances.

Swales's chapter "Moral Confusion and the Comedy of Ambiguity" examines *Professor Bernhardi,* a play that is called a comedy because it concerns the interplay of moral argumentation with the context of argumentation. Since a moral utterance is conditioned by its context, it is unlikely that one solution to a problem would apply across the board. Swales chooses to focus on Bernhardi's actions stemming from his refusal to allow the priest to administer last rites to the dying girl. Wishing to keep her suffering at a minimum, Bernhardi is shocked that the priest has awakened the girl from her final drug-induced euphoria, for this guarantees a death neither happy nor blessed.

The two versions of morality in the play, according to Swales, are instinctive humanity and the morality of the social organization. Bernhardi's conviction that the most moral thing is to alleviate suffering is not universally correct, but the right one according to his interests and training in the ethics of the medical profession (61). He acts first as a physician, not as a private individual or a Jew, as the papers claim. Regardless of his certitude, Bernhardi's choice must take the morality of the social organization into consideration (59), which Swales calls the outer sector of morality. This sector affects the local circle of family, friends, and work, as well the realm of the social and political order (65). There are dilemmas beyond the hospital room to consider, suggests Swales. Bernhardi believes he sacrifices his integrity by allowing his decision to become heroic for the sake of a political cause or for the good of the Elisabethinum Hospital. It is not enough to be consistent in his intuitive decision, because Bernhardi fails to carry through his decision to the outer moral dimensions. His very resistance to the tainted public sphere shows his moral inadequacy, Swales believes, because that sphere demands more than private consistency. Integrity comes only through compromise for the greater good, but Bernhardi has compromised in the wrong direction — "between the complete withdrawal of a man skeptical of any positive action or statement on a problematic issue and the reformer who is prepared to stand for certain values and for their recognition in the world around him" (64). To take any stand at all means to follow through with it. It seems incongruous, though, that no one in the play is qualified to indict Bernhardi with a clear conscience. What makes the play a comedy is that the truth is spoken by the opportunist politician Hofrat Winkler, the person least qualified to do so (64). While Schnitzler stresses the imminent corruptibility of both language and action in the public sphere, bold speech and action remain necessary evils.

One place Swales finds a pragmatic standard, precisely because it is existential, is at the conclusion of *Traumnovelle,* where Fridolin and Albertine hear their daughter's laughter and face the new day with the unresolved confusion of their mutual revelations: "Schnitzler can offer no more than Camus's assertion at the end of *La Peste,* a conviction wrung from the depths of negation and despair, that the business of everyday living is a worthwhile process, one to which the individual must assent" (78). This existential component corresponds to Reinhard Urbach's view that when moral codes fail to result in improved life, they become fair game for the satirist. Doubtful whether individuals and societies can improve themselves, Schnitzler uses satire not to suggest improvements, but to destroy illusions.[25] Urbach argues that Schnitzler's depictions of the roadblocks to individual freedom do not remove hope altogether from the equation, but that the satirist becomes the optimist *ex negativo.*[26]

Overcoming Impressionism: Ernst Offermanns, *Arthur Schnitzler: Das Komödienwerk als Kritik des Impressionismus* (1973)

Also paying attention to *Professor Bernhardi* is Ernst Offermanns, whose book *Arthur Schnitzler: Das Komödienwerk als Kritik des Impressionismus* (1973) is a close examination of impressionism in Schnitzler's works.[27] Before tracing his interpretation of the play, however, it is important to review a few of his remarks about impressionism, beginning with his explanation of Schnitzler's philosophical essay "Der Geist im Wort und in der Tat" (Mind in Word and Deed), first included in 1927 in *Buch der Sprüche und Bedenken* (Book of Sayings and Second Thoughts), which contained aphorisms and observations from the twenties and was incorporated into *Aphorismen und Betrachtungen* in 1967. Schnitzler begins his musings with two diagrams on facing pages. On the left page, he shows two triangles sharing a horizontal axis, but with one pointing upward and one pointing downward. At points on the "celestial" top triangle are affixed those careers of mind associated with continuity and good memory: prophet, poet, statesman, historian, for example. The "infernal" reflection of the triangle in the bottom half depicts those careers for which continuity is troublesome: politician, journalist, litterateur, for example. On the facing page is the same diagram, but associated with careers of deed: heroes, leaders, and scientists come out favorably vis-à-vis their infernal counterparts of swindlers, dictators, and quacks. Underneath the explorers (positive), with their definite quests, are the aimless adventurers (negative) whose actions come to represent for Schnitzler the negative typology of the impressionistic lifestyle: "Der negative Typ lebt ohne das Gefühl von Zusammenhängen, das Gestern ist tot für ihn, das Morgen unvorstellbar, nur im Raum vermag er sich auszubreiten, er hat im wahren Sinne des Wortes keine Zeit, daher seine Ungeduld" (The negative type lives without any sensation of connections, yesterday is dead for him, tomorrow unimaginable, only in space can he spread out, he has in the true sense of the word no time at all, hence his impatience).[28] The present tense for negative types has slipped into constant transition. Positive types, on the other hand, possess a sense of continuity that promises an awareness of responsibility in the present. If impressionism is a collective neurosis, negative types are accordingly more susceptible to it.

Explaining this typology is Offermanns's first task. Nearly a decade earlier, he had compiled the materials and commentary for a 1964 edition of *Anatol*.[29] At that time, he had attributed the loss of the unified self to the autonomous personality.[30] He had also attributed Anatol's impressionism to the general decay of values that included the traditional metaphysical, moral, and societal order. The subject had no binding standard to oppose the stimulations of the moment to keep itself anchored in reality. The Anatol phenotype, Offermanns argued, is best described by Schnitzler's term "kernlos": an irresolute conglomerate of impressions, it lacks a unifying center and shifts itself according to moods.[31] Without a trajectory of identity, including a healthy memory and goals for the future, the lonely and restless self literally has "no time," attempting to overcome emptiness by expanding into surrounding space (Offermanns 1973, 9). Impressionism thus converges with imperialism: Anatol is an adventurer because his discontinuous ego fails to overcome isolation from the social environment, and the women he conquers are solely the territorial screen on which he projects his adventures. Skepticism, hypochondria, and the inability to forget are experiences that further poison the impressionist (10).

Offermanns then describes the genesis of impressionism in terms of dissolution and acceleration. In the history of consciousness, for example, impressionism can be traced to the dissolution of Christian-idealist metaphysics into positivism, and of historicism into extreme subjectivity (10). That is, the hierarchical narratives of religion and nation have lost their credibility as unifying forces, and the individual is alone in the void with relativism. In practical economic terms, industrialization and urbanization contribute to the increase and complexity of impressions individuals are forced to process. In addition, the laws ruling the marketplace stipulate speed, novelty, and a redefinition of private and public, work and relaxation. In the political realm, liberal influence and standards of reason become weaker as previously marginalized groups such as anti-Semitic Christian Socialists and Slavic nationalists gain influence. Sensuality, moods, and art become the refuge for liberals, and this is another reason for impressionism: it functions as an arena of chosen protest (in response to historical forces, not as a victim of them) against the increased banal uniformity of labor and the reduction of all experience to matters of labor (10–11). Whether as a label to apply to others or to oneself, impressionism is another word for decadence. For both the cause and effect of the "feuilletonization" of reality, finally, Offermanns holds the press responsible (12).

Drawing on Hermann Broch's idea in his essay "Hofmannsthal und seine Zeit" (1948) that Vienna defined the center of the European value-vacuum, Offermanns argues that after 1900, Schnitzler's impressionistic dramas become progressively critical toward the spirit of the epoch, and not simply reflective of it. The one-acts are appropriate for reflecting the lack of development in the hero: life is seen as a series of interchangeable episodes (12). This is true of *Reigen* (1900) no less than of *Anatol:* both cycles echo Nietzsche's idea of cyclical return. Offermanns finds that all figures are subject to an unmitigated determinism that weakens any critical impulse, but that Schnitzler's demand for truthfulness can be deduced dialectically from its absence. The burlesques *Der grüne Kakadu* (1899) and *Zum großen Wurstel* (1905) emphasize the marionette-character of existence, even parodying Schnitzler's own themes and motives, but his self-irony signals a change from both cycle and burlesque to comedy. This departure is determined by a shift in his view of freedom and determinism and a more intensive criticism of impressionism. *Der einsame Weg* represents the first straightforward analysis of the impressionistic type (13). After examining that play briefly, Offermanns explores the permutations of the comedy of impressionism: the instances and ethical ramifications of the "negative type" in Schnitzler's dramas.

Offermanns's discussion of *Professor Bernhardi*, his sixth chapter, occurs under the rubric of the collision of individual and politics in the elegiac comedy. Offermanns asserts that understanding Bernhardi entails knowing something about the politician Flint and the priest. Flint is a nihilist who embodies impressionism by ignoring the past and seizing opportunistically upon the mood of the moment (95). His goals fit his worldview of productivity, which means staying busy for the sake of some generality or greater good. At first glance, this seems the opposite of the passivity one would associate with the impressionist. But common to all impressionists, including Flint, is the loss of ego, because the mood of the moment has squashed the protests of memory-based conscience (95). Were his private convictions constant, Flint's public performances as a political actor would negate them. But being ephemeral instead, each new conviction simply replaces the one before it, whether expressed privately in front of Bernhardi or proclaimed enthusiastically before Parliament. Active impressionism is the ability of the deft rhetorical "sportsman" to achieve his intended effect.

The pendulum of Flint's convictions, says Offermanns, swings with each new situation. Bernhardi convinces Flint to take up his cause before Parliament, but more appealing to Flint than the rightness of the cause is the prospect of manipulating opinion and stylizing the issue into a struggle of light against darkness. Because the initial support was not authentic, it is not against Flint's fickle character to end up suggesting — as he hears disapproval of his initial views — that Bernhardi perhaps be cited for a religious disturbance. Conscience requires facing up to conflict, but in Flint the stronger impression prevails (96–97). If Flint acts according to the moment, the cleric is far less flexible, acting only under the auspices of unchanging ideology. Both fail to achieve a credible autonomy, however, by separating their private views from their public statements. What is more, both markedly avoid concrete moral action by falling back on the phrase: "in einem höheren Sinn" (in a higher sense), an abstraction that loses no time ushering in concrete injustice (97).

As far as Bernhardi himself is concerned, Offermanns places the accent differently than Rey and Swales. Bernhardi's case-by-case morality allows him to avoid both extreme flexibility and rigidity. His morality originates in a negation of evil that does not branch out into positive maxims or ethical generalizations. It suffices for him to be "wahrhaftig" (98: consistent) and thus avoid being maneuvered into a "Rollenexistenz" not his own. He will neither endorse the programs of the liberal newspaper nor allow it to fight his battles (99). He demands precise, consistent thought and fidelity to one's past — unlike Anatol, for example, or Sala in *Der einsame Weg* (100). After discussing Bernhardi's failed attempt at dialogue with forces akin to rubber or granite (103), Offermanns completes his description of Bernhardi, whose fledgling steps take him beyond passivity, as the type of reactive hero who represents Schnitzler's attempt at dramatic rebirth. Bernhardi speaks brokenly and indecisively, hesitating, questioning, objecting, and even cooling his anger such that his surroundings appear comical and impel a retreat into his career (104–5). He himself is comical only in the sense that Schnitzler has reversed the function of the comical figure in its form popular until Lessing: instead of singling out one figure made laughable by his wrong actions, Schnitzler's play calls itself a comedy because of the constellation that gives rise to individualistic behavior ridiculed by a society made up of Flints (106). Ultimately Bernhardi claims the heritage of Lessing's *Nathan der Weise,* but unfortunately times have changed. Unlike Lessing, Schnitzler cannot hinder the worst of patriarchal ideology through a coalition of reason, faced as he is with an entire society bent on irrationality (107).

For Offermanns, the comedy ends without the usual resolution of dramatic tensions. Still, there is a flicker of hope in Bernhardi's resigned posture. *Der einsame Weg* ends with the possibilities of decadence; *Fink und Fliederbusch* with an image of total leveling and conformity to the system. But within the chaos of relativism and half-truths is nevertheless an exemplary individual conscious of the right thing and attempting to achieve it (108). Schnitzler's stated belief, after all, is that the world has been advanced more by those more right than righteous, by doubters more than dogmatists of all parties (109).

The historical implications are clear for Offermanns. In Flint's case, the concept of any character development whatsoever is inapplicable, except when history weds sentimentality to his brutal but empty work ethic to develop fascism (96). The sportsman and the fanatic are the fateful types who will come into their own in the First World War and beyond (97). "Im Spiel der Flints ist die Barbarei angelegt, und die Flints bereiten sich vor, die Mörder der Bernhardis zu werden" (105–6: The Flints have laid the foundation for barbarism and are preparing to become the murderers of the Bernhardis).

Fräulein Else, Bourgeois: Manfred Diersch, *Empiriokritizismus und Impressionismus: Über Beziehungen zwischen Philosophie, Ästhetik und Literatur um 1900 in Wien* (1973)

During the seventies, at least, Offermanns's work met with scholarly approval within the Schnitzler fold; in his research review Seidler expresses his wish that Offermanns's analysis of Schnitzler's comedies be duplicated with respect to the stories.[32] At roughly the same time, GDR scholar Manfred Diersch was working carefully on his own analysis of impressionism to arrive at quite different conclusions regarding its genesis and composition. Diersch's thesis is that empiriocriticism and impressionism are not attributable to some *Zeitgeist* circa 1900, but to concrete historical-material conditions for which Schnitzler's imperialistic class is responsible. Unfortunately, Diersch's supple criticism becomes a foregone conclusion when he explores the shortcomings of every ideology but his own. While his observations illustrate the remarkable convergence of views in the early seventies concerning Schnitzler's ethics, his Marxist conclusions distance him from the prevailing humanist view of Schnitzler.[33]

The following summary applies to Diersch's critical method, his remarks on the novella *Fräulein Else,* and his conclusions about *fin-de-siècle* Viennese literature in general. His thesis of similarities in the writings of Mach, Bahr, and Schnitzler is a bold one, but beyond his introduction, I limit this summary to the discussion of Schnitzler, where Diersch's interpretation is clearly informed by the chapters on Mach's empiriocriticism and Bahr's impressionist aesthetics that precede it.

Diersch has chosen Mach to represent empiriocritical philosophy, Bahr the aesthetics of impressionistic literature, and Schnitzler impressionistic literature as a whole. Every style of writing and painting corresponds to a style of thinking. Diersch must make sense of empiriocriticism to the extent that the questions arising from its worldview were the same as those of impressionist aesthetics, and vice versa. The next step is showing how the impressionist interpretation of human reality influenced the content and form of literary production. To Diersch, the internal principles of the monologue novella *Fräulein Else* illustrate Bahr's impressionist aesthetics, although Diersch does not explain his decision for *Fräulein Else* over *Leutnant Gustl*, which was published precisely during the height of Bahr's and Mach's popularity at the century's turn (7–8). Bahr, Mach, and Schnitzler exemplify false bourgeois consciousness through worldviews determined by their concrete material station in society. At the core of their epistemology lies positivism, a specific form of bourgeois philosophy that has developed in tandem with the imperialistic society of Austria-Hungary (10–11). Diersch hopes his investigation on the genesis of positivism will shed light on the bourgeois ideology it has spawned in the present (12). Just as decadence has been a deprecatory label, so positivism must brace itself for another round of abuse, having last served Körner's purposes as the negative corollary to expressionism.

At first glance, says Diersch, it appears that *Fräulein Else* is another installment of Schnitzler's sociocritical exposure of hypocritical bourgeois morality, of the contradiction between the façade of respectability and actual depravity (84–85). Everything revolves around money: anyone in Else's world with enough of it can afford the luxury of a good reputation (85). Lest we think Else is the victim of her parents and Dorsday in becoming a purchasable object, Diersch reminds us that Else's monologue is full of longing for love and uninterrupted pleasure and thoughts of death, even before the fateful letter from her mother arrives requesting Else beg Dorsday for money to bail out Else's father from a longstanding gambling mess (85). Harboring the wish to be a hussy, she has already made a point of undressing with her shades open, even before Dorsday requests a private viewing of her body in return for providing the requested financial help (86).

Love, fidelity, and friendship are not binding components of Else's world. She and her family live behind the masks demanded by their societal positions, making impossible the reciprocal trust necessary for authentic community (87). According to Diersch, sexuality in this milieu is an alienating force granting only momentary pleasure. With life meaningless except for a few sensations that count as residual values, all human qualities appear infinitely adapted (88–89). Else's view of death as the sole certainty resembles Ernst Mach's view that the death of individual perception means the end of everything; death functions both to intensify her hedonism and to promise release from it (89). The lack of objective moorings, ethics, and trust makes any decision strenuous, and the pressure from the outside (Dorsday and her parents) corresponds with her own internal pressure to reach a decision (90–91). Without a doubt, Else is the machine-ego that according to Mach is unsalvageable due to the lack of any immanent meaning whatsoever in her life (92). All this is proof that Else is scarcely a simple victim of immoral external factors: "Mit der Annahme objektiver Maßstäbe, an denen Gut und Böse *innerhalb* der Novelle zu messen wären, setzt die Interpretation etwas

voraus, was in seiner Auflösung zu zeigen, gerade ein Anliegen der Novelle ist" (93: By accepting objective standards by which good and evil
could be measured within the novella, criticism postulates precisely the
thing whose dissolution the novella is trying to prove). This is a corrective to William Rey's sunny estimation of Else (and Marcolina in *Casanovas Heimfahrt*) as two of the purest embodiments of feminine freedom
ever created by Schnitzler.[34]

Diersch notes correctly that the inner monologue form ("psychoste-
nography") is the most adequate response to Bahr's call for converting
the impressionistic view into literature and for objectifying the state of
the soul (94). In addition, Schnitzler provides extra motivation for the
plot by describing Else's weakened physiological state, also a volatile
catalyst for a labile psyche (95). On the level of language, Else's thoughts
are shown through free association: not surprisingly, noun phrases,
coordinating conjunctions, ellipses, and question marks predominate
(100). All information about time and place is subject to change: we see
the landscape through Else's consciousness, for example, a source that
changes the information it delivers according to mood (97). Memories,
fantasies, and emotions bounce the reader from place to place, and Else's
monologue changes occasionally into a dialogue with herself (102).

Else's pointillist consciousness is reflected in the atomization of the
text. But Diersch extrapolates from the text back to Schnitzler, suggesting that Else serves to reflect Schnitzler's own writing habits. Busy
watching his characters develop, Schnitzler never has a preconceived
notion of how a text will end, for he too is dependent on impressions.
Moreover, the absence of concepts in the text signifies Schnitzler's distrust of them. Schnitzler preferred case studies to generalizations, but felt
the loss of adequate explanations of experience. Like Else, Schnitzler
feels radically alone, recording in his works a series of impressions that
announce the loss of meaning (107). His output therefore arrives in the
same philosophical place as Mach's empiriocriticism and Bahr's call for
a "new psychology" (108). Schnitzler's form shapes reality as a subjective, psychic phenomenon. Else's microscopic introspection indicates the
dissolution of personality from the inside out. The problem is that any
general ethical statement one is compelled to make must be adapted to
fit the current mood and psyche of the heroine, thus remaining tied to
her subjective reality rather than to the social one (108–9).

If Else is nothing but an ensemble of impressions; if the norms that
could be used to judge this view of life have become inconsistent; if every
individual is held prisoner in her own world without meaning (110),
does this make Schnitzler a nihilist? If we are shown a consciousness laid

bare from the inside out, in which communication is broken and subjective knowledge rendered automatically suspect, is there any hope beyond skepticism? Diersch's verdict reads like Urbach's: Schnitzler is the dialectical moralist showing dissolution in concrete life sectors, not the apologist for ethical norms argued for generally (111).

For the reader with the understanding for it, *Fräulein Else* makes transparent that Else's loss of meaning is a criticism of the world from which she stems, and this means Schnitzler is not nihilistic (114). Schnitzler's complete works show the ground from which his moral skepticism and philosophical relativism grew, but the social sphere he depicts is limited. It is not enough to explain the objective agreement of his views with Mach and Bahr by personal contact or intellectual influence alone. Instead, the explanation arrives after the chapter on Schnitzler's snapshot of Else's interior monologue, when Diersch turns from discussing disorientation in the self to address the symptoms of societal malaise more directly, presenting Schnitzler as a prisoner of bourgeois decadence, not its liberator.

Vienna's impressionism (from roughly 1890–1914) rested on material factors unacknowledged by Schnitzler, Mach, and Bahr (although Bahr began as a Marxist). What these thinkers were experiencing was not a universal loss of meaning and purpose, but a specifically Austrian loss of traditional liberal values within a growing apparatus of state imperialism. Quoting Marx and Engels, Diersch attributes Schnitzler's sense of isolation to the alienating effects of labor (146–47). Aesthetic isolationism keeps captive those impressionists such as Schnitzler who attempt to transcend their society, because the problems they address come packaged with imperialism.

If Bahr complains of breakdown in the individual or in the art work, lamenting how money, fashion, popularity, and novelty determine a work's success more than its content does, he nevertheless fails to pinpoint the problem central to capitalism itself. The symptoms of failure are not a sign that an intrinsically healthy system has spun slightly out of orbit: it is foolish to talk about the misapplication of something already unhealthy at its core. Unfortunately, the symptoms that should enable Bahr to escape the system only lead him back into it. Diersch is astonished that writers like Bahr and Schnitzler deliver accurate descriptions of decadent values without determining their imperialist cause (151). The objective causes for alienation from self, community, and workplace derive from the bourgeois perspective inside the imperialistic relations of production (155). After 1890, this perspective was the decay of a liberalism once considered unalterable. The message of freedom, progress, law, and humanism as universal and eternal was really the class-specific property of the economically liberal (157).

A specifically Austrian decadence comes from a long feudal tradition, multi-nationalism, a heightened sense of the Baroque, and the prominence of the theater in public life (159–63). One sign of decadence is anti-Semitism, a symptom of a decayed humanistic ideal visited upon impressionists. The simple economic explanation supplied by Engels is that anti-Semitism was the reaction of medieval, declining social classes against modern society with its large-scale capitalists and day laborers, and was therefore a perversion of feudal socialism. Large-scale capitalism at the end of the nineteenth century had irritated the petite bourgeois, the guild laborers, and shopkeepers — classes indeed left over from the Middle Ages — to the point of hunting for a scapegoat (164).

Thinking they were experiencing the loss of all meaning, impressionists were only experiencing what was visible through an imperialistic grid. The distaste that disenchanted liberals had for idealism and abstractions should have been aimed at the clichés of bourgeois capitalism (166). The loss of the whole and its comfortable reassurances was experienced by impressionists who had the luxury to consider this loss. Decadence was inevitable not because of moral breakdown or the loss of liberal ideals, but because the imperialistic motor had begun to move the monarchy toward self-destruction. In other words, the impressionists had confused cause and effect. Breakdown of values was a sign of decadence, but not its cause. What was ultimately responsible was the volatile mix, for liberals, of economic gains and political losses. Diersch reads impressionistic aestheticism ultimately as a reflection of the conflicts of imperialistic reality in a bourgeois consciousness that was experiencing the transition to imperialism in turn-of-the-century Vienna (171).

To sum up: following the dark decades of the thirties and forties, the rebirth of Schnitzler criticism began slowly in the fifties and gathered speed with the 1962 centennial of Schnitzler's birth. An association, its journal, and new editions of his works did much to encourage Schnitzler scholarship. Schnitzler seemed particularly suitable for moral investigations — a remarkable fact, when we remember the accusations of his decadence, moral relativism, and nihilism. The new critical generation insisted on observing a Schnitzler of expanded scope and ethical vigor, where the emphasis was on free will instead of determinism. Advocates of Schnitzler such as William Rey, Martin Swales, and Ernst Offermanns proclaimed his criticism of impressionism — he was not the same as his characters. Freedom held sway over determinism in Schnitzler's characters, who to embolden their sense of ethical purpose had to at least believe in the existence of free will.[35] Diersch, for his part, criticized Schnitzler's imperialistic worldview using GDR-style Marxism. Whether humanist or Marxist, these scholars found much in Schnitzler that had to do with the "right" way to live, in statements of value and truth, authenticity, and responsibility. Ethics show through in any enterprise intent on documenting, uncovering, and pointing the finger at suppression: any "is" situation requiring a better "ought." The history of Schnitzler's misunderstanding and rediscovery is a reminder of how urgently criticism was needed to decode these ethical messages and thus offer alternative responses to his texts.

Notes

[1] In Europe, Vienna produced five dissertations on Schnitzler after the Second World War, with Germany following suit with five during the fifties, but none became cornerstones for scholarship.

[2] Herbert Seidler, "Die Forschung zu Arthur Schnitzler seit 1945," *Zeitschrift für Deutsche Philologie* 95 (1976): 567–95, here 576.

[3] Herbert W. Reichert, "Arthur Schnitzler and Modern Ethics," *Journal of the International Arthur Schnitzler Research Association* (1963): 21–24, here 21.

[4] Frederick J. Beharriell, "Arthur Schnitzler's Range of Theme," *Monatshefte* 43/7 (November 1951): 301–11.

[5] Oskar Seidlin, introduction, *Der Briefwechsel Arthur Schnitzler — Otto Brahm,* ed. Seidlin, 2nd ed. (Tübingen: Niemeyer, 1975), xxix.

[6] Quoted in Klaus Kilian, *Die Komödien Arthur Schnitzlers: Sozialer Rollenzwang und kritische Ethik* (Düsseldorf: Bertelsmann Universitätsverlag, 1972), 49.

[7] Richard Allen, "Arthur Schnitzler's Works and their Reception: An Annotated Bibliography" (Diss., U of Michigan, 1964), 73–74.

[8] Robert O. Weiss, "Arthur Schnitzler's Literary and Philosophical Development," *Journal of the International Arthur Schnitzler Research Association* 2/1 (1963): 4–20, here 11–13.

[9] Arthur Schnitzler, *Aphorismen und Betrachtungen,* ed. Robert O. Weiss (Frankfurt am Main: Fischer, 1967), 20.

[10] Quoted in Allen, "Annotated Bibliography" (1964), 77.

[11] Weiss, "Literary and Philosophical Development," (1963), 17; Josef Körner, *Arthur Schnitzler: Gestalten und Probleme* (Zürich: Almathea, 1921), 11.

[12] Jeffrey B. Berlin, *An Annotated Arthur Schnitzler Bibliography 1965–1977: With an Essay on the Meaning of the "Schnitzler-Renaissance"* (Munich: Wilhelm Fink, 1978), 1.

[13] Arthur Schnitzler, *Entworfenes und Verworfenes: Aus dem Nachlaß,* ed. Reinhard Urbach, vol. 6 of *Gesammelte Werke* (Frankfurt am Main: Fischer, 1977).

[14] Berlin, *Bibliography* (1978), 10.

[15] Kurt Bergel, introduction to *Studies in Arthur Schnitzler,* ed. Herbert W. Reichert and Herman Salinger (Chapel Hill: U of North Carolina P, 1963), 2.

[16] Weiss, *Literary and Philosophical Development* (1963), 5.

[17] Seidler, "Forschung seit 1945" (1976), 572.

[18] Seidler, "Forschung seit 1945" (1976), 569.

[19] Weiss, *Literary and Philosophical Development* (1963), 6.

[20] William Rey, "Beiträge zur amerikanischen Schnitzlerforschung," *German Quarterly* 37/3 (1964): 282–89, here 282–83.

[21] William H. Rey, *Arthur Schnitzler: Die späte Prosa als Gipfel seines Schaffens* (Berlin: Erich Schmidt Verlag, 1968), 12.

[22] Martin Swales, *Arthur Schnitzler: A Critical Study* (Oxford: Clarendon Press, 1971), 52.

[23] William Rey, "Das Wagnis des Guten in Schnitzlers *Traumnovelle,*" *German Quarterly* 35/3 (May 1962): 254–64, here 255.

[24] Frederick J. Beharriell, review of *Arthur Schnitzler: A Critical Study,* by Martin Swales, *Journal of English and Germanic Philology* 72 (1973): 424–28, here 425.

[25] Reinhard Urbach, *Schnitzler-Kommentar zu den erzählenden Schriften und dramatischen Werken* (Munich: Winkler, 1974), 46–48.

[26] Urbach, *Schnitzler-Kommentar* (1974), 48.

[27] Ernst L. Offermanns, *Das Komödienwerk als Kritik des Impressionismus* (Munich: Fink, 1973).

[28] Schnitzler, *Aphorismen und Betrachtungen* (1967), 142.

[29] Ernst Offermanns, "Materialien zum Verständnis der Texte," in Arthur Schnitzler, *Anatol,* ed. Offermanns (Berlin: Walter de Gruyter & Co., 1964), 165–80.

[30] Offermanns, "Materialien"(1964), 165.

[31] *Aphorismen und Betrachtungen* 53–54, quoted in Ernst Offermanns, *Arthur Schnitzler: Das Komödienwerk als Kritik des Impressionismus* (Munich: Fink, 1973), 9. See also Horst Thomé, "Kernlosigkeit und Pose. Zur Rekonstruktion von Schnitzlers Psychologie," *Text & Kontext* 20: 62–87 (1984), and Anna Stroka, "Der Impressionismus in Arthur Schnitzlers 'Anatol' und seine gesellschaftlichen und ideologischen Voraussetzungen," *Germanica Wratislaviensia* 12/76 (1968): 97–111.

[32] Seidler, "Forschung seit 1945" (1976), 588.

[33] Manfred Diersch, *Empiriokritizismus und Impressionismus: Über Beziehungen zwischen Philosophie, Ästhetik und Literatur um 1900 in Wien* (Berlin: Rütten & Loening, 1973).

[34] See Rey, *Späte Prosa* (1968), 33.

[35] Swales, *Arthur Schnitzler: A Critical Study* (1971), 73.

4: Emancipation and Sociohistorical Approaches

THE LAST CHAPTER DESCRIBED the investigations resulting from the momentum of the 1962 centennial of Schnitzler's birth: the present chapter addresses the time frame of scholarly activity surrounding the fiftieth anniversary of his death, celebrated in 1981, and is underpinned by a particular theme and mode. The theme is emancipation, and while it is possible that any author's works can be queried concerning the level of freedom they reveal concerning class, race, and gender, this is particularly true in Schnitzler's case. To scholars of the late seventies and eighties, his works invited a mode of sociohistorical analysis that shifted the critical spotlight from aesthetic concerns to questions of content. The historical backdrop for Schnitzler's works began to be clarified by an audience mostly unfamiliar with the specific constraints on emancipation during Schnitzler's time, although well-acquainted with the vocabulary of emancipation in the present.

Granted, sociohistorical inquiry is in some respects always about uncovering the status of emancipation in literature; in other respects, investigations driven by concerns of emancipation do not always address the historical backdrop. For the examples that follow, however, the convergence of mode and theme becomes explicit. Also apparent is how the various combinations of race, class, and gender make productive a discussion of the institutions such as fraternities, salons, and the military, as well as of the class-crossing practice of dueling.

Limits of the Fraternity:
Gotthold Lessing's *Ernst und Falk* (1778)
and Schnitzler's *Traumnovelle* (1925)

The first sociohistorical approach to be examined here is found in Hartmut Scheible's books, *Arthur Schnitzler in Selbstzeugnissen und Bilddokumenten* and *Arthur Schnitzler und die Aufklärung* (1977), an extensive examination of emancipation in the middle class, particularly of its Jews.[1] In his introduction to the second work, of concern to us here, Scheible discusses the two extremes of Schnitzler scholarship: Blume, who subsumes Schnitzler's worldview under nihilism, and Rey, who subsumes Schnitzler under moral harmony. Scheible questions Rey's insistence in *Arthur Schnitzler: Professor Bernhardi* (1971) that Schnitzler's negativism is eclipsed by his affirmation of the cosmos and that the religious element preserves the play from thematic superficiality.[2] Scheible sees Rey's somewhat philistine remarks as an example of ahistorical approaches wherein humanism turns inhumane by overlooking Schnitzler's depiction of pre-fascist dispositions as the rotted product of the declining bourgeoisie (*Aufklärung*, 9). Diersch makes more sense to Scheible because he derives Schnitzler's content and form from the historical and economic situation, but his project suffers from a Marxist approach made rigid by the terms "empiriocriticism" and "impressionism" (*Aufklärung*, 9–10).

Scheible does not intend to add "Aufklärung" to the list of restrictive labels such as "süße Mädel," "versunkene Welt," or "Nihilismus." Instead, he hopes to make visible a historical perspective in which to view Schnitzler. This perspective, the Enlightenment, has not been tapped sufficiently as a resource for understanding an author whose works contain the impulse of ideas formed early on in the *Bürgertum*, works written long after these ideas had become ideologies (*Aufklärung*, 10). Scheible sets the stage for his discussion by retelling Schnitzler's parable about transcendental beings, representing pure ideas, who visit the earth (*Aufklärung*, 10–11). Received at first as leaders, these sublime incarnations of ideas would soon be degraded to "Überzeugungen," which for Schnitzler translates better as ideologies than as convictions. Soon the beings would have been degraded to servants whose garments the humans would use to make flags for their causes. The final war year of 1918 in which Schnitzler wrote "Parabel" is the focal point for Scheible's observations. It is also the year *Casanovas Heimfahrt* appeared: the story of the aging adventurer who has written a bigoted pamphlet against Voltaire and is on his way home to Venice, where he will end his days denouncing everything once important to him. With corruption and self-destruction, Casanova represents the approaching end of the bourgeois era (*Aufklärung*, 8).

Due to the loss sustained by liberal concepts during the First World War, Scheible disagrees with Rey's uninterrupted trust in those concepts. Before the cataclysmic events that inspired Schnitzler to write "Parabel," Schnitzler had suggested that since the feudal monarchy would be in shambles following the war, the work of peace treaties should aim at assuring the triumph of democracy over absolutism. If easily-influenced individuals could not be improved, then at least their organizations could

(*Aufklärung,* 12–13). The problem is that during the war Schnitzler failed to see that the liberal doctrine of balance for competing interests had been broken by a bourgeoisie no longer believing it possible to attain the unity, equality, and solidarity spelled out in its slogans (*Aufklärung,* 13).

According to Max Horkheimer, the nineteenth-century "Dogma der Interessenharmonie" originated in the eighteenth-century optimism about the future.[3] But then the trust in a balanced scorecard of individual interests was shattered by an era of economic transformation producing the kind of irrational vulgarities that Professor Bernhardi must suffer. The most embittered Schnitzler becomes about ideas degenerating into ideologies is in his diary entry of June 3, 1919, where he comments on the stipulations of the Versailles Treaty being equivalent to "die Lüge an sich — ohne Zweck, ohne Witz, ohne Sinn, ohne Größe — die erleben wir zum ersten Mal" (*Aufklärung,* 14: the pure lie — without purpose, wit, meaning, greatness — this we're encountering for the first time). This is the moment the liberal worldview of Schnitzler, Freud, and so many others crashes to pieces, turning the optimistic belief in progress into recidivism (19–20).

Scheible offers a fascinating perspective of Enlightenment principles of freedom, rationality, and brotherhood by first linking the origins of the middle class with the secret of freemasonry, for which Gotthold Lessing's (1729–81) *Ernst und Falk: Gespräche für Freimaurer* (Ernst and Falk: Conversations for Freemasons, 1778) provides the text. The thesis is that secret lodges developed to provide a realm of privacy removed from the power claims of the absolutist state. In a zone free of politics, the lodges offered middle-class rationality a temporary safe "lodging" (*Aufklärung,* 88–89). Any rituals the lodge offered were secondary to the secret they served to protect, which was really no secret at all, but common knowledge that could be arrived at independently. Paradoxically, the goal of the secret was to make itself obsolete in proportion to the inroads that reason made into society, because a free society would no longer require secrecy (*Aufklärung,* 89–90). The secret was to dispense with the adjective "good" in "good deeds." If reason could become reconciled with nature and integrated into it, no one would hesitate to perform deeds for the greater good. To that end, reason needs to stop insisting on having the last word in transcending nature (*Aufklärung,* 90–91).

In *Ernst und Falk,* Lessing asserts that freemasons have forgotten their historical function. Their rituals were necessary as long as reason claiming universal validity had not been realized or had hardened into a coherent ideology. If the ritual could reify itself, the secret ran the risk of becoming an end in itself. Because the true secret of freemasonry was its very function, it was impossible to express. A reified ritual diluted the secret into secretive acts that could indeed be expressed, but at the expense of the ritual's originally-intended universality. If one forgot the historical function of freemasonry, it was likely that its signs of freedom would freeze into pure ritual and forfeit progressiveness (*Aufklärung*, 94).

Nineteenth-century historicism perfected the tendency of the bourgeoisie to view itself ahistorically, making it relinquish its claim to universal reason. Now, the function of the secret was reversed, for instead of expanding universal reason, it screened off the circle of initiates from intruders. What is more, given the fact that most of "good" society now made up the ranks of the lodge — those whose boredom and need to be busy creates a class (by default, thus negatively), according to Lessing — it is clear that the reification of the ritual is determined by the restoration of the feudal hierarchy! Out of an institution of progressive citizenry with a historical purpose, the lodge became an elite circle determined by the feudal worldview. The parole of freedom and equality was a lie spoken only by the wealthy few (*Aufklärung*, 94–95).

This, then, is how Scheible explains Lessing's explanation of the connection between freemasons and middle-class impulses for autonomy. In the next step, the aristocratic secret society in Schnitzler's *Traumnovelle* is in Scheible's view a foil to the freemasons, and he connects the password of the former with the parole of the latter.[4] In the mansion where Fridolin does not and cannot belong, the signs of feudal behavior include song, costumes, cavalier clothing, and the inveterate demarcation of insiders from outsiders (*Aufklärung*, 95–96). We are left guessing about what holds the society together, for here the secret has degenerated into secrecy as the society's organizational principle, which makes apparent only the mechanisms of discipline at work within it (*Aufklärung*, 97). Remarkably, the masked "orgy" that takes place whenever the society meets contains nothing Dionysian to remove prohibitions, but instead remains a half-hearted petit-bourgeois ritual producing the kind of barbarism with which such groups as the German Nationalists were rewarded in full a few years after the *Traumnovelle* appeared (*Aufklärung*, 98).

The distinction between private and public space, symbolized by the lodges, experienced its greatest corruption in the decline of liberalism under Vienna's anti-Semitic mayor Karl Lueger (1844–1910). Lueger's opportunistic anti-Semitism played to mob instincts in public and was conveniently forgotten during games of tarot with his Jewish friends in private. This inconsistency was reason for Schnitzler to wonder in his autobiography whether it was ever possible to distinguish politics from private convictions.[5] *Traumnovelle* was proof that anti-Semitism had moved its accent from religion more broadly to race, and in the novella racism and masks appear together: the three masked cavaliers who interrogate Fridolin for dropping his mask wear the black, yellow, and red colors of the German Nationals. This anti-Semitic group, splitting from the radicalism of Georg von Schönerer's adherents, was also set apart by its pseudo-religious costumes and feudal behavior.[6] Fridolin's outsider status thus resembles that of Professor Bernhardi, or of Heinrich Bermann's father in *Der Weg ins Freie,* who could credit such groups for ruining his political career. Still, Hertha Krotkoff insists that instead of making the exclusive society a symbol for exclusion of the Jews in the Austro-Hungarian Monarchy, one should read the society's exclusiveness as symbolic of any situation in which outsiders seek acceptance to closed social circles.[7]

This is a case where erring on the side of caution is unnecessary, because Jews found themselves increasingly the outsiders, not the least in the student fraternities mentioned in the novella.[8] In his book *Jewish Origins of the Psychoanalytic Movement,* Dennis Klein begins by citing Oskar Ehrenberg's view from *Der Weg ins Freie* that any Jew who loves his country the way his father did has to be considered a tragicomic figure, given the discrepancy between the liberalizing epoch of the seventies and eighties and the situation by the turn of the century.[9] Klein emphasizes the eagerness, trust, and zeal of Jewish assimilation according to Lessing's secret of universal reason — even after the German liberals had begun to close ranks under fire in the late nineteenth century. Jews remained faithful to the spirit of the freemasons, despite being expelled from the societies that had worked for their emancipation. Ironically, anti-Semitism, the nightmare of Lessing's hopes in *Nathan der Weise* (1779), forced Jews to restrict their goal of universal liberation to themselves. Rejected in their efforts to shed their status as the chosen people, liberal Jews implicitly assumed a messianic vanguard for leading the way to universal redemption. The universal struggle of the Enlightenment became by default the Jewish struggle.

Just as the freemasons gathered privately in protest of absolutism, so the B'nai B'rith lodge emerged in response to anti-Semitism. One cannot help but notice that the values of the lodge overlapped the humanistic message of the Old Testament stressed by Samuel Hammerschlag, Freud's religion teacher at the Gymnasium. A Jewish point of view meant belief in "the root and origin of the theory of the free, autonomous personality and the innate rights of man" (Klein, 42). According to Hammerschlag, anything uniquely bestowed by "origin, language, or religion" was meaningless if it remained provincial, ignoring the goal of universal emancipation (Klein, 43). As with freemasonry, the secret of Judaism was to work toward the greater good, with history pointing the way to the exits of the temple at such time as the temple's function of advancing universal exodus became obsolete. The uneasy question, of course, concerned the feasibility of dismantling the refuge of B'nai B'rith for people like Freud, who joined its Vienna chapter in 1897. Society documents applauded emancipation from Enlightenment ghettos, with Lessing, Rousseau, and Voltaire serving as the moral ancestors (Klein, 78). Marginalized by German Nationals and other faction groups, Jewish liberals continued worshiping Enlightenment gods, attuned to increased rhetoric of a German chosen race: an ironic instance of fringe groups borrowing a discourse of identity from each other. Struggling with its own sectarianism, B'nai B'rith welcomed isolation from hostility while regretting its necessity (Klein, 78).

Klein's conclusion that Austrian anti-Semitism was simply a derivative of the timeless accusation — Jews are never at home, but are rootless wanderers — leads to a cautious assessment of the metaphors of space and wholeness. Klein asserts that "the basis of the feeling that psychoanalysis was a Jewish mission of redemption is thus found in the early stages of assimilation" (32). Recalling Lessing, one could say that Freud's impulse for wholeness derived from the secret that became exclusive. Now, under the protection of a society where he felt he belonged, he could work toward unlocking the secrets of the psyche. The Psychoanalytic Movement constituted a freedom of movement for the soul, regardless of constraints on outward mobility. Ludwig Braun attributed Freud's psychoanalytic success to his Jewish quality of wholeness: "He felt that because Freud refused to devote himself to Zionism, to religious piety, or to any other partial expression of Judaism, he was 'genuinely Jewish,' a *Ganzjude*." Freud's discernment of wholeness helped him see "that the mind and soul of every person have the same organization" — a quality accelerating his success in the quest for psychic wholeness (Klein, 85).

The enthusiasm with which Freud was welcomed into the B'nai B'rith inspired him to become its champion and savior. After the lodge celebrated his seventieth birthday in 1926, he wrote to Schnitzler that he had been claimed by the Jews for themselves and treated like a Chief Rabbi or national hero.[10]

Long before 1926, of course, Freud had indeed found his niche in the Jewish society of his choosing, one different from the feudal society in *Traumnovelle* and all the exclusivity it represented. About the novella, published the year of Freud's much celebrated seventieth birthday, Freud had wished to share his thoughts with Schnitzler: "P.S. Über Ihre Traumnovelle habe ich mir einige Gedanken gemacht."[11] Schnitzler never made the effort to discover what Freud thought about his novella.

Der Weg ins Freie: Roadblocks to Freedom

In the case of the Austrian middle class of Schnitzler's era, the lines of emancipation connected class with race: liberal Jews had ample reason to endorse rationality, freedom, and justice. Even when during his lifetime Schnitzler's works appeared to be timeless statements of love and death, they were understood much better when one appreciated the inseparability of psychological nuances from historical costumes. The reason for examining the major criticism on the novel *Der Weg ins Freie*, much of which coincides with the anniversary of Schnitzler's death in 1981, and some that extended well beyond it, is to show how examples of sociohistorical criticism raise the critical status of the novel to a level undreamt of by Schnitzler's contemporaries. It was as though the novel had been waiting for just this mode of criticism. The novel, of course, is about its own reception: why Schnitzler would be dismissed by his contemporaries on the basis of his Jewish ancestry. Within its pages, Schnitzler was providing the ideological reasons it would not be well-received, even though he considered it among his best achievements.

Again, the theme of emancipation is served by the mode of social history. On the basis of investigations by Klaus Laermann (1977), Detlev Arens (1981), Egon Schwarz (1981, 1982, and 1985), Norbert Abels (1982), Norbert Miller, (1985), Wolfgang Nehring (1986), and Andrea Willi (1989), four major points of the novel are explored here: geographical delineation, the unity of psychology and sociology, the sociological composition of impressionism, and the impossibility of emancipation (not always the same as assimilation) in an era of Zionism and anti-Semitism.

Laermann's chapter on *Der Weg ins Freie* (Janz and Laermann, 1977) is the most comprehensive delineation of how geography comments on social standing. A map of Vienna shows the distance between the first-district apartment of the protagonist Georg von Wergenthin and the home of his middle-class girlfriend Anna Rosner in the fourth district. When not in his own apartment, outdoors, or at the Rosners',

Georg can be found at the Ehrenbergs', whose exclusive apartment borders Schwarzenbergpark in the third district. Less occasional are his visits to the artist Bermann in an eighth-district suburb, and to Nürnberg in a dilapidated section of the inner city (first district).[12]

Missing in Schnitzler's sampling of social groups are representatives of the court, centers of industry and trade on the Ring, and those outcroppings of workers' dwellings found not only in the city center, but also in Hernals, Ottakring, Neulerchenfeld, Fünfhaus, Margareten, and Favoriten to Simmering. Because any planned trysts with Anna in Salmannsdorf require Georg to pass through such areas, Schnitzler's lack of commentary must only reflect Georg's lack of interest. Though the exclusion of the working poor appears unpardonable, the novel's intention is to examine the political and psychic constitution of the Viennese bourgeoisie, particularly its Jews, in the first years of Christian-Socialist rule. The situation of the Wergenthin, Ehrenberg, Rosner, and Golowski families, as well as primarily Jewish artists and writers, is at stake there.[13]

Building on Laermann's remarks, Egon Schwarz approves of the connections identified between place and social position, calling this the aura of the milieu. In his view, the novel takes on an added dimension once one understands the aura as extension of personality, for only then does the purely spatial become atmospheric and mythic. Reading Schnitzler armed only with a glossary of local references is to miss an important point, warns Schwarz, who reads these references as pointing beyond the local Viennese charm toward the thesis that in every character Vienna's political forces have reached the fringe, overpowering the liberal center.[14] As for the ignored lower social classes, Schwarz believes that Schnitzler is thereby criticizing himself, admitting his ignorance of the plight of Eastern Jewish petty merchants and laborers settling in Leopoldstadt and Brigittenau. At the Zionist Conference in Basel that precedes the novel's action, Leo Golowski reports having experienced the tangible longing of these poorer Jews for their own homeland. Heinrich Bermann's rejoinder is that the fiction of *Vaterland*, demanding the subject's patriotic allegiance to the state, pales in the face of *Heimat*, that sense of local belonging for which no feelings of solidarity are required of Jews or Christians. Shared persecution was not a reason to align oneself with similar fates.[15]

Despite this attention to the details of Vienna's districts, Schwarz notes in an article on the aristocracy that social reality in Schnitzler's works appears via a detour into the psyche, a realm he defines as the sum of the compromises that instinctual life has negotiated with social relationships in the family and the state. A physical map is obviously insufficient for exploring this realm. Nor does Schnitzler's commentary on the mutation of the aristocracy appear as programmatically as in the works of his Austrian predecessors Marie von Ebner-Eschenbach and Ferdinand von Saar. Schwarz is not surprised that Schnitzler's close concentration on the psyche allows him to infiltrate social structures.[16] A social issue such as anti-Semitism has its own psyche, to which Schnitzler devotes more attention than to its political and social side, as Schwarz cites from Schnitzler's autobiography.[17] Nevertheless, in choosing to endorse, with Wolfgang Nehring, sociohistorical approaches to works such as *Leutnant Gustl* so as to preserve the stringent effects of those works, Schwarz comes to disagree with Cedric Williams's statement that Schnitzler's concerns are solely psychological.[18]

Wolfgang Nehring sees the novel as the most appropriate response to the perennial accusation that Schnitzler was an apolitical writer. A story of both love and social relationships, the novel even supports much non-literary historical research about the situation of Viennese Jews at the turn of the century.[19] Nevertheless, like Schwarz, Nehring insists that even in this novel, second in political content only to *Professor Bernhardi* four years later, the reader experiences only indirectly such events as universal suffrage, the election loss of the liberals, and the takeover of city government by Lueger's Christian-Socialist backers. Threatened by the same political trends, Jews spend time with other Jews. Schnitzler projects external events onto the characters, who arrive at their individual life paths through struggling with the events. Thus Schnitzler remains first of all a psychological writer, an observer of souls more than politics, though treating all issues concurrently.[20]

With sociohistorical criticism having encouraged commentary on the novel's geographical sectors and on psychology's underpinning of even the most blatant political utterances, the next step is Detlev Arens's insistence on identifying the factors contributing to Georg's impressionistic posture. Arens disputes Gottfried Just's assertion that Schnitzler is incapable of transcending the condition he was depicting. Just's ahistorical judgment not only neglected Schnitzler's development as a writer, but also the weighty fact that sentimentalism was typical for the epoch.[21] In Arens's view, correctives to Just are found in the studies of Swales, Scheible, and Friedbert Aspetsberger, all of which delineate the social determination of the impressionistic type.[22] Especially significant is Aspetsberger's focus on convention as the fossil remains of social orientation, from which result the conflicts attributed to indignation or "Entrüstung."[23]

An indication of the importance of historical background is the close attention the research pays to the events of 1897, a year to whose events Norbert Abels, a student of Hartmut Scheible, dedicates an entire chapter.[24] In her investigation of the novel's initial reception, Andrea Willi calls the year 1897 a paradigm for the impending fundamental political and societal changes in the monarchy, not to mention the end of the monarchy itself.[25] She recalls, for example, that the language edicts passed by Minister President Badeni declared Czech and German to have equal footing in Bohemia and Moravia; and that Badeni endorsed to the Kaiser the Christian-Socialist mayor Karl Lueger, signaling for all practical purposes the end of liberalism. Gustav Klimt and his colleagues formed the Secession that year; Freud was busy with his book on the interpretation of dreams, *Traumdeutung;* and heated discussions took place the following year about admitting women to university study.

The salon continued as a persistent nexus of declining liberal discourse. In the novel, it is the Ehrenberg salon and its representatives of the aristocracy, politics, and the military to which Georg enjoys access. Putting him within easy reach of aristocracy (Demeter Stanzides), upper-middle class (Dr. Stauber), and petty bourgeoisie (Anna Rosner), Georg's mobility is a metaphor of flux that applies to the entire social order, each group of which is wearing a token uniform to disguise an empty interior (Willi, 101–2). Officers and aristocrats seem to play at politics, as though it were a theater liberals had abandoned for the real theater, with its recognizable national heroes. More out of necessity, Jews too have to play at representing something considered an exception to their norm. This usually means an exceptional effort in every sense (107).

The diversity of social groups the salon fosters cannot conceal the boundaries between them. Offering a chapter on the Jewish salon's origins in the era of Moses Mendelssohn (1729–86), Norbert Abels surmises that the enlightened division of politics and morality in the secret lodges persisted among those whom societal mechanisms of exclusion forced into the salons — a new ghetto. — As already suggested, the anti-Semitic association of Jews with freemasons was not coincidental (Abels, 119). According to Abels, the failed relationship between Georg and Anna (class differences) corresponds to the failed relationship between Georg and his Jewish friends (ethnic differences); the salon fails to live up to its ideal of judgment-free community (131). Abels ends his chapter on the salon by claiming that the Jewish salon of the late nineteenth century prefigured the internment of those unwilling to shout along at the Nuremberg rallies (120).

Andrea Willi is not so pessimistic. While the salon may not usher in ultimate liberation, Georg and Heinrich still engage in substantive conversations by venturing beyond its walls into less constricting social space. Their bike tours, hikes, and coffeehouse visits all illustrate a physical movement matching their intellectual vibrancy. For short moments, representatives of different groups suspend their differences, bridging their chasms in ways that society at large will not permit (107). Willi's willingness to concede growth in the friendship between Georg and Heinrich indicates a reading that refuses to conform all interpretation to awareness of the coming terror.

Perhaps the most important contribution of sociohistorical engagement with the novel is the discussion of assimilation and Zionism, particularly the roadblocks Schnitzler sees in the path of each Jew's "Weg ins Freie." Schwarz points out that political antipathy toward the Jews increased when social Darwinism joined forces with the religious, economic, and cultural hostilities already present. After the market collapse of 1873, it was easy to mobilize large segments of the population, especially the Catholic Church, against the Jews, while smuggling a number of other evils into the accusation that Jewish financial speculation with non-Jewish money had caused the fall.[26] Schnitzler devotes several pages of his autobiography to ensuring that his future readers have a grasp of how widely anti-Semitism extended its nets. He writes about how it was impossible for Jews in the public eye to ignore their ethnic origin; instead, Jews were forced to choose the least problematic stereotype of first impressions: oversensitive, overly bold, impudent, shy, or paranoid. Remaining unfazed under a nonchalant demeanor was not an option, Schnitzler claims, unless one could remain unfazed while watching skin being slit open by a contaminated razor.[27]

A variation on the theme is Willi's dissertation, written almost a decade after the full-length investigations of Detlev Arens and Norbert Abels, which suggests understanding assimilation in the novel by connecting it directly with its historical scenery. Using a review in the *Allgemeine Zeitung des Judentums,* a newspaper considered liberal at the time, she first summarizes its supposedly enlightened arguments and then locates the reviewer's parallel character in the novel. Ludwig Geiger, the reviewer, critiques the novel in a manner reminiscent of the fictional Dr. Stauber, whose constant message to Georg is that assimilation demands a heightened sense of duty from Jews. Geiger's review intones that the road to freedom is not in the frequent hikes Georg takes nor in Leo Golowski's Zionism, but rather in the fulfillment of duty in the present, where respect for oneself and one's predecessors unites with trust in the future. A reference to the role of Enlightenment Jew Moses Mendelssohn completes the thought (Willi, 111–12).

Having linked the interests of the real journalist Geiger and the fictional Dr. Stauber, Willi adds another voice to the mix of patriarchal liberalism: Raoul Auernheimer's feuilleton on the novel, appearing in Vienna's *Neue Freie Presse*. Auernheimer's remarks are significant because they perpetuate clichés of Schnitzler's womanizing in the effort to avoid direct discussion of anti-Semitism, a subject this newspaper considered taboo. In her critical reading, Willi disagrees with Daviau's claim that Auernheimer promoted Schnitzler by intentionally profiling his depictions of things Austrian in order to secure his reputation from anti-Semitic attacks. In her view, neglect of anti-Semitism produces overcompensation in other areas, which ultimately invites clichés promoting anti-Semitism. For this reason, even well-meaning critics produce criticism having little to do with the novel (Willi, 119). Willi believes that if the feuilleton permits aesthetic and narcissistic withdrawal, it reproduces on a formal level what it attempts on the level of content. Specifically, it suppresses the loss of political power and feigns a continued effective presence of the nobility, all the while silencing the "Jewish Question." The feuilleton leaves a dubious impression of its author, based as it is on opportunism or transient effect. As we have seen, the feuilletonist of his day writes quickly in order to escape his own conscience (Willi, 121–22). It is difficult to imagine silence in the press on an issue so large — not just as a policy, but specifically in a review of *Der Weg ins Freie*.

Whatever Jews helped develop as an arena for participation was replaced by a system that called for their exclusion. Abels points out that the Jewish posture of ethics and morality was an extra trait the non-Jewish population could not assimilate. Whenever Jews humanely told the truth in art, it was threatening because it exposed the lies and aggression of its recipients, and it is in this light that one can make sense of Arnold Schönberg's compositional dissonances (Abels, 11). Because the so-called "Jewish question" was not a question the Jews posed in the first place, their eagerness to "answer" the question had no positive effect on non-Jews (Abels, 12).

Norbert Miller claims that Salomon Ehrenberg's pessimism about the chances of assimilation is no match for his hatred of feudalism, against which he makes a point of flaunting his Jewish solidarity. In this respect this wealthy factory owner manifests traits of Seligmann Hirsch in Ferdinand von Saar's short story of the same title, after whom he may have been modeled.[28] Tragically, Salomon's world view, by which he interprets refeudalization as dangerously erasing liberal gains and all that he stands for, sets him at odds against his son Oskar, who would like to convert to Catholicism to enjoy a semblance of life as the aristocrat he pretends to be now. Oskar must remain an unbaptized sycophant out of fear that his father will keep him out of his will.[29] It comes to a scandal between father and son, however, as Salomon one day sees Oskar tipping his hat to young Catholic aristocrats leaving church. After receiving a hard slap from his father, Oskar does the honorable thing by attempting suicide. His attempt ends in failure, and minus an eye he embarks on travels abroad with Prinz von Guastella.

Almost to a fault, the father-son conflicts in the novel develop around the ways in which *fin-de-siècle* sons fail to measure up to paternal expectations.[30] Generational conflict in the novel should not lead to the conclusion that Schnitzler spurns any chance of Jewish assimilation. He and most of his characters are assimilated, after all. Rather, as Nehring points out, the issue of integrity hinges on whether the Jews accept their origins or conform opportunistically to the non-Jewish norm. Schnitzler is clear that he rejects Oskar Ehrenberg's "road into the open," for Oskar represents the hope that bourgeois assimilation can occur via refeudalization.[31] Despite its loss in real power, the Austro-Hungarian nobility, with its popular behavioral norms, still could trump a suspiciously wealthy middle class. One of the most blatant statements of refeudalization Schnitzler scholars point to is the notorious *Waidhofener Beschluß*, whose exact wording Schnitzler includes in his autobiography. This anti-Semitic declaration arose to counter Jewish successes in the *Mensur*, the fencing duels of student fraternities. In 1896, German-Austrian students declared Jews unworthy of giving or receiving satisfaction on the basis of inherent dishonor, an expression of sentiment already present during Schnitzler's student years in the early eighties.[32]

Schnitzler himself shrugged off the ethnic and religious side of his own Jewish origin, but could not admire the Jew who chose the route of renegade or snob. The renegade was a Jew such as Karl Kraus or Alfred Polgar who sought baptism; the snob was one whose attempts to measure up to aristocratic standards always fell short or assumed tragicomic proportions. In his friend Hugo von Hofmannsthal Schnitzler could see this trait at its most pronounced, because it was a sickness he had endured for a time himself.[33] Schnitzler's time at university and in the army, if it had not cured him of the belligerence that controlled those arenas, had at least allowed him to see through it. The character Oskar understandably suffers from a snobbery derived from his lacking the essential renegade component of baptism. Willi stresses that the function of baptism for Georg von Wergenthin is to be a guarantee of greater objectivity in his Jewish friends — while in practice it really guarantees the uncritical acceptance of prejudices.[34] Skepticism is privileged because Schnitzler suspects baptism can be nothing more than an escape route from responsibility.

Like Willi, Abels uses the notion of *Schein und Sein* to underscore the false security of denying one's Jewish origin.[35] The persistent message of his book is that the integrity of accepting one's origin offers little consolation if the road into the open is paved with anti-Semitic barricades, some of them erected by Jews. This realistic note surfaces in Norbert Miller's essay as well. Miller echoes Salomon Ehrenberg's sober observation that no amount of assimilation or willing subjection can stop the racist slide into barbarism and the economic scapegoating of minorities. Consequently, Salomon's inner distance to Judaic rituals is not reason enough to play his renegade card, particularly if such a solution only buys a little time while sacrificing integrity.[36]

The uncompromising self-knowledge of the elder Ehrenberg is reason enough for him to challenge the cynicism of Nürnberger, who justifies his disregard for baptism by claiming never to have felt Jewish in the first place. Long before slapping his son Oskar, Salomon has reminded Nürnberger to count on feeling offended if someone knocks off his hat after noticing his rather Jewish nose. The point Miller draws is that regardless of the caricatures of Salomon and of his predecessor Seligmann Hirsch, both fathers remain more attuned than their children to political tragedy. They recognize the subjective moment in caricature: those in power control how much the Jews are allowed to ignore the images of themselves.[37]

Beyond his scorn of renegades and snobs, Schnitzler rebels against forced solidarity of race, often visible in the diminished respect of self and others of the so-called "Esoijuden" — those Jews who, after discovering their fellow train passengers are also Jewish, are likely to sigh, take off their shoes, and stretch their feet out onto the empty seat across from them. When not around Jews, however, the Jewish community exhibits its lack of self-respect through its readiness to do penance. The psychology of self-hatred depends on accepting as truth the statements others have made about a particular individual or group. Once accepted by Jews themselves, anti-Semitism can flourish unchecked.[38] This realization of Heinrich Bermann is offered in the full knowledge of his own inclinations toward self-hatred. His haunting talent for understanding at least explains how resolute action is almost impossible for him and for his characters. An example of self-hatred in one less self-aware is Berthold

Stauber, whose attempts to overcome the specter through love, science, and politics all end in failure.[39]

If there is any alternative to refeudalization or problematic assimilation for Jews, Salomon Ehrenberg is unaware of it, choosing instead to follow Zionism, despite the problems it offers in sharp relief. Most scholars dismiss the hopes of Zionism in the novel with the same alacrity they perceive in Schnitzler's dismissal of any political solution — something like Bernhardi's reluctance to become the spokesman of the Zionists in *Professor Bernhardi*. Willi is an exception. For her, Zionism represents a new ethical and aesthetic ideal. For example, the move of the Golowski family from the comfortable first district to the impoverished second district of Leopoldstadt is an occasion for Leo to examine his Jewishness in light of his new surroundings. His social descent forces him to be concerned for the problems of strangers who are beginning to look more like his own people. Willi interprets Leo to be in the throes of the linguistic crisis of Schnitzler's epoch, especially in the way in which he challenges the indifferent, ornamental tone of the conversations between himself and Georg. Unlike Lord Chandos in Hofmannsthal's famous "Brief," Leo does not relinquish language entirely, but employs it skeptically. The quest for sincerity and meaning in language resembles the search for a space in which Leo's fellow Jews can realize their ambitions. It is more for their sake than for his own that Leo is impassioned with Zionism.[40]

Although Leo cannot prevent his family's economic and thus geographical fall from social grace, he can at least indemnify himself through a successful duel. Leo has little control over the circumstances leading to his challenge of his superior officer, but he can expect more equal treatment in the duel, including a suspension of difference in rank. As long as he is still allowed to duel, and as long as a military norm holds sway over a civic code, the military norm also suspends the racial code. Compensating for their lack of respect elsewhere by commanding respect in the military, Jews could employ sanctioned violence in the cause of honor, however fleeting this honor turned out to be for Jews historically as a whole. Dueling places Leo outside the law, but he was already outside the law because it did not protect him against Sefranek's hazing. This parallel military structure supercedes the civil structure unofficially and thus with more compulsion, giving Leo at least the chance for private justice. Leo knows his solution remains private, but the irrationality of anti-Semitism provokes irrational responses.[41] Despite what he believes is praiseworthy in Zionism as a whole, Leo can vent his private frustration only by dueling. This is the exact reverse of Professor Bernhardi's situation: Bernhardi wants the situation resolved on a private level and detests becoming the champion of the Zionists. This fact recalls Russell Berman's insight that "individual consciousness is always undercut by some more profound structure" such as economic organization or the unconscious.[42] It is worth keeping in mind that besides harboring psychoanalysis and socialism, Vienna also inspired the Zionism of Theodor Herzl, made necessary precisely because of the forces unleashed by the unconscious. Leo's case shows the obstacles over which he has no control: he may choose to respond rationally to those obstacles through political action. His control over psychology is as loose as that over politics, however. Politics and psychology are mutually contaminating, as Berman puts it when discussing the two "different" themes of the novel.[43]

As a temporary solution to anti-Semitism, the duel fares better in Schnitzler's eyes than mass baptism. As mentioned, few options existed for Jews in the wake of the 1896 Waidhofen Resolution. Another Jew who frequents the Ehrenberg salon, the former officer Willy Eißler, wears his Jewish pride in plain view: his dueling scars prove he has settled scores willingly and successfully with anti-Semites. Endorsing Leo's action as a model for improving the lot of Jews in Austria, Eißler nevertheless fails to realize, unlike his author, that the individual road to the open is losing its credibility under political irrationality. One example of an inflammatory slogan — "Was der Jude glaubt ist einerlei, in der Rasse liegt die Schweinerei" (It matters little what the Jew believes, he's contaminated by race) — shows the extent to which anti-Semites obliterate distinctions and view Jews solely as racial representatives. Abels notes that such banality seals off all routes for social rehabilitation.[44] After Waidhofen, the duel is less a chance at revenge or justice or even blind anger than a convenient channel, like anti-Semitism, for aggression.[45]

The novel is crammed full of conversation. Standpoints of integration and Zionism are propagated, debated, and criticized, but almost always for the sake of self-persuasion. Insecurity and contradiction provide for concessions in all positions.[46] Schwarz considers an important sign of Schnitzler's ambivalence the conversation in which Leo Golowski argues for the return of Jews to Palestine and Heinrich Bermann responds just as passionately against it.[47] Leo wants to shift the focus away from the fate of Jewish officials, reserve officers, and lecturers, all of whom must endure double standards, to the image of the Jews he had seen in Basel pining for a sense of belonging and feeling welcome somewhere. Heinrich makes clear that his allegiance rests neither with German nationalists nor with Zionists, no matter what he shares with the latter, for even mutual suffering fails to create solidarity with those normally at a distance. Nationalism and religion of any kind leave him bitter. *Vater-land* is a politically expedient term for which he reserves cynicism, whereas feelings of *Heimat* designate a right to that homeland.[48] Schnitzler understands both points of view, showing how political reality and individual psychology undermine one's convictions. More ratic a socialist than her brother is a Zionist, Therese Golowski's politic aspi-rations are so inconsistent as to be theatrical. This goes for Behold Stauber as well, thus reflecting Schnitzler's skepticism of pinning opes on political activity for redressing any situation in Austria, not jus nti-Semitism. Jews such as Willi Eißler, Heinrich Bermann and Else En-berg see their courses of action rendered impossible by their own co-sitions and the historical moment. Their powerlessness shows its s resignation and cynicism.[49]

The interpretations of *Der Weg ins Freie* examined here show importance of reading with a map, in order to identify the location social groups in reality and their correspondences in the novel. T gives clues toward understanding the psyche of rich and poor Jews, example. The salon is the place that shows the liberal center in the pro ess of disintegration at the time of the novel. But Schnitzler is not pr marily an author of milieu alone, and any comment on historical costum must include the stirrings in the psyche underneath. Schnitzler is no apolitical, but he would rather merge political discourse with persona disposition. Social history also helps identify the social determinants of impressionism less judgmentally than the earlier critical modes that lo-cated it in, and limited it to, moral shortcomings. Georg's sentimentality is society-wide. Finally, the scholarship recognizes Schnitzler's concern that future readers understand why both assimilation and Zionism repre-sented as much a dead-end as self-hatred, when one became surrounded by anti-Semitic sentiment.

Analysis of Dueling

In the introduction to the 1977 book (cited already with respect to *Weg ins Freie*) that for both launched their professorships in Germany, Rolf-Peter Janz and Klaus Laermann claim their job is not to reconstruct the social givens of 1900 Vienna so much as to analyze the historical content of individual works as well as the historicity of aesthetic forms, taking into account the situation of the Viennese bourgeoisie reflected by those forms, especially where that class wanted little to do with them.[50] In his chapter on *Anatol*, Janz characterizes his sociohistorical method as more value-free and reliable than the criticism of impressionism we have considered in the previous chapter. He objects to Offermanns's reference to the Anatol type as the culmination of nihilism left behind by the disintegration of metaphysical, moral, and societal order. Quite simply, to believe that Anatol has no guilty conscience ignores Anatol's painful awareness of seceding from fidelity and goal-directed rationality. A sociohistorical analysis can better demonstrate that it is precisely the impressionist's claim of "konsequente Indetermination" (consistent indetermination) that reveals his embeddedness in the social conventions he trying to resist (Janz/Laermann, 79). What is more, the rhetoric of "Wertzerfall" (decay of values) assumes the presence of an intact order ting to decay in the first place. Better to interpret Anatol not as the sequence of moral decline and ego disorientation, but as a figure en freedom by Schnitzler to ignore reality until it catches up with him, gain and again. It is because ethical norms loom large that Anatol attempts to dispense with them, with the result that failure only makes him more painfully aware of them (79). As symbol of the wealthy bourgeois *rentier*, Anatol is always attempting two escapes: from bourgeois constraints into adventure, and from political reality into aestheticism (15–16). Janz appropriates Diersch's thesis without mentioning him. The impressionist is unable to choose from the unlimited possibilities for action, although they are at his disposal as they are for the bourgeois in the era of imperialism (80). Janz asserts that Anatol's broken perception of time results in his dysfunctional manipulation of the territory in which he finds himself: all is subject to his economic control.

Although not addressed in *Anatol*, one of the consequences of amorous adventure is the duel, one of the most persistent feudal structures to weather the liberal attempt to renounce unpredictability and privilege. The chapter "Leutnant Gustl," written by Laermann, begins with the evidence that military proprietors of honor operated with extralegal *Faustrecht* attuned to its own brand of logic. The scandal of *Leutnant Gustl* in militaristic and anti-Semitic papers originated in the lament of the damage done to the esteem of the Austro-Hungarian Army by a Jew ignorant of Aryan honor (Janz/Laermann, 110). Those scandalized misunderstood the novella as criticizing the army, dueling, and anti-Semitism. Indignation was due to a guilty conscience from reading the transcript of the thought life of a lackluster infantry lieutenant (111). This was the novella's modernity: proferring disillusions rather than the glory dreamt of by an officer. Internal monologue, employed for the first time in German literature, best registered the gap between external and internal honor (112). Any Gustl under the honor code obeys the hegemonous superego made up of the eyes of society (115). In the incessant monologue of memory fragments and sexually aggressive associations, it is made clear that the lieutenant is incapable of sustained reflection, and the reality of suicide is forgotten in the constant drift toward trivialities or sexual musings (118).

The chapter "Zur Sozialgeschichte des Duells" elucidates the weighty responsibility of "Satisfaktionsfähigkeit," the privilege and obligation to issue or be issued a duel challenge. Dueling, a surrogate of armed class struggle, is the grim responsibility the upper classes must accept to remain cordoned off from the lower classes (Janz/Laermann, 133). Because Gustl has been prevented by the baker from responding violently to his reprimand, and because he must guarantee the efficacy of his privilege, violence must turn inward in the form of suicide. Until the result of violence is witnessed, honor, the foremost determinant of truthfulness and even personhood, is suspended. The archaic notion is that the source of law vanishes with the law, and that each personal law is obliged to answer to the personal law of another. The outcome of executing one's right delivers the automatic verdict on the situation, as in an ordeal. The dismissal of reason from the process is evident in the promptness stipulated for moving from insult to restoration. Quick reprisal was necessary because an insult was considered a stain not only on the officer, but also on all his peers. When justice is raised to duty, rational misgivings have no place except for a "Rechtsverdreher" such as the lawyer Gustl has challenged to a duel (136). The duel surpassed civil penal codes in intricacy and variation, and its visible outcome, whether injury or death, rendered more concrete satisfaction than could a term in jail, never mind whether the one offended received justice or death (137). As already seen, it proved expedient for Leo Golowski in *Der Weg ins Freie* to gamble on dueling as a chance at punishing his anti-Semitic commanding officer for hazing received (153–54).

Around 1900, dueling also served to keep a standing army combat-ready. Bellicosity was an officer's necessary trademark, not contingent on the declaration of war. Still, to reduce the duel to a venting function avoids its richer sociohistorical dimensions, Laermann argues, and to call Schnitzler dead-set against dueling misses the thesis against compulsory dueling in *Freiwild*. Schnitzler himself declined to challenge or accept challenges, leading to his loss of officer's patent when he refused to challenge the author of an article in *Reichswehr* at the time *Leutnant Gustl* was published.

Laermann reminds us that in *Freiwild*, Karinski, who has been given the insulting slap by Rönning, has the right as the injured party to shoot first in a duel by pistols (Janz/Laermann, 141). Rönning's refusal of the challenge does not automatically shame him as a civilian the way Karinski would be shamed had he refused as an officer. Rönning is, however, a marked man deprived of honor and the freedom of movement, and by reaching for his gun when Karinski blocks his path effectively shows himself a victim of the militaristic norm of compulsory dueling, albeit in a more spontaneous form (142). Any justification of compulsory dueling ignores the fact, however, that it stood originally in opposition to the state's monopolistic claim to power (143). Violence was the prerogative of the state, not the individual, as is evident from early seventeenth-century edicts. Laermann has no doubt that dueling spread in reaction to the centralizing of a state power apparatus. Prohibitions became necessary because the feudal nobility, compensating for its political loss of sovereignty by its skill in weaponry, was refusing to be placed into regiments of a standing army, so accustomed was it to defending land on the basis of contract (143–44).

Enforcing the prohibitions was another story, both in absolutism and in the duel's migration into the *Bürgertum*. The development of honor councils is proof of a change from the pressure the state originally brought to bear against the duel to the pressure it exerted to ensure its execution, for now the weapon reinforced what the uniform represented (Janz/Laermann, 144–45). Better to duel and be briefly incarcerated than lose one's rank for cowardice. Wives would at least receive a pension for husbands killed in confrontation (146).

The duel transmitted militarism into society to the extent that reserve officer positions were factored into the armed forces with the Dual Monarchy from 1868 on, bringing the educated middle class under the sway of codes originally foreign and perhaps even detestable to them. Schnitzler's focus on compulsion rather than militarization shows his unawareness of the scope of the problem, despite the fact that militarism lay at the core of compulsory dueling. That his civilian figures show a half-hearted acceptance of the conventions thwarting their version of the law sends a clear signal about the real patterns of power in *fin-de-siècle* Austria (Janz/Laermann, 147). Military solutions are non-solutions to their bourgeois problems, which usually concern adultery, as we see in *Liebelei* and *Das weite Land* (148). It was less the fact than the discovery of adultery that brought about a duel challenge, because reputation and appearance outweighed fidelity and actual marital harmony (151). The fear of a discovered affair translated into female hysteria, as *Liebelei* shows (152).

Wealth, education, and family name were factors eclipsed by the duel's effectiveness for marking the distinctiveness of the ruling class.

Laermann's chapter convincingly presents a feudal institution in decline that nevertheless promoted the "Selbstnobilitierung" of the middle classes. Emancipation in the form of civil laws intended to curtail residual feudalism was bypassed. All in all, this is criticism that views the socio-logical content of Schnitzler's works as equal to the authority of "non-fiction" for discerning the importance of dueling.

Emancipation for Women?

A year after the publication of Janz and Laermann's book, Brigitte De-Lay noted in a review of Barbara Gutt's *Emanzipation bei Arthur Schnitzler* (1978) that Gutt's cutting-edge discussion of emancipation benefits from Schnitzler's diary, letters, aphorisms, and fiction, and has led Gutt to appreciate Schnitzler's ability to lampoon and overturn roles imposed upon women. Emancipation for Gutt means the ability to be-come fully human, whether female or male, just as it means the successful assimilation of socially marginalized groups such as the Jews.[51]

Schnitzler's advocacy of women results from his ability to notice par-allels between the "Frauenfrage" and the "Judenfrage": as one himself marginalized, he could ask how self-identity was possible in an increas-ingly anti-individualistic, Christian-Aryan, male-dominated society.[52] Forced assimilation and the struggle for emancipation is common to the women of Jewish or non-Jewish race and religion: "In diesem Sinne sind alle Schnitzlerschen Frauengestalten Jüdinnen oder genauer: Juden" (Gutt, 130: In this sense all of Schnitzler's female figures can be consid-ered female Jews, or more precisely Jews).

With respect to the "Frauenfrage" of Schnitzler's time, Gutt notes that the women in his readership considered him to be their advocate for social justice, as seen by his frequent invitations from women's reading clubs to read from his works (166–67). The reading horizon of Austrian women spanned a wide range of literary works, from Nietzsche's misog-yny to Ibsen's naturalism, and the fact that Schnitzler depicted both indicates the breadth of his vision, explaining as well the dichotomous reception of his works (168).

Gutt proposes the Swiss writer Max Frisch (1911–91) as proof that Schnitzler's literary successors give similar attention to women's libera-tion. Frisch has played out Schnitzler's observations about female superi-ority and considered the consequences for both sexes. Even so, Schnitzler disciples are necessary to continue his message, because his own works continue to resonate with Germany of the 1970s. Gutt's thesis is that the success of the television adaptations of some of

Schnitzler's works has not only reflected a Schnitzler renaissance, but also helped to cause it (173). There is nothing wrong with Urbach's suggestion that the prosperity of today's audiences can be compared with that of the Schnitzler audiences before the First World War.[53] More importantly, though, according to Gutt, Schnitzler's works resonate because of the renewed interest in the "Frauenfrage" some eighty years after it was first topical (175).

Converting novellas and plays into television dramas revives old questions of the adequacy of the medium, but most audiences can be trusted to focus on the message. The astounding result is that the cliché of charming, melancholy Anatol has been abandoned to the benefit of recognizing the psychological appropriateness of marital problems from the woman's point of view. When the ZDF, for example, subtitled its 1971 production of *Zwischenspiel* "Die neue Ehe" (The New Marriage), reviews noted an expansion of the emancipation discussion from Ibsen's *Nora,* and that female protagonist Cäcilie appeared extraordinarily emancipated for a 1906 plot (Gutt, 178). A version of *Spiel im Morgengrauen* (Daybreak, 1926) in 1974 gained recognition because Leopoldine avenged herself in emancipatory fashion, and in 1975 the star of *Fräulein Else* came across as hiding more intelligence and wit under her forced female behavior than all the men surrounding her (179). Gutt is careful to point out that Schnitzler's works carried more than mere enlightenment or elitist literary value. Both scheduling (he is shifted from the late program to the more popular family and holiday scheduling) and viewer statistics prove sensational success; for example: "*Das weite Land* wurde vom ORF am 1. Weihnachtstag (25.12) 1969 um 20.15 h ausgestrahlt, vom ZDF am Ostersonntag (29.3) 1970 um 20.15 h (Sehbeteiligung 29%, Index +3)" (180).

Gutt concludes that the rediscovery of Schnitzler via any medium is attributable to the interdependent factors of his radical modernity and of the German audience's nostalgic perception of the "guten alten Kaiserzeit" (180–81). There is also the significant possibility that progressive literature from the turn of the century is so appealing because nothing like it exists in the present to which women can turn (181). Whatever one thinks of her premise, Gutt's 1978 Berlin dissertation is clearly one of the first to benefit from the swell of liberation discourse and to alert German-speaking scholars to the need for systematic study of the women in Schnitzler's works.[54]

According to Renate Möhrmann, Gutt is the first to notice that Schnitzler was writing specifically about women's conditions in the attempt to improve them.[55] Möhrmann notices that recognition of

Schnitzler's reluctance to give us *Hausfrau* and *femme fatale* — instead depicting anti-heroes who refuse to filter reality through the eyes of their husbands — is an insight that has been obstructed by at least two female scholars with their own agendas: Georgette Boner, whose 1930 Zürich dissertation "Arthur Schnitzlers Frauengestalten" mystifies femininity into archetypal Dionysian and Apollonian categories, both of which bypass any question of intellect; and Susanne Polsterer, whose 1949 Vienna dissertation "Die Darstellung der Frau in Arthur Schnitzlers Dramen" warns youth and foreigners about Schnitzler's false statements concerning the female psyche. Concerned to reinstate the reputation of Viennese women, Polsterer castigates Schnitzler while remedying the damage done by his female caricatures.[56] However, Willa Elizabeth Schmidt was the first to notice Schnitzler's emancipatory potential. Four years before Gutt, her 1974 Wisconsin dissertation "The Changing Role of Women in the Works of Arthur Schnitzler" charts a progression from "Existence for the Man" to "Attempts at Coexistence" to "Woman in her Right."[57]

Both Möhrmann and Alfred Doppler[58] argue that a change in female depiction is evident from 1900 onward, and both choose as their examples *Märchen* (1893), *Frau Berta Garlan* (1900), and *Therese: Chronik eines Frauenlebens* (1928). In the third version (1902) of Schnitzler's drama *Märchen*, for example, he has changed the ending from one in which Fanny has a breakdown to one in which she tells Fedor firmly to leave. The change does not signal emancipation directly, but it does switch the narrative perspective to a female one. Schnitzler becomes less concerned about how men regard women than about showing the emancipatory potential in women's models of community.[59] To Möhrmann, the failure of *Märchen* at its premiere was not due to moral licentiousness, with which it was charged, but to the inability of the third act to satisfy the audience's appetite for a happy ending. Once the "Märchen" about dual morality becomes reality, the prospect of love is only a memory. Schnitzler's refusal to give the Viennese audience what it expected composed the sociocritical potential of the play, but it was not advisable to choose the easy way out, as was suggested by star Adele Sandrock: if not a wedding, then give the audience a suicide. Schnitzler reaps praise for avoiding the cathartic effect of sentiment and theatrics, which would have reinstated aesthetic order while ignoring its prolongation of societal disorder.[60]

Another example of women finding their voice is the novella *Frau Berta Garlan*, in which Schnitzler's use of the internal monologue reflects his interest in the psychology of his characters and their society.[61]

Berta's internal monologue reveals the collision of her innate human needs with societal norms, and of her search for fulfillment with the reified view of women as sex objects. Doppler admires Schnitzler's ability in the monologue to pinpoint the mechanisms of suppression.[62] For Möhrmann as well, Berta is the prisoner of her family's unnatural and conventional views on sexuality and marriage.[63] Her misery makes the liberating impulse of the *süße Mädel* (sweet girls) all the more understandable, for there is a positive element of choice in choosing younger and more attractive men.[64] Schnitzler research has tended to focus on the exploitation of the *süße Mädel,* overlooking the fact that suburban girls were free to pursue their desires and were not, like Bertha, obliged to settle for men finally ready to settle down. The element of choice places these sentimental young women beyond being prohibited erotic freedom (bourgeois wife) on the one hand, or being expected to offer purchasable sex (prostitute) on the other.[65]

Schnitzler's novel *Therese* receives special attention. Composed as a trivial adventure novel, its chronicle of Therese's experiences never strays beyond her consciousness.[66] This is Schnitzler's way of settling accounts with the world of *Anatol* decades before, as the male characters in the novel remain unmoved by the inhumanity they either cause or do nothing about, but this time there is nothing at all humorous about it.[67] Nevertheless, *Therese* depicts liberation within loss. Despite her dismal status as governess, Therese begins to emancipate herself from double standards, shrugging off the expectations of her female role in her attempt at life as a private teacher. Her failure only confirms that Schnitzler has delivered an authentic chronicle. In addition, Schnitzler disenchants the mother-child relationship by loosing motherhood from biological moorings. Therese's attachment to the children she must look after exceeds her fondness for her own son, because she has been forced to place him in the care of others in order to earn a living.[68] In this depiction, Schnitzler thus anticipates the sociological finding that women are about more than biological needs, and in this novel he functions as their advocate.[69]

In the late eighties, Ulrike Weinhold is perhaps the best example of the revolt of the feminist daughters against the fathers in Schnitzler scholarship. Her 1987 article on Schnitzler and female discourse[70] offered evidence of a productive feminist shift in thinking on Freud that was not so much a demise of the Freudian model as an about-face from doing positivistic detective work. Freud was no longer the sole authority, but was a player within the criticism that included misogynists or racists of varying degrees such as Otto Weininger (*Geschlecht und Charakter* [Sex and Character, 1903]) or Paul Julius Möbius (*Über den physiologischen Schwachsinn des Weibes* [On the Physiological Feeble-Mindedness of Woman, 1900]). To feminists such as Weinhold, structures of hysteria, narcissism, and exhibitionism ought not to be regarded as largely female abnormalities to be diagnosed and explained, but as symptoms of male discourse. Those with a Freudian perspective could scarcely help considering a work such as *Fräulein Else* pathological, but this interpretation, arrived at by mostly male scholars, is too simple.

Bourgeois discourse of the late nineteenth century emphasized female nature over female intellect. A woman's political silence suited her reduction to the function of an appealing body meant to refresh men returning from the ugly business of civilization. Beauty was conferred by the male glance, while the myth of woman-as-seductress survived by shrouding sexuality in mysterious "otherness." Projecting a lack of female intellect fostered the perception that sexually overdeveloped women required male moral parameters, a view encouraged by Freud's postulation of a super-ego less developed in women. Refusing a woman the capacity of reason prevented any healthy assessment (Weinhold, 113–15).

Within this state of female determinedness, Schnitzler shows that male discourse of the female is insufficient in situations where discourse is exposed as something other than the reflection of reality. When Katharina suddenly leaves Albert in the short story *Die Fremde* (The Stranger, 1902), Albert is left standing with the remnants of his fixed image of her, and commits suicide. Her abrupt strangeness frees her from the way Albert has always thought of her, because a woman's first step toward autonomy is the one that frees her from male-determination (Weinhold, 115–17). This escape from male discourse remains tricky, because Schnitzler cannot envisage what should follow that first step, according to Weinhold: "Die Frau erscheint bei ihm als diejenige, die sie nicht ist, jedoch nicht als mehr" (119: Woman appears in his works as that which she is not, but not as anything more). Without autonomy, there is bound to be constant estrangement of partners, but one should remember that Schnitzler was diagnosing the crisis of his time and not just the women in it (120).

Schnitzler's skepticism of language's adequacy to describe reality was not shared by Freud. Rather than seeing illness as a fundamental questioning of existing order, Freud diagnosed repression as an inescapable component of individuals confronting civilization. For Freud to question scientific discourse would have required relinquishing the concept of ego and superego, his tools for investigating the desires of the unconscious.

Assuming the necessity of defining the authentic female psyche, Freud's failure stemmed from never questioning the prevailing discourse of "common sense." Because morality was a male domain, men had to keep in check the predominant sexual aspect of women in order to save them from themselves (Weinhold, 121).

Applied to *Fräulein Else*, this means that no record of Else's thoughts can take us outside the bounds of male-determined discourse. As long as she is first and foremost a body, no amount of Else's memories, fantasies, and immediate worries to which we are privy can offer proof of her autonomy. Regardless of her irritation toward her parents, Dorsday, and everyone else blamable for her breakdown, any discursive movement toward alternatives must falter in clichés and fall silent. Silence is both a refusal to play by the rules and an inability to formulate an alternative. Her exhibitionism cancels out her own claims for eroticism and ends in scandal. In the final analysis, says Weinhold, Else's "hysteria" requires quotation marks, because it is a social disease (129). Weinhold's issue with treating Else as a case study that identifies Oedipal causes for her behavior is that it ignores *a priori* entrapment in medical discourse. Interestingly, the focus on discourse repeats the claim psychiatry had made against organic medicine when it said hysteria may call for therapy, not drugs. The feminist position argues that the battle against hysteria may call for therapy, but the war requires an examination of psychiatric categories inherited from traditional medicine. Until allowed to represent herself, woman is still only a body. Identify the repression as sexual, and one removes the symptoms, said Freud. Identify the causes for repression, say feminists like Weinhold, and one may discover that the cure has perpetuated the disease.

Notes

[1] Hartmut Scheible, *Arthur Schnitzler in Selbstzeugnissen und Bilddokumenten* (Reinbek bei Hamburg: Rowohlt, 1976) and Hartmut Scheible, *Arthur Schnitzler und die Aufklärung* (Munich: Fink, 1977). The latter is referred to subsequently in the text as *Aufklärung* and page number.

[2] William Rey, *Arthur Schitzler: Professor Bernhardi* (1971), 21, quoted in Scheible, *Schnitzler und die Aufklärung* (1977), 8–9.

[3] Max Horkheimer, "Geschichte und Psychologie," in *Kritische Theorie: Eine Dokumentation,* ed. Alfred Schmidt, vol. 1 (Frankfurt am Main: Fischer, 1968), 14.

[4] This point is made by R. K. Angress, review of *Arthur Schnitzler und die Aufklärung,* by Hartmut Scheible, *Monatshefte* 71 (1979): 347–48.

[5] *Jugend in Wien,* 146–47, quoted in Scheible, *Aufklärung* (1977), 39.

[6] Hertha Krotkoff, "Zur geheimen Gesellschaft in Arthur Schnitzlers *Traumnovelle*," *German Quarterly* 46 (1973): 202–9, here 207.

[7] Krotkoff, "Zur geheimen Gesellschaft" (1973), 208.

[8] On nationalistic "Bummels," see *Jugend in Wien*, 151–55.

[9] Quoted in Dennis B. Klein, *Jewish Origins of the Psychoanalytic Movement* (Chicago: U of Chicago P, 1981), 1.

[10] Quoted in Klein, 85. Although Klein does not mention it, Freud is received in much the same way as Schnitzler's fictional Professor Bernhardi, who is made a spokesman of a Zionism he has not chosen, and who cannot forget the rowdy yells linking Jews with Freemasons: "Nieder mit den Juden! Nieder mit den Freimaurern!" (Schnitzler, *Professor Bernhardi* [*DW* 6, 213]).

[11] Freud to Schnitzler, 24 May 1926; Sigmund Freud, "Briefe an Arthur Schnitzler," ed. Heinrich Schnitzler, *Neue Rundschau* (1955), 100.

[12] Rolf-Peter Janz and Klaus Laermann, *Arthur Schnitzler: Zur Diagnose des Wiener Bürgertums im Fin de siècle* (Stuttgart: Metzler, 1977), 155.

[13] Janz and Laermann, *Zur Diagnose des Wiener Bürgertums* (1977), 160–61.

[14] Egon Schwarz, "Milieu oder Mythos? Wien in den Werken Arthur Schnitzlers," *Literatur und Kritik* 163–64 (April-May 1982): 22–35, here 25–26.

[15] Egon Schwarz, "Arthur Schnitzler und das Judentum," in *Im Zeichen Hiobs: Jüdische Schriftsteller und deutsche Literatur im 20. Jahrhundert*, ed. Gunter Grimm and Hans-Peter Bayerdörfer (Königstein: Athenäum, 1985): 67–83, here 81.

[16] Egon Schwarz, "Arthur Schnitzler und die Aristokratie," in *Arthur Schnitzler in neuer Sicht*, ed. Scheible (1981), 54–70, here 55–57.

[17] Schwarz, "Judentum" (1985), 69.

[18] Schwarz, "Aristokratie" (1981), 68 n 6.

[19] Wolfgang Nehring, "Zwischen Identifikation und Distanz: Zur Darstellung der jüdischen Charaktere in Arthur Schnitzlers *Der Weg ins Freie*," in *Kontroversen, alte und neue: Akten des VII. Internationalen Germanisten-Kongresses (Göttingen 1985)*, ed. Albrecht Schöne, vol. 5, *Auseinandersetzungen um jiddische Sprache und Literatur: Jüdische Komponenten in der deutschen Literatur* (Tübingen: M. Niemeyer, 1986), 162–70, here 162–63.

[20] Nehring, "Identifikation und Distanz" (1986), 163–64.

[21] Detlev Arens, *Untersuchungen zu Arthur Schnitzlers Roman Der Weg ins Freie* (Frankfurt am Main: Lang, 1981), 33.

[22] See Martin Swales, "Nürnbergers Novel: A Study of Arthur Schnitzler's *Der Weg ins Freie*," *Modern Language Review* 70/3 (1975): 567–75 and Friedbert Aspetsberger, "Arthur Schnitzlers *Der Weg ins Freie*," *Sprachkunst* 4/1–2 (1973): 65–80.

[23] Arens, *Untersuchungen* (1981), 34.

[24] Norbert Abels, *Sicherheit ist nirgends: Judentum und Aufklärung bei Arthur Schnitzler* (Königstein: Athenäum, 1982).

[25] Andrea Willi, *Arthur Schnitzlers Roman Der Weg ins Freie: Eine Untersuchung zur Tageskritik und ihren zeitgenössischen Bezugen* (Heidelberg: Carl Winter Universitätsverlag, 1989), 96.

[26] Schwarz, "Judentum" (1985), 68.

[27] Quoted in Abels, *Sicherheit* (1982), 15.

[28] See Norbert Miller, "Das Bild des Juden in der österreichischen Erzählliteratur des Fin de siècle. Zu einer Motivparallele in Ferdinand von Saars *Seligmann Hirsch* und Arthur Schnitzlers Roman *Der Weg ins Freie*," in *Juden und Judentum in der Literatur*, ed. Herbert Strauss and Christhard Hoffmann (Munich: Deutscher Taschenbuch Verlag, 1985), 172–210.

[29] Schwarz, "Judentum" (1985), 79–80.

[30] Russell A. Berman, introduction to *The Road to the Open*, by Arthur Schnitzler, trans. Roger Byers (Berkeley, CA: U of California P, 1992), vii–xvi, here xii.

[31] Nehring, "Identifikation und Distanz" (1986), 167.

[32] *Jugend in Wien*, 152. See also Andrew Wisely, *The Discourse of Honor and Dueling in the Works of Arthur Schnitzler* (New York: Lang, 1996), esp. 167–203.

[33] Schwarz, "Judentum" (1985), 75–76.

[34] Willi, *Untersuchung zur Tageskritik* (1989), 126.

[35] Abels, *Sicherheit* (1982), 96.

[36] Miller, "Bild des Juden" (1985), 201.

[37] Miller, "Bild des Juden" (1985), 202.

[38] Schwarz, "Judentum" (1985), 69.

[39] Willi, *Untersuchung zur Tageskritik* (1989), 163–64.

[40] Willi, *Untersuchung zur Tageskritik* (1989), 183.

[41] Willi, *Untersuchung zur Tageskritik* (1989), 195.

[42] Berman, introduction to *Road* (1992), viii.

[43] Berman, introduction to *Road* (1992), ix–x.

[44] Abels, *Sicherheit* (1982), 115.

[45] Abels, *Sicherheit* (1982), 116.

[46] Nehring, "Identifikation und Distanz" (1986), 165.

[47] Schwarz, "Judentum" (1985), 80–81.

[48] Quoted in Schwarz, "Judentum" (1985), 80–81.

[49] Nehring, "Identifikation und Distanz" (1986), 161.

[50] Janz and Laermann, *Zur Diagnose des Wiener Bürgertums* (1977), xiii.

[51] Brigitte DeLay, review of *Emanzipation bei Arthur Schnitzler*, by Barbara Gutt, *MAL* 14/1–2 (1981): 141–43.

[52] Barbara Gutt, *Emanzipation bei Arthur Schnitzler* (Berlin: Volker Spiess, 1978), 125.

[53] Reinhard Urbach, *Schnitzler-Kommentar zu den erzählenden Schriften und dramatischen Werken* (Munich: Winkler, 1974), 7, quoted in Barbara Gutt, *Emanzipation bei Arthur Schnitzler* (1978), 174–75.

[54] See also Friedrich Knilli, "Lieutenant Gustl — ein k.u.k. Antisemit aus bundesrepublikanischer Sicht," in *Literatur in den Massenmedien — Demontage von Dichtung?* ed. F. K., Knut Hickethier and Wolf Dieter Lützen (Munich: Hanser, 1976), 139–64.

[55] Renate Möhrmann, "Schnitzlers Frauen und Mädchen. Zwischen Sachlichkeit und Sentiment," in *Arthur Schnitzler in neuer Sicht,* ed. Scheible (1981), 93–107, here 95–96.

[56] Möhrmann, "Schnitzlers Frauen" (1981), 94.

[57] Möhrmann, "Schnitzlers Frauen" (1981), 95.

[58] Alfred Doppler, "Der Wandel der Darstellungsperspektive in den Dichtungen Arthur Schnitzlers. Mann und Frau als sozialpsychologisches Problem," in *Arthur Schnitzler in neuer Sicht,* ed. Scheible (1981), 41–59.

[59] Doppler, "Wandel der Darstellungsperspektive" (1981), 46–47.

[60] Möhrmann, "Schnitzlers Frauen" (1981), 98–100.

[61] Doppler, "Wandel der Darstellungsperspektive" (1981), 47.

[62] Doppler, "Wandel der Darstellungsperspektive" (1981), 51.

[63] Möhrmann, "Schnitzlers Frauen" (1981), 102.

[64] Möhrmann appreciates Rolf-Peter Janz's thorough analysis in Janz and Laermann's *Arthur Schnitzler: Zur Diagnose des Wiener Bürgertums im Fin de siècle* (1977) of the *süssen Mädel,* because Janz realizes the liberating moment of ignoring reigning sexual conventions. Möhrmann continues Janz's argument (101).

[65] Möhrmann, "Schnitzlers Frauen" (1981), 103–4.

[66] Doppler, "Wandel der Darstellungsperspektive" (1981), 54.

[67] Doppler, "Wandel der Darstellungsperspektive" (1981), 56.

[68] Möhrmann, "Schnitzlers Frauen" (1981), 104–5.

[69] Möhrmann, "Schnitzlers Frauen" (1981), 106.

[70] Ulrike Weinhold, "Arthur Schnitzler und der weibliche Diskurs. Zur Problematik des Frauenbilds der Jahrhundertwende," *Jahrbuch für Internationale Germanistik* 19/1 (1987): 110–45.

5: Schnitzler and Freud: Uncanny Similarities?

IN HIS 1919 ESSAY "Das Unheimliche," Sigmund Freud described the uncanny as the sudden revelation of that which has long remained hidden.[1] "Uncanny" also describes the sensation when psychoanalysis has laid bare the determining forces that have besieged the patient. According to Michael Worbs, Freud knew what he was talking about. His long avoidance of meeting Schnitzler was an attempt to avoid the shock caused by the suddenly familiar, because he had been noticing in Schnitzler for some time those aspects in himself that had been left undeveloped, whether by choice or circumstance. Seeing his *Doppelgänger* Schnitzler would be an uncanny reminder of decisions he had made and subsequently repressed.[2]

In his letter of May 14, 1922 extending congratulatory wishes on Schnitzler's sixtieth birthday, Freud attributes his avoidance behavior to his "Doppelgängerscheu," because Schnitzler's discoveries through intuition and self-observation are uncanny correlates to his own clinical observations:

> Ihr Determinismus wie Ihr Skepsis — was die Leute Pessimismus hei-
> ßen — Ihr Ergriffensein von den Wahrheiten des Unbewußten, von der
> Triebnatur des Menschen, Ihre Zersetzung von den kulturell-
> konventionellen Sicherheiten, das Haften Ihrer Gedanken an der Pola-
> rität von Lieben und Sterben, das alles berührte mich mit einer un-
> heimlichen Vertrautheit.[3]

> [Your determinism as well as your skepticism — what people call
> pessimism — your ability to be moved by the truths of the unconscious
> and by the instincts of human nature, your dissection of cultural-
> conventional certainties, the way your thoughts adhere to the polar-
> ity of loving and dying — all of that touched me with an uncanny
> familiarity.]

It was a two-way street, Heinz Politzer claims: both the poet in Freud and the researcher in Schnitzler had resisted the confrontation with their unfulfilled selves.[4] With the reasons ultimately unverifiable, the fact remains that Freud's disclosure fueled the eagerness of Schnitzler scholars to explore the thematic links between the two medical doctors.

Freudian Approaches in the Fifties and Sixties

Before the letter became a recognized artifact of sorts in 1955, Victor A. Oswald, Jr. and Veronica Pinter had in 1951 already accessed the unpublished correspondence to supply one of the first post-Reik Freudian interpretations of Schnitzler, attempting to prove on the basis of *Fräulein Else* that Schnitzler was not a pupil of Freud's.[5] "On Freud's own authority," they wrote, "we must regard Schnitzler as an independent master of depth psychology, and it should henceforth be indisputable that an understanding of depth psychology is requisite to any complete interpretation of the men and women who people Schnitzler's work" (280). With Freud and Schnitzler thus on equal terms, Oswald and Pinter nevertheless collapse the novella into a case study of Else as a hysterical neurotic and incestuous exhibitionist stalled in narcissism, whose introverted libido forgoes relationships in favor of gratification alone (281–82). Her own death-wishes express her hope to be free of psychic conflicts and to atone for the death-wishes she harbors for others (282), and her collapse after presenting herself naked causes a hysterical disturbance of visual paralysis (287). Maintaining that Else's attitudes and actions are explicable through Freud alone, the authors concede that *Fräulein Else* makes important statements about family, society, and civilization (287–88).

Supporting this Freudian reading, Frederick Beharriell shows how Schnitzler's unfinished text "Frühlingsnacht im Seziersaal" (Spring Night in the Dissection Room, 1880) clearly anticipates Freud's views.[6] Because it appears long before Freud's studies on hysteria and dreams, the text can be said to demand a psychoanalytical interpretation, to be distinguished from a Freudian one (1953, 84). The main precepts of Freud's dream theory can be identified in the plot of Schnitzler's story, in which a medical student is in love with a girl, Christine, without knowing it. By projecting his love onto the friend he believes is her lover, this student supplies proof that Schnitzler has anticipated Freud's view: namely, that a dream-ego often hides behind strangers to identify with them, because dreams are always egoistic (87). The friend stands for the dreamer's repressed sexuality and fulfills his wish to be the one dancing the wild dance with Christine. The fact that the dreamer has been to a dance the day before his dream also illustrates Freud's idea of day residues well before Freud labeled them such (87).

The letters Schnitzler received from Freud, published by his son Heinrich in the *Neue Rundschau* in 1955, fueled another article by Beharriell, nine years after his first article.[7] This time, Schnitzler anticipates Freud's views not only concerning infantile trauma — in *Der Sohn* (The Son, 1892), a son kills his mother with an ax because he has never forgotten her look of rejection — but also with respect to the etiology and treatment of hysterics: the posthumous story *Der Empfindsame* (The Sensitive Man, 1895) depicts a man's suicide when he finds out his sexual favors have functioned as a cure suggested to restore his lover's singing voice (Beharriell, 1962, 727). Other anticipated elements Beharriell mentions are nymphomania in *Die Verlobte* (The Fiancée, 1891), "ambivalent feelings toward the other man" in *Der Witwer* (The Widower, 1892–1893), a stream-of-consciousness technique that parallels free-association in *Der Andere* (The Other Man, 1889), and a patient's resistance to treatment in *Paracelsus* (1895), which Freud explicitly acknowledges in "Fragment of an Analysis of a Case of Hysteria" (728–29). This last play, linked thematically with *Der Schleier der Beatrice* (1899) and published while Freud was finishing *Traumdeutung*, contains the poetic equivalent of Freud's project: "Doch Träume sind Begierden ohne Mut / Sind freche Wünsche, die das Licht des Tags / Zurückgejagt in die Winkel unsrer Seele, / Daraus sie erst bei Nacht zu kriechen wagen" (726–27: Yet dreams are longings without courage / Bold wishes that the light of day / Chases back into the corners of our soul, / From which they dare creep out only at night).

In addition to Beharriell's proof of Schnitzler's anticipation of Freud, the Schnitzler centennial year of 1962 also brought Richard H. Lawson's interpretation of *Leutnant Gustl*, which resembled Oswald and Pinter's reading of *Fräulein Else*.[8] Like Oswald and Beharriell, Lawson insists the psychological level take precedence over a superficial level of interpretation fixated on Gustl's caste honor. Gustl's Oedipus complex is obvious and extreme, and his duels manifest his own death wish (6). According to Lawson, the quarrel between the baker and Gustl occurs only in Gustl's mind (7–8). Because Gustl suffers from a pervasive castration fear, the ostensible seizure of the saber reduces Gustl to impotence, in effect turning the baker into a father-figure (8). The doctor Gustl must duel is also a father-figure, because his remark that Gustl was forced to leave the Gymnasium severs Gustl from his mother (17). Gustl's suppressed incestuous affection for his mother is expressed in his preference for older women (12–13). Meanwhile, his sister Klara plays the surrogate mother role (16).

Thanks to his psychiatric training, Robert Weiss feels qualified to document the various psychological sufferings of Schnitzler's characters. Having discussed in 1958, in a study based on his 1955 dissertation, the paranoid schizophrenia of Robert in *Flucht in die Finsternis* (Flight into

Darkness, 1931),[9] his subject ten years later spans Schnitzler's complete works, for which he tabulates thirty-two psychoses.[10] The main figure of *Fräulein Else,* for example, manifests a psychotic break caused by "schizoid personality, prepsychotic; insoluble conflicts; anxiety and guilt neurosis," the symptoms of which include an "incident of exhibitionism; hysteric paralysis; suicide to escape insoluble conflicts" (396–97). For the psychopath Franz Fabiani in *Therese: Chronik eines Frauenlebens,* Weiss notes his diagnosis: "Defective personality; early criminal tendencies; liar, thief, truant, forger, incorrigible; lacks conscience completely; alcoholic; blackmailer; promiscuous; repeated criminal acts; panderer; robs his own mother, kills her in the process" (393).

Weiss's charts, based on authorities from the forties and early fifties, contain neither psychoneurosis nor borderline cases, although he includes "manifestations of constitutional psychopathy," which he explains is characterized "chiefly by personality defects, lack of insight, lack of social responsibility" and which "does not respond significantly to psychoanalysis or hypnotherapy" — leaving psychopathology essentially without any known treatment (400, n. 12). A "Freud-less Freudian," by virtue of conclusions similar to but independent of Freud's systems, Schnitzler presents major psychoses in a way that as late as 1968, the time of Weiss's writing, had not been challenged by professional advances in psychiatry (378–80).

Such are the typical Freudian terms one encounters in this selected set of Freudian studies. This generation of Freudian criticism would encounter similar resistance, though from less strident quarters, as Theodor Reik's 1913 vanguard study *Arthur Schnitzler als Psycholog.* The more acceptable intrinsic or "werkimmanent" criticism of the IASRA disputed the notion that Schnitzler would tag Else a "hysterical neurotic."[11] Jeffrey Berlin restated William Rey's assertion of fifteen years earlier that the Schnitzler-Freud *Doppelgänger* association was long dead, with Schnitzler's debt to Freud no more and no less than Freud's debt to him.[12] Old works and old methods, Freudian criticism included, could be left behind in the search for new game, for it was clear that genius transcended historical context and the social world. Without a doubt, this death pronouncement on psychoanalytical interpretation was premature.

Fiction versus Freud

In a long article of 1974, Bernd Urban advises recalling Freud's reluctance to take credit for many of his discoveries, since Freud believed that new ideas in science often appeared either as old ideas with a new twist or as having identifiable predecessors.[13] In fact, according to Freud, psychological investigation itself was necessary for calling to mind long-forgotten sources of so-called original ideas.[14] The idea of mutual intellectual influences, occurring laterally rather than in a linear fashion, seemed a more productive way to credit sources. Instead of arguing whether Freud or Schnitzler was first to pounce on certain psychological truths, one should favor this notion of common intellectual domain, Wolfgang Nehring argues.[15] He points out that Gustl and Else are examples of free association that ends without self-awareness and self-realization. One should distinguish between the psychoanalyst, who rediscovers the principles of the human soul in a work of art, and the poet, who leaves a situation ambiguous enough to invite different explanations: "In this case the fixation on unequivocal principles would be a falsification of a work. The Freudian interpretation of Schnitzler did not always avoid this danger." [16] For Nehring, any critic is welcome in the textual house built around its author's intention, but Freudians especially must admit that the psychology they offer is not necessarily that of the author. Nehring considers Lawson's study as an example of oversimplifying the affinity between Schnitzler and Freud in using Oedipus to understand *Leutnant Gustl.*[17]

Martin Swales, too, regrets that Lawson's study sacrifices the wider social context of *Leutnant Gustl,* much the same way that Robert Weiss's analysis of psychiatric elements in *Flucht in die Finsternis* misses the novella's ambiguities of narration.[18] No matter how captivating the case study, literature takes precedence. Granted, Freud's and Breuer's case studies of hysteria depict abnormal conditions, but Schnitzler's characters are more than patients.[19] Take the narrator in *Flucht in die Finsternis,* for instance, who seems to be blocking the reader from full access to the protocol of Robert's degeneration, even though the novella is largely in the third-person form. We remain uncertain whether Robert is schizophrenic, wondering whether Schnitzler is delivering Robert's subjectivity or some other objectivity. The narrator will not admit which, or even change grammar to signal a switch in perspective.[20] This ambiguity is quite different from Freud's patients being diagnosed under a system postulating a feasible cure.

Two other widely-read investigations of *Flucht in die Finsternis* using Freudian terminology — by Hans-Ulrich Lindken in 1982 and Heide Tarnowski-Seidel in 1983 — were also perceived as warping the nature of the text.[21] Speculations concerning whether Robert's insanity comes about by disposition or environment are misplaced, complained Michaela Perlmann in 1987. The continued insistence of Schnitzler scholars on measuring literature according to psychopathology went against Schnitzler's own concern that the novella's unmistakable focus on mental illness was becoming a threat to its artistic legitimacy.[22]

In a paper given in 1981, Swales ventures that part of Freud's "Doppelgängerscheu" in averting a meeting with Schnitzler had to do with Schnitzler's insistence on historicity. "Seine Majestät das Ich" is a timeless formula sufficient for Freud, but Schnitzler's kings require concrete historical costumes to lift them out of myth. One should know that Oedipus was not just a son and husband, but a king as well.[23] If Schnitzler's historicity grounds his characters in modernity, his psychology ensures that his themes endure. Psychology always serves the interest of Schnitzler's sociocritical observations, manifesting itself in the gestures and habits of his characters. A simple comparison is Schnitzler's *Leutnant Gustl* with Hofmannsthal's *Märchen der 672. Nacht*. Psychoanalysis is indeed appropriate for interpreting Hofmannsthal's fable, because the fable reads as a dream containing the repressed impulses of a protagonist whose familial status is more important than his professional legacy. Servants who surround the merchant's son have no social or ethical characteristics, but serve merely to illustrate the state of his soul (Swales 1982, 56).

Leutnant Gustl, on the other hand, cannot be done justice by an ahistorical Freudian approach, because Schnitzler's lieutenant is anchored in the linguistic and social norms of the Austro-Hungarian army. Satire in the inner monologue shows Gustl's inability to transcend those habits of thought. Any investigation of Gustl's sexual vanity, hatred toward Jews and socialists, and condescension toward women needs to acknowledge a psychic constitution that has been thoroughly socialized (Swales 1982, 58). For Schnitzler's contemporaries, dealing with his works from a psychoanalytical viewpoint, no map is necessary to point the way in a primarily internal landscape. The fact that Janz and Laermann provide a map of Vienna and explain the society behind dueling makes all the more confusing their attribution of Gustl's predicament to a castration complex (Swales 1982, 57, 61).

Janz's Freudian analysis of *Leutnant Gustl* spans eight pages, and the scene of contention is the one in which Gustl's comrade Wiesner startles him awake from a nap in the nude on a hot afternoon. Gustl's scramble for the saber next to him sends Wiesner into a fit of laughter. If not already associating phallus and saber, Janz argues, the scene at least conveys a symbolic castration in the baker's ability to prevent Gustl from drawing his saber. Janz connects Gustl's phallic symbols to anti-Semitism and sadism, but also to homosexuality. If, for example, Gustl enjoys having a Jew support the mistress they share, it is because his jealousy includes a homoerotic component — according to Freud an interest in the men who have already slept with her.[24] In the officer corps, Gustl can experience his latent homosexuality only through comradeship. In the corps or in civilian spheres, a homoerotic phallic competition exists, and all staring contests, even in the concert that begins the novella, are substitute phallic competitions. Gustl's pride in his own glance — a lover had once commented on his beautiful eyes — makes it imperative he win all such contests.[25] Fixing the other with his glance prevents his own castration, and dueling is his contraphobic reaction to a deep-seated castration anxiety that parallels his anxiety at dropping in status in the judgmental public eye. His duels dispose of traumatic situations called up almost at will, and with manhood intact he strengthens his standing among the punishers.[26]

Michaela Perlmann also cites Schnitzler's disagreement with many tenets of psychoanalysis, and locates Scheible, Worbs, and herself in the category considering psychology subsidiary to literature: in other words, psychology explains the universal with the goal of an objective scientific theory, while literature describes singular observation with the goal of a subjective aesthetic statement.[27] The following discussion of medical knowledge shows how Schnitzler and his critics progress from case-study approaches — the positivism of Freud — to a more intricate and ethical psychological approach. In following this progression, I also note Schnitzler's criticism of the physicians that are among his favorite and most frequent characters.

Knowledge and the Semi-Conscious

Freud and Schnitzler were more than dilettantes in the expertise of the other. Schnitzler was trained under many of the same authorities as Freud, notably the psychiatrist Theodor Meynert (1833–92) and the physiologist Ernst Brücke (1819–92). Following five years at the General Hospital from 1885–88, he then assisted his father at Vienna's *Poliklinik* until Johann Schnitzler's death in 1893, editing the *Internationale Klinische Rundschau,* the medical journal that his father founded.[28] Here he reviewed no fewer than six of Freud's excellent translations between 1886 and 1892 of writings of Jean Martin Charcot (1825–93) and Hippolyte Bernheim (1840–1919) that dealt primarily with hysteria and hypnosis. An extensive discussion of Freud's translation of Charcot's *New Lectures on the Sicknesses of the Nervous System, Especially on Hysteria* in 1887 reveals Schnitzler taking Freud's side against the Viennese medical establishment, but his engagement was for hysteria research, not for Freud's specific version thereof.[29] Schnitzler's only real fascination with medicine was in its form as psychiatry, in which functional nerve maladies eluded traditional prescriptions,[30] and his only free-standing essay was "Über funktionelle Aphonie und deren Behandlung durch Hypnose und Suggestion" (On Functional Aphonia and Its Treatment through Hypnosis and Suggestion, 1888), which applied his hobby of hypnosis to his father's specialty area of laryngology. He demonstrated that hypnosis was useful for curing aphonia, for example, and even relied on it to perform a nose operation without anesthetic on a young girl — one of the many public experiments he carried out in the polyclinic. Still, Schnitzler found hypnosis unreliable and increasingly troublesome ethically, in much the same way that Freud was moved in 1892 to replace hypnotic technique with free association.[31] All this makes clear that what Freud in the *Doppelgänger*-letter attributes to Schnitzler's intuition is traceable to the medical training that overlapped with his own, especially Schnitzler's more than theoretical knowledge of the developments in hysteria and hypnosis research.[32]

The seed of Schnitzler's discontent and disenchantment with the Viennese medical establishment lies in what William Johnston has described as the atmosphere of "therapeutic nihilism." At the University of Vienna Medical School, it was becoming apparent that the knowledge that could be gleaned from patient histories was precluding interest in the real health needs of the patients.[33] Justly concerned, Schnitzler contributed a treatise to his father's journal in 1889 that described scientific knowledge parting ways with ethical responsibility. The confidence he had in the medical knowledge of the incoming cohort of physicians did not necessarily extend to confidence in their love for humanity.[34]

Walter Müller-Seidel cites this treatise in challenging Mark Luprecht's assertion that the cynicism nineteen-year-old Schnitzler felt regarding the existence of true compassion remained his life-long credo.[35] Luprecht supports his assertion with a passage from Schnitzler's diary of nine years earlier (29 April 1880), in which Schnitzler assumed that interests of the ego were incompatible with compassion. Schnitzler's reasoning then was that it was difficult enough to meet the needs of one's own ego, and this 1880 statement becomes proof for Luprecht of Schnitzler's subservience to the value vacuum postulated by Hermann Broch — a touchstone unfortunately no longer tacitly valid by 1990.[36] Luprecht's use of the diary to make this assertion ignores all other entries that enumerate Schnitzler's own compassion toward others (not limited to family and friends) and the compassion he noticed in others, particularly his brother Julius. Besides, holding Schnitzler to an adolescent statement ignores his later assertion of the freedom of choice, which would counteract Luprecht's thesis.

Indeed, the debate over determinism and free will remains primary in the discussion of ethics emerging from the critique of an impressionism that most scholars refused to attribute completely to factors beyond individual control. A Schnitzler aphorism from 1927 uses the psychological vocabulary of repression to emphasize the need for individual care of the psyche: "Ein Schicksal mag äußerlich abgetan sein, es bleibt immer noch Gegenwart, solange wir es noch nicht völlig verstanden haben. Erst wenn es geheimnislos für uns wurde, haben wir das Recht, es Vergangenheit zu nennen."[37] If "fate" is not processed into knowledge, one runs the danger of its haunting one's present and remaining the favorite justification for action or lack thereof. Without demystification, experience remains volatile, but its causes may precede even conscious memory.

Schnitzler's short story *Der Sohn* (1889), a trauma case study told from a physician's point of view, reflects Freud's and Breuer's tracing of disputed male hysteria symptoms to early childhood trauma. Like Charcot, Schnitzler considered trauma an event suffered passively, while Freud described how repression actively intervenes to prevent one from processing the event.[38] Schnitzler's physician in the story remarks on the uncertainty of "wie wenig wir wollen dürfen und wieviel wir müssen,"[39] an uneasy balance of modal verbs that reflects the tension of choice and constraint and changes little over Schnitzler's lifetime. That infant shock can fund later crimes is the theme of his late novel *Therese* (1927), while the question of choice and constraint factors into *Flucht in die Finsternis* (1931).

Because for Freud natural laws applied to all events, including so-called chance or coincidence, determinism was never in question, and Schnitzler's similar medical training allowed him to concur that in most cases free will was a chimera.[40] Mark Luprecht explains Schnitzler's initial reluctance to believe the deterministic-materialistic view he encountered in medical school in Hermann Helmholtz's essays on forces and energies. The message from Schnitzler's aphorisms — the arena that expressed his philosophical struggle most directly — was that it was fatalistic to accept determinism alone, but arrogant to accept free will by itself. So long as no one asked him to prove it, his pragmatic stance was that the denial of free will ushered in absurdity, and that it was best to reject dogma of any kind, whether from religion or science.[41] As Freud stated in his letter of 1922, the affinity between the men appeared to be the skepticism and determinism informing their common treatment of love and death, dissection of conventions, and focus on instinctual drives.[42] Both men had enough humanity to claim a working space between therapeutic nihilism and metaphysical speculation. In that space, the writings of both reflected their profound appreciation for literature.[43]

Most scholars mention Schnitzler's assertion in a 1930 interview with George Viereck to the effect that making sense of life requires acting to all intents and purposes as if one had free will.[44] Kenneth Segar, who named his article on *Traumnovelle* "Determinism and Character," writes that Schnitzler's aphorisms assume that free will must translate into a feeling of responsibility. The issue is made more significant by Schnitzler's grappling with free will and determinism within psychoanalysis during the time he was polishing *Traumnovelle*. His response to Freud's *Das Ich und das Es* (The Ego and the Id, 1923) conveys his general attitude. Segar explains that Schnitzler found Freud's subdivision of the ego into superego and id to be unnecessary, because he believed people simply had egos that looked more like ids than superegos, or more like superegos than ids. Schnitzler's version provided no moral alternative if individuals were unable to control what was predominant in them, because some would be predetermined to do more good than others. Segar recalls similar deterministic factors from another text of this period: *Der Geist im Wort und der Geist in der Tat* (1927), where Schnitzler suggests that an individual's mental constitution is an *a priori* inflexible trademark. For Segar, Schnitzler is a determinist lurking behind a moralist, because ethics mean nothing if they are dependent on how much superego or id happens to be present in an individual.[45]

Not surprisingly, one particularly productive period of skepticism toward systematic determinism came during Schnitzler's second period of interaction with Freud's circle shortly before the war, because he was busy reading what Theodor Reik was writing about him and his works. Skepticism sharpened into pointed criticism by the time he met Freud in 1922. When Freud explained that the pond in Schnitzler's recently completed manuscript *Der Gang zum Weiher* (1921, published 1926) was symbolic for the experience of birth, Schnitzler noted in his diary the propensity of inventors for becoming the slaves of their ideas.[46] In fact, ambivalence toward Freud the genius and megalomaniac became a trademark of his private writings. Schnitzler always preferred to remain in the world of the explicable as long as possible, but without inviting confrontation with those who like Reik insisted on the universality of experiences such as incest fantasies.[47]

Between 1904 and 1925, Schnitzler's own specific responses to orthodox psychoanalysis took the form of aphorisms, which were published
from his notes as "Über Psychoanalyse."[48] He challenges the apparent
arbitrariness of dream symbols, over-determination (whereby a single
mental event is interpreted as the final common path of many forces),
and the idea that sexuality supercedes all other determining causes for
behavior. The opposite of Freud's libido concept is not for Schnitzler the
death wish — he wonders why it should not rather be the desire to harm
others. In addition, Schnitzler notices a tendency in many persons to do
good rather than the one to do harm for which Freud is always seeking
confirmation.[49]

The views on determinism held by Freud and Schnitzler influence
their mapping of the levels of conscious. Schnitzler labels the area between conscious and unconscious the *Mittelbewußte* — the mid- or semi-
conscious, where most events of the psyche occur. This labeling allows
a flexible classification of unconscious thoughts and stimuli, without
leading completely into the realm of drives and consequently of speculation.[50] To this intermediate region he consigns more meaning than does
Freud, recommending that analysts pay more attention to it than to the
unconscious.[51] Furthermore, it is the poet's task, not the analyst's, to
mark the divisions between conscious, semi-conscious, and unconscious
as sharply as possible: "Das Unbewußte fängt nicht so bald an, als man
glaubt, oder manchmal aus Bequemlichkeit zu glauben vorgibt."[52]

The inevitable consequence of paying more attention to an area of
one's psyche subject to control is that more responsibility is expected for
one's actions. Seeing precisely this question of responsibility driving
Schnitzler's distinction, Scheible cites for support the construction of
Traumnovelle, which reflects the model of a semi-conscious in which
impulses travel both upward and downward, as though in a rail switching
yard.[53] Fridolin cannot escape accountability for his actions, regardless of
the fluid transitions among the levels. Scheible also makes the important
point that even Freud's *Das Ich und das Es* admitted the need for an
intermediate stage, diminishing somewhat the importance of the unconscious. Whenever questions of responsibility came into play, pure facts
fell silent, and this was where Freud admitted that a work of art completed what scientific theory was incapable of explaining. The truth of a
life, Albertine insists in *Traumnovelle,* cannot be fully comprehended by
adding up the sequence of its events.[54]

Schnitzler's protests against orthodoxy take the personal form of the
aphorism, a form known for its suspicion of categories. Perlmann notes
that an aphoristic challenge of a Freudian treatise grants the author a

measure of freedom. Like the scientific aphorisms of the mature Goethe, the aphorisms of the mature Schnitzler watch scientific developments through a skeptical lens.[55] Freud's generalizations did what science was supposed to do, while Schnitzler's aphorisms insisted on encapsulating the contradictions of experience.[56] But whether orthodox or skeptical, both men are convinced, as Friedrich Hacker points out, that one must be unmasked if one is to be helped. Consciousness means having a voice in one's production instead of remaining a slave to instinct.[57]

To understand one's tendency to drift toward a marionette existence is the first step in fighting for autonomy, Hacker insists, to which Thomé provides a more psychological explanation in his research review and separate studies. Yet Thomé, too, ends up calling this insight existential. Attempting to describe impressionism in terms of the semi-conscious, Thomé finds that the essential problem is not immediately moral or societal (though it becomes so) but psychological. In the semi-conscious, the subject is susceptible to half-conscious clichéd behavior ("Verhaltensklischees") that substitutes for fully conscious world-orientation.[58] It is the escape taken to avoid the pain of inner and outer reality that becomes morally questionable. For non-pathological cases, Schnitzler assumes that reaching the full conscious requires a psychic exertion. Crisis, or the point of unmasking, is usually the motor that propels the subject from "Gesellschaftlichkeit," or unreflective role-playing, to autonomy of the mature ego.[59] In *Traumnovelle,* the point about unmasking is driven home when Albertine places Fridolin's mask from the costumier's shop on his pillow to greet his return from a night spent in the secret society. This is the apex of a process that has turned Fridolin's impressionist doctoring into a matter of life or death, resulting — this is the implicit hope — in genuine concern for the patients as deserving human beings separate from his own ego.

Before that uncanny moment of silent challenge by the mask on his pillow, Fridolin has personified the concerns about therapeutic nihilism raised in Schnitzler's treatise on professional commitment. Dr. Adler, who grants him access to the corpse of his unknown rescuer, is more humane than he, for Fridolin's curiosity about the corpse is not scientific, but erotic.[60] Not as committed to his craft as the pathologist, Fridolin measures success by the number of patients he can see in two hours, and his questionable commitment is borne out by the text. Albertine smiles and strokes his hair when he announces his plans to resume his research, knowing his contributions to science are as paltry as his attention span is short. Fridolin's decision for the practical side of medicine over the academic side, which the narrator has us believe rests on a need for comfort, veils his mediocre academic qualifications, and does not simply accord with his bourgeois tastes. It is obvious that Fridolin feels inferior even to those he scorns, such as Marianne's future spouse Dr. Roediger, a history lecturer, and is not nearly as socially committed as doctors who live up to their calling. Noticing a man on a park bench in need of money, he expresses his fear of responsibility by rationalizing that giving to this one man will indebt him to all of Vienna's homeless thousands. Lackluster engagement is shown by his arriving too late to save the prostitute Mizzi, and by his failure to intervene against Gibiser's exploitation of the girl Pierrette at the costume shop.[61]

Schnitzler's doctors are usually negligent, lascivious, and honor-crazed. Dueling, already seen to be a "symptom" of middle-class feudal aspirations, is the ritual most incongruent with the Hippocratic Oath. No matter how farcically Schnitzler paints physicians as service personnel, principals, or seconds at duels, the fact remains that they are encouraging rather than trying to stop bloodshed.[62] His criticism also implicates the positivist medical establishment for refusing to acknowledge and treat psychic disturbances. This is shown especially in Dr. Copus's inability to treat a case of hysteria in *Paracelsus* (1898).[63] The establishment was particularly reticent about accepting male hysteria. As noted in the last chapter, in Weinhold's category of discourse about the female, the male scientist determined the aberration, with the outcome that even the etymology of hysteria resisted an etiological application to men.

Judging by Fridolin's diagnoses of hysteria in *Traumnovelle*, it is possible to date the novella's origins in a medical tradition no earlier than 1895, when Freud's and Breuer's studies on hysteria appeared. In his study of the novel, W. G. Sebald draws attention to Fridolin's house-call on Marianne, whose years of domestic service have her exhibiting a form of domestic hysteria.[64] Like Marie from *Der Ruf des Lebens*, Marianne, haggard and pale, is slowly withering from constant housework and the care of her father, which includes night stints.[65] Her lips, narrow as though from unspoken words, reflect the aphonia that it had once been Schnitzler's business to cure through hypnosis — but it also suggests her mute protest against a hysteria brought on by her environment. To one so affected, not even the relief of the end to her father's pain can lighten the sentence of male-determined captivity. According to a Freudian reading, Marianne's father has died from natural causes and from Marianne's death wishes. Fridolin supports Marianne, liberates her, and serves as her accomplice in the patricide for which she yearned so long.[66] In Sebald's view, Marianne's fate, the neuralgic point of her hysteria, is sealed when Fridolin nods to Dr. Roediger as he leaves her in his care.

Somehow, the hysterical manifestations of female longing are less constitutional than the symptoms of a life determined by male governance.[67] Marianne has no chance for the sort of catharsis made famous by the Anna O. case, in which the woman was able to overcome her symptoms once Freud's colleague Breuer had helped her attribute them to the strain of caring for her ailing father.[68]

If hysteria is a psychic response to a conceptually rigid world, as Weinhold argued concerning *Fräulein Else,* then it should be preventable. At least a few of Schnitzler's physicians thus needed to examine themselves. Müller-Seidel reminds us that the protagonist of *Doktor Gräsler, Badearzt* (1914) fails to recognize the pain that compels his sister to take her life while he is snoozing over a scientific journal.[69] Would he have seen the problem, had she been his patient? In like fashion, Fridolin's visit to Marianne only continues a pattern of rigid concepts he has begun at home. There he takes issue with Albertine's reminder that her rights count as well, especially with respect to honesty. To her rhetorical question, What would have happened, had she been the first to search for love, she adds a frustration directed at men in general: "Ach, wenn ihr nur wüßtet" (Oh, if only you men knew). The right to mutual honesty extends to mutual sexual satisfaction: claiming a space in which the wife is neither Madonna nor whore.[70] The novella shows Fridolin's revenge on Albertine for her usurpation of the male's right of infidelity. Men of Schnitzler's class have their juvenile flings and still expect a virgin bride.

Dependent on male diagnosis, then, hysteria shows bourgeois women a step removed from the male subservience to ideals considered fundamental, but really perpetuating self-interest. The solution to hysteria clearly does not lie in therapy alone, given its questionable etiology. Without assuming that Schnitzler advocates his narrator's stance, one can surmise that the narration of *Traumnovelle* leaves assumptions of power unchallenged. Fridolin's point of view is no more objective than a first-person account, and delivers at best only more disguise. Scheible recalls a study from 1891 called "Die Braut," where Schnitzler's male narrator purports to fill in the gaps of a female narrative he has taken over. What the narrator and unwary reader consider objective narration is really evaluation, of course, and the paternalistic corrective of an "untrustworthy" account passes for reality. The clues are not even all that subtle: in one spot, a we-pronoun assumes universal acceptance of the norms of the male readership. The narrator describes a man seeking a nice girl of good background who as a wife will provide the virtuous contrast to the erotic adventures of his youth.[71]

Dreams

It was argued that Scheible's 1977 book *Arthur Schnitzler und die Aufklärung* placed both Freud and Schnitzler under the legacy of the Enlightenment and described where its idealism compromised with liberal historical reality at the end of the nineteenth century. The rationalism of Enlightenment as an end in itself was construed to be at a political and psychological dead-end. By 1908, Schnitzler has his autobiographical figure Heinrich Bermann in *Der Weg ins Freie* assert that understanding offered little counsel for feelings or actions: "Es schützt uns nicht vor Leid, nicht vor Ekel, nicht vor Vernichtung. Es führt gar nirgends hin" (Scheible 1977, 68: It offers no protction from suffering, repulsion, or annihilation. It leads nowhere). If understanding ignores the instincts, they find gratification irrationally, as Scheible hastens to point out. Scheible notes that Schnitzler's interest after 1900 changes from case studies, in which psychology is an end in itself, to interactive ethics, in which psychology illumines the nature of relationships the nature of relationships — a change Scheible calls the most significant in Schnitzler's creative output (67).

It is the dream that provides knowledge of the self beyond the range of consciously applied reason, partly because it arises from a region that, unlike the semi-conscious, resists manipulation. In Scheible's view, the dream's ability to capture hidden affects rectifies the dangers of rational analysis. It functions as a knowledge medium that forces us to rethink its traditional misuse in literature "als bloßen Vorwand für unverbindliches Fabulieren" (73: as a mere excuse for loose fabricating). Take the difference between *Zwischenspiel* and *Traumnovelle:* in the former, the truth is that Amadeus decides on complete honesty at the point when his erotic interest in Cäcilie is low. As the man, he decides the future for their relationship, and his wife is left responding with the silence of stage gestures, as Schnitzler demonstrates so well. The medium of language, still determined by male norms, does not necessarily remain more reliable than Cäcilie's non-verbal language. In *Traumnovelle*, though, it is the visible partnership on the level of gesture and form that offers hope for the couple, despite what they say to one another. Like Swales, Scheible finds that dream depictions have a different purpose in Schnitzler's ruthless exposure of self-deception than in, for example, Hofmannsthal's feudalistic worldview. He also sees nothing wrong with applying Freudian categories to dream texts in which the sociohistorical context is not of primary significance (70–71).

Perlmann, similarly, distinguishes between the dream, which offers knowledge, and the semi-conscious, which favors the *erlebte Rede* narrative perspective of the dreamlike, in which external events are told solely through the perspective of the protagonist, yet in the third person. This distinction allows her to recognize Fridolin's narrator as rewriting reality from beginning to end as dreamlike or a matter of fate and thus to excuse his actions. A passage such as "wie von einer unsichtbaren Gewalt fortgetrieben" (as if driven by an invisible power) might be a cipher for Fridolin's own cowardice and weakness. Because fiction forms his cognitive horizon, what happens to him is frequently a comic reminder of the novels he has read. The *erlebte Rede* ought to persuade the critical reader to take Fridolin's statements with a grain of salt. Not surprisingly, Perlmann disagrees with Michael Imboden's view that the dreamlike nature of the night's events can be traced to Schnitzler's intention of depicting the paranormal; she sees it rather as the effort to depict Fridolin's semi-conscious. The hazy connections between science and occult are made by his characters, not by Schnitzler himself.[72]

Considering his dreams of possible interest to others, Schnitzler assembled his dream transcriptions from 1875–1927 into a kind of diary that is part of his unpublished works.[73] The dreams are mostly about death, sex, and writing, with the death motif prominent enough to be woven into what Perlmann calls Schnitzler's two most important literary dream depictions: *Fräulein Else* and *Traumnovelle*.[74] Schnitzler noted that reading Freud's *Traumdeutung* shortly after its appearance in 1900 caused him to dream more and to analyze his dreams more precisely. He dreamt frequently about Freud between 1912 and 1922, probably due to frequent discussions with Freud's followers between 1912 and 1914. 1922, the year he divorced Olga and met with Freud, contains the most dream records (seventy-one). Schnitzler dreamt of being Freud's patient two years before their dinner at Freud's home.[75] After the visit he dreamt more and interpreted more concisely, having received a gift edition of lectures from Freud.[76] Their unplanned Berchtesgaden encounter of 16 August 1922, predicted by a dream, is recorded in a diary entry in which Schnitzler describes having felt invited "über allerlei Untiefen meines Schaffens (und Daseins) mich mit ihm zu unterhalten — was ich aber lieber unterlassen will" (to discuss all manner of deep creative processes with him — which I'd rather not do).[77]

Ulrich Weinzierl traces this attraction and repulsion to Schnitzler's disappointment that Freud could not relieve the sadness of Schnitzler's recent divorce.[78] Behind Schnitzler's suspicion of the talking cure lay disappointment that he was not its beneficiary. Mutual respect, seen in

Freud's mention of reciprocal congratulations and in each man's habit of sending new publications as "revenges" to the other,[79] was a precondition for at least partial confession: Weinzierl notes that Freud confessed to similarities with Richard Beer-Hofmann and Josef Popper-Lynkeus as well.[80] It was Schnitzler's fault the relationship never really developed after the first meeting in 1922, as Freud remained ever the wooing party.[81] More dreams of Freud followed his daughter Lili's suicide, and he pictured himself in Freud's examination room expressing the pain of losing Lili, with Freud in turn revealing the loss of his daughter (Sophie, at age 27).[82]

As shown in the discussion of Reik, Schnitzler declared his own psyche off-limits for analysis, unless on his terms. The dream Schnitzler had about Reik's encroaching intimacy[83] leads Weinzierl to question Schnitzler's trust in a self-analysis that supposedly transcended external appraisal. To be sure, such gifted "Aufrichtigkeit" (honesty) was indebted to intuition (as Freud mentioned in his letter), medical training, and the discipline of a diarist. But Weinzierl, himself a journalist and biographer of Schnitzler's caustic critic Alfred Polgar, insists Schnitzler was mistaken in believing he knew all that much about himself. The only explanation for not exploring his dreams more thoroughly is that he was afraid to acknowledge the gaps in his self-knowledge. Weinzierl cites a diary entry showing Schnitzler's failure to associate a dream of flying with another explicitly sexual dream.[84] He also disagrees with Perlmann's thesis that in Schnitzler's dreams dogs stand for his critics.[85] To Weinzierl, wary contact with affectionate, nipping dogs and his fear of rabies obviously represent Schnitzler's unbridled sexual instinct, homoeroticism, and fear of sexually transmitted diseases. He sees still another denial of homosexual desire in Schnitzler's admiration for the Prussian writer Fritz von Unruh (1885–1970).[86]

Weinzierl was echoing what Scheible had noticed with respect to the autobiography *Jugend in Wien:* Schnitzler's limited dream interpretation reproduces a mixture of discretion and suppression, as though the expression of fears might make them come true.[87] Ironically enough, Weinzierl's analysis of Schnitzler follows directly on his description of Schnitzler's misgivings at being the object of analysis. In his analysis, he responds to Schnitzler's response to Reik, saying in effect that the semiconscious cannot possibly supply adequate self-knowledge, else why have psychoanalysis at all? Weinzierl uses his knowledge of Freud to attempt a fairer biographical assessment than either silence about philandering or the opposite extreme of myth-building could do. It was to this latter danger than another biographer native to Vienna, Renate Wagner, was susceptible with her 1981 biography.[88] But Weinzierl does not "out" Schnitzler so much as nudge him from the privileged position he has held, subject only to criticism more suitable for fragile museum pieces. Weinzierl is fair, neither accusatory like criticism that pronounces Schnitzler decadent through and through, nor overly-adulating in the way Lee Jennings rightly describes the many "melioristic tendencies" resulting from attempts to overturn the image of decadence.[89]

As another Viennese scholar, Konstanze Fliedl, reminds us, the forbidden desires Reik notes in Schnitzler's writings are not incriminating in themselves, unless one forgets them (not: unless one carries them out). Fliedl marks the shift in Schnitzler's texts from the question of guilt of fantasized crime, be it patricide or incest, to the self-deceiving claim of memory failure.[90] This touches Schnitzler's main objection that psychoanalysis left the region of the semi-conscious too quickly for the unconscious, and that the patient too easily fulfilled the therapist's prophecies. Fliedl focuses on Schnitzler's aversion to the excuse that repression or memory loss provided, and on his correction of it. The excuse of lost memory does not cause irresponsibility so much as it results from it. Her point is that individual memory loss can lead to societal amnesia, for, to believe Schnitzler's experiences, a person without memory is attracted to an even more dangerous memory-less collective.[91] Best echo Schnitzler's view that we are all murderers in our minds, and make fairly good detectives of ourselves.[92]

Schnitzler's dreams rarely intruded into his works except as patchwork ideas, but his works often inhabited his dreams. He maintained a distance from psychoanalytical categories, even when his dream subject was the limits of psychoanalysis itself. Perlmann notes that typical elements of psychoanalytic dream interpretation are lacking in his dreams: primarily the revealing of unconscious wishes that are satisfied in dreams, the reference to dream laws such as condensation, displacement, and depiction through symbols, and especially the recourse to infantile roots.[93] Schnitzler had few objections to Freud's wish-fulfillment theory. Like the English psychologist Havelock Ellis (1859–1939), he affirmed the compromise between physiological and psychoanalytical dream sources, regularly noting somatic sources such as ear pain for his dreams, or insisting that the sensation of falling was traceable to a disturbance of inner-ear balance during more fitful sleep.[94] The interpretations of his dreams contain little about infantilism, sex, and phallus. A dream about flying would not signify sexual arousal if accompanied by anxiety, for example, would typically convey the fear of losing respect. Water dreams were considered less memories of birth than indications of something erotic. Like other Freud critics such as Carl G. Jung (1875–1961), Schnitzler argued that Freud spent too little time discussing the manifest content of dreams. Schnitzler tries to make the interpretation fit the dream, instead of placing the dream into an interpretive category.[95]

The dreams in Schnitzler's works function to convey what his characters hide from themselves, thereby undermining their claims. In *Frau Berta Garlan,* for example, the narrator gives the reader insight into motives unknown to Berta due to her illusionary directions while awake.[96] In *Der Weg ins Freie,* Georg's dreams are transparent self-indictments, as Reik explained. The first expresses his guilt for harboring death wishes toward his own son, for his infidelity to Anna, and for his indecisiveness in his career and relationships. The second, on the heels of the first, expresses a wish-fulfillment that whisks away both the fear of dying in a duel with the husband of his recent lover, and his guilt about irresponsibility.[97]

One could argue that there are elements of Georg's dreams that appear in Albertine's dream about herself and Fridolin, and in the plot of *Traumnovelle* as a whole. This is surely no coincidence, since Fridolin and Georg are cut from the same cloth. Perlmann makes the important point that Schnitzler the poet begins his questions in the moral dimension of dreams, which Freud the scientist completely ignores. Even more important to Schnitzler, knowing one's hidden desires as expressed in dreams seems to be how to overcome them in the social realm.[98] Responsibility makes up the first pillar of his dissent with psychoanalysis, and distaste for system-thinking is the second. Schnitzler chooses the illumined path whenever possible, because it means recognition of what one is hiding, not what is hidden from view, and forces a response to the problem in the here and now, not deferring to a search for its etiology.

Notes

[1] Sigmund Freud, "The Uncanny," trans. Alix Strachey, *Psychological Writings and Letters,* ed. Sander L. Gilman (New York: Continuum, 1995), 120–53, here 126.

[2] Michael Worbs, *Nervenkunst: Literatur und Psychoanalyse im Wien der Jahrhundertwende* (Frankfurt am Main: Athenäum, 1988), 180. Reprint, Frankfurt: Europäische Verlagsanstalt, 1983.

[3] Freud to Schnitzler, May 14, 1922; Sigmund Freud, "Briefe an Arthur Schnitzler," ed. Heinrich Schnitzler, *Die Neue Rundschau* 66 (1955): 95–106, here 96–97, also quoted in Worbs, *Nervenkunst* (1988), 179.

[4] Heinz Politzer, "Diagnose und Dichtung: Zum Werk Arthur Schnitzlers," in *Das Schweigen der Sirenen: Studien zur deutschen und österreichischen Literatur* (Stuttgart: Metzler, 1968), 112.

[5] Victor A. Oswald, Jr. and Veronica Pinter Mindess, "Schnitzler's *Fräulein Else* and the Psychoanalytic Theory of Neuroses," *Germanic Review* 26 (1951): 279–88.

[6] Frederick J. Beharriell, "Schnitzler's Anticipation of Freud's Dream Theory," *Monatshefte* 45 (1953): 81–89, here 81.

[7] Frederick J. Beharriell, "Freud's Double: Arthur Schnitzler," *Journal of the American Psychoanalytic Association* 10/4 (1962): 722–33.

[8] Richard H. Lawson, "A Reinterpretation of Schnitzler's *Leutnant Gustl,*" *Journal of the International Arthur Schnitzler Research Association* 2/1 (1962): 4–19.

[9] Robert O. Weiss, "A Study of the Psychiatric Elements in Schnitzler's *Flucht in die Finsternis,*" *Germanic Review* 33/4 (1958): 251–75.

[10] Robert O. Weiss, "The Psychoses in the Works of Arthur Schnitzler," *German Quarterly* 41/3 (1968): 377–400.

[11] Robert Bareikis, "Arthur Schnitzler's *Fräulein Else:* A Freudian Novella?" *Literature and Psychology* 19/1 (1969): 29.

[12] Jeffrey B. Berlin, *An Annotated Arthur Schnitzler Bibliography 1965–1977. With an Essay on the Meaning of the "Schnitzler-Renaissance."* (Munich: Wilhelm Fink, 1978), 2.

[13] Bernd Urban, "Arthur Schnitzler und Sigmund Freud: Aus den Anfängen des Doppelgängers. Zur Differenzierung dichterischer Intuition und Umgehung der frühen Hysterieforschung," *Germanisch Romanisch Monatsschrift* 24/2 (1974): 193–223, here 196.

[14] Urban, "Aus den Anfängen des Doppelgängers" (1974), 197.

[15] Wolfgang Nehring, "Schnitzler, Freud's Alter Ego?" *MAL* 10/3–4 (1977): 179–94, here 193 n 27.

[16] Nehring, "Alter Ego" (1977), 190.

[17] Nehring, "Alter Ego" (1977), 191.

[18] Martin Swales, *Arthur Schnitzler: A Critical Study* (Oxford: Clarendon Press, 1971), 123.

[19] Swales, *Critical Study* (1971), 124.

[20] Swales, *Critical Study* (1971), 127–30.

[21] See Hans-Ulrich Lindken, "Zur Ätiologie und Semiotik des Wahns in Schnitzlers *Flucht in die Finsternis,*" *Text und Kontext* 10/2 (1982): 344–54, and Heide Tarnowski-Seidel, *Arthur Schnitzler: Flucht in die Finsternis: Eine produktionsästhetische Untersuchung* (Munich: Fink, 1983).

[22] Michaela Perlmann, *Der Traum in der literarischen Moderne: Untersuchungen zum Werk Arthur Schnitzlers* (Munich: Wilhelm Fink, 1987), 168.

[23] Martin Swales, "Schnitzler als Realist," *Literatur und Kritik* 161/162 (1982): 52–61, here 60.

[24] Rolf-Peter Janz and Klaus Laermann, *Arthur Schnitzler: Zur Diagnose des Wiener Bürgertums im Fin de siècle* (Stuttgart: Metzler, 1977), 121.

[25] Janz and Laermann, *Zur Diagnose des Wiener Bürgertums* (1977), 123.

[26] Janz and Laermann, *Zur Diagnose des Wiener Bürgertums* (1977), 124–25. Like Swales, Horst Thomé wonders how orthodox interpretations can surface, especially after the presumed demise of the Freudian paradigm; see Horst Thomé, "Sozialgeschichtliche Perspektiven der neueren Schnitzler-Forschung," *Internationales Archiv für Sozialgeschichte der Deutschen Literatur* 13 (1988): 158–87, here 172.

[27] Perlmann, *Traum* (1987), 16–17.

[28] Worbs, *Nervenkunst* (1988), 196.

[29] See Ulrich Weinzierl, *Arthur Schnitzler: Lieben, Träumen, Sterben* (Frankfurt am Main: Fischer, 1994), 66–67, and Worbs, *Nervenkunst* (1988), 204–6.

[30] Worbs, *Nervenkunst* (1988), 208.

[31] Worbs, *Nervenkunst* (1988), 209.

[32] Worbs, *Nervenkunst* (1988), 208–10.

[33] William Johnston, *The Austrian Mind: An Intellectual and Social History 1848–1938* (Berkeley: U of California P, 1972), 223.

[34] Walter Müller-Seidel, *Arztbilder im Wandel: Zum literarischen Werk Arthur Schnitzlers* (Munich: Verlag der Bayerischen Akademie der Wissenschaften, 1997), 21.

[35] Mark Luprecht, *What People Call Pessimism: Sigmund Freud, Arthur Schnitzler & Nineteenth-Century Controversy at the University of Vienna Medical School* (Riverside, CA: Ariadne Press, 1990).

[36] Luprecht, *What People Call Pessimism* (1990), 145.

[37] This 1927 aphorism is quoted in Heinz Politzer, "Diagnose und Dichtung: Zum Werk Arthur Schnitzlers," in *Das Schweigen der Sirenen: Studien zur deutschen und österreichischen Literatur* (Stuttgart: Metzler, 1968) 110–41, here 113.

[38] Worbs, *Nervenkunst* (1988), 236–37.

[39] Quoted in Politzer, "Diagnose und Dichtung" (1968), 113.

[40] Worbs, *Nervenkunst* (1988), 194, 197.

[41] Luprecht, *What People Call Pessimism* (1990), 124–27.

[42] Nehring, "Alter Ego" (1977), 182.

[43] Perlmann, *Traum* (1987), 21.

[44] Kenneth Segar, "Determinism and Character: Arthur Schnitzler's *Traumnovelle*," *Oxford German Studies* 8 (1973): 114–27, here 117. See also Worbs, *Nervenkunst* (1988), 198–99.

[45] Segar, "Determinism and Character" (1973), 120–21.

[46] Schnitzler, diary entry of 18 August 1922, quoted in Worbs, *Nervenkunst* (1988), 220.

[47] Theodor Reik, *Arthur Schnitzler als Psycholog* (Minden: Bruns, 1913), 141.

[48] Arthur Schnitzler, "Über Psychoanalyse," *Protokolle: Wiener Halbjahresschrift für Literatur, bildende Kunst und Musik* 2 (1976): 277–84.

[49] Segar, "Determinism and Character" (1973), 118–19.

[50] Perlmann, *Traum* (1987), 38.

[51] Segar, "Determinism and Character" (1973), 119.

[52] Arthur Schnitzler, *Aphorismen und Betrachtungen,* 455, quoted in Perlmann, *Traum* (1987), 37.

[53] Hartmut Scheible, *Arthur Schnitzler und die Aufklärung* (Munich: Fink, 1977), 102.

[54] Scheible, *Aufklärung* (1977), 104.

[55] Perlmann, *Traum* (1987), 41.

[56] Worbs, *Nervenkunst* (1988), 258.

[57] Friedrich Hacker, "Im falschen Leben gibt es kein richtiges," *Literatur und Kritik* (1982), 36–44, here 44.

[58] Thomé, "Sozialgeschichtliche Perspektiven" (1988), 163.

[59] Thomé, "Sozialgeschichtliche Perspektiven" (1988), 164.

[60] Perlmann, *Traum* (1987), 183.

[61] Perlmann, *Traum* (1987), 184.

[62] Müller-Seidel, *Arztbilder im Wandel* (1977), 23–24.

[63] Müller-Seidel, *Arztbilder im Wandel* (1977), 24–25.

[64] W. G. Sebald, "Das Schrecknis der Liebe: Überlegungen zu Schnitzlers *Traumnovelle,*" *Merkur* 39/2 (February 1985): 120–31, here 122.

[65] See Urban (1974), 211 n 85.

[66] Sebald, "Schrecknis der Liebe" (1985), 123.

[67] Sebald, "Schrecknis der Liebe" (1985), 123.

[68] Quoted in Urban, "Aus den Anfängen des Doppelgängers" (1974), 211.

[69] Müller-Seidel, *Arztbilder im Wandel* (1977), 26.

[70] See also Scheible, *Liebe und Liberalismus* (Bielefeld: Aisthetis, 1996), 179–80.

[71] Quoted in Hartmut Scheible, *Liebe und Liberalismus* (1996), 177. See also Marianne Knoben-Wauben, "Ambivalente Konstruktion der Weiblichkeit: Das Bild der Frau aus der Sicht des Wissenschaftlers Sigmund Freud und des Dichters Arthur Schnitzlers," ed. Guillaume van Gemert and Hans Ester, in *Grenzgänge: Literatur und Kultur im Kontext* (Amsterdam: Rodopi, 1990), 279–96.

[72] Perlmann, *Traum* (1987), 190–91.

[73] Werner Welzig, "Der Traum: Ein Text," epilogue to *Arthur Schnitzler: Tagebuch* (vol 8: 1923–26), 487–96, here 496. See also Worbs, *Nervenkunst* (1988), 210–11.

[74] Perlmann, *Traum* (1987), 27.

[75] Weinzierl, *Lieben, Träumen, Sterben* (1994), 72.

[76] Worbs, *Nervenkunst* (1988), 219.

[77] Quoted in Weinzierl, *Lieben, Träumen, Sterben* (1994), 74

[78] Weinzierl, *Lieben, Träumen, Sterben* (1994), 75.

[79] Freud, Letters to Schnitzler of 14 May 1912, 3 August 1926, and 5 July 1928, in "Briefe an Arthur Schnitzler" (1955), 95, 99, 100.

[80] Weinzierl, *Lieben, Träumen, Sterben* (1994), 8–79.

[81] Worbs, *Nervenkunst* (1988), 221. Worbs records seven meetings, the last one occurring on December 1926. It was not, as Hausner writes, due to Schnitzler's

misgivings about psychoanalysis. Hausner is merely speculating when identifying Freud's dogmatism (which Stefan Zweig mentions) as the cause for Schnitzler's failure to seek out Freud's company after the dinner in Freud's apartment on June 16, 1922 (Henry Hausner, "Die Beziehungen zwischen Arthur Schnitzler und Sigmund Freud," *MAL* 3/2 [1970]: 48–61, here 55). "While Freud did not approach Schnitzler out of fear of too great a similarity, Schnitzler avoided Freud due to his opposing views" (56). Hausner correctly stresses Freud's wooing of Schnitzler, especially in the years of contact (in person 1922–1926, thereafter only by letter) (57).

[82] Perlmann, *Traum* (1987), 23, 25.

[83] Schnitzler, diary entry of July 8, 1913, quoted in Konstanze Fliedl, *Arthur Schnitzler: Poetik der Erinnerung* (Vienna: Böhlau, 1997), 449.

[84] Weinzierl, *Lieben, Träumen, Sterben* (1994), 82.

[85] Weinzierl, *Lieben, Träumen, Sterben* (1994), 82.

[86] Weinzierl, *Lieben, Träumen, Sterben* (1994), 84–85.

[87] Hartmut Scheible, "Diskretion und Verdrängung. Zu Schnitzlers Autobiographie," *Frankfurter Hefte* 25 (1970): 129–34.

[88] Renate Wagner, *Arthur Schnitzler: Eine Biographie* (Vienna: Molden, 1981).

[89] Lee B. Jennings, "Schnitzler's *Traumnovelle* — Meat or Poison?" *Seminar* 17/1 (1981): 73–82, here 74.

[90] Fliedl, *Poetik der Erinnerung* (1997), 463.

[91] Fliedl, *Poetik der Erinnerung* (1997), 464.

[92] Fliedl, *Poetik der Erinnerung* (1997), 465.

[93] Perlmann, *Traum* (1987), 29–30.

[94] Perlmann, *Traum* (1987), 52.

[95] Perlmann, *Traum* (1987), 61.

[96] Perlmann, *Traum* (1987), 105.

[97] Reik, *Schnitzler als Psycholog* (1913), 186–90.

[98] Perlmann, *Traum* (1987), 94.

6: The Task of Memory: The Diary Project

IN BREADTH AND CONSISTENCY, Schnitzler's diary is among the most significant of German and European literature. In 2000, the Austrian Academy of Sciences finished its project of publishing the ten 400 to 500 page volumes of Schnitzler's diary, having started in 1981 to bring order to his entries between 1879 and his death in 1931. Predictably, easier access to the diary confirmed the suspicion that Schnitzler brooded over concerns far more multifarious than love and death, something astute readers had known for decades. Beyond serving to support interpretations of texts or to prove Schnitzler was capable of diversity, the diary became an object of scrutiny in its own right, reflecting a determination, especially in Vienna, to prove that this man's legacy was worth preserving. The discipline demanded by such prolific journal writing could alter the image of a man so long considered impressionistic before the First World War and out of step afterwards. What has been shown to be consistent and trustworthy is, after all, worth preserving. In the scholarship that discusses Schnitzler the diarist and autobiographer, or in the biographical approaches that rely on these genres, an ambivalent fascination has emerged not always to the liking of Schnitzler aficionados. The turn toward non-fiction has shone the spotlight more brightly on Schnitzler's complexity, but also on his pathologies.

The Diary Project (1981–2000)

Schnitzler's diary wrote predictability into his life as a bulwark against the unpredictable. Made credible by excruciating self-honesty, the diary became his anchor against an experience of slippage rivaling that of his characters. With religion a false comfort and critical recognition on the decline, Schnitzler's hope for immortality was to preserve his reflection in the diary for future generations. What began as explorative became a necessary daily confession and self-judgment of greater resonance than the rituals Schnitzler noticed in Judaism or Christianity. To hope for an end to melancholy was too optimistic, but the diary offered at least the means for its daily management. Such an anchorage for Schnitzler in the face of transience and death cannot be overstated.[1]

The existential pathos of Schnitzler's daily biography is only one aspect of the diary. When the first two volumes of Schnitzler's diary appeared in 1985, Horst Thomé hailed the opportunity scholars had for correcting speculation about Schnitzler and his cultural context. The diary would nourish the investigation of those "microsystems" yielding objective knowledge of literature and society. With its short notations devoid of commentary, it could be relied upon to channel social reality itself. Moreover, the diary would eliminate philological guesswork by serving as a window on the evolution of texts to creative maturity. Thomé looked forward to reinvigorated investigations in the manner of Michael Worbs, who had mined the diary for Schnitzler's knowledge of Freud's theories and ambivalence toward Freudian psychoanalysis. In short, the diary's many uses promised to reproduce the effect the Zürich Archives had on Thomas Mann scholarship.[2]

Suggestions for how to use the diary are provided by Werner Welzig in his epilogues to each diary volume. Welzig, professor at the University of Vienna in charge of the diary project during its entirety, condenses a main theme from the span of years in question and suggests ways of reading Schnitzler's life in dialogue with his time.[3] Thanks to its huge database, the diary can document the social formation of the self and excel as a chronicle of sexuality, marriage, family, and *fin de siècle* Viennese roles.[4] The epilogue for the years 1920 to 1922, for example, examines the vocabulary of confrontation Schnitzler uses during his separation and divorce from his wife Olga. Another epilogue features dream vocabulary for the years 1923 to 1926, and for the volume 1917 to 1919 Welzig proposes that the references to billiards, poker, and guessing games be used for writing a cultural history of games peculiar to Schnitzler's milieu.[5] During Schnitzler's prime bicycling years of 1893 to 1902, it is the influence of technology on self-identity that captures Welzig's attention. The intoxication of acceleration, fashion, and class statements influence Schnitzler's description of the world as seen from a bicycle saddle. Here, casual descriptions of new technology invite the reader to consider long-familiar technology with a wonder befitting its initial reception through Schnitzler's eyes.[6]

Considered as a literary genre, writes Horst Thomé, the diary offers little reason to revise the Schnitzler image already provided from his correspondence and autobiography. But Thomé envisions even more comprehensive investigations into the importance of the bicycle, the granting of literary prizes, changes in theater habits, censorship, boundaries of tolerance, possibilities of the media, and the progress of technology in everyday life.[7] The diary's extensive data could stimulate a sociohistorical examination of the physicians, artists, and intellectuals it mentions, in order to hypothesize about social interaction in an increasingly anti-Semitic Vienna. How did Jews in various levels of assimilation communicate with non-Jews, and how did the artistic elite relate to institutions such as the army, the administration, the scientific community, and the stock market? The cross-section of a life is a history of private life, providing glimpses into rules for all modes of relationships, social rituals, themes of polite conversation, and the use of leisure time.[8]

Rather than focusing so narrowly on the material of Welzig's epilogues and Thomé's microsystems, most diary investigations have been content to discuss the obvious. This is no working journal or *journal intime,* but more a chronicle in the style of Goethe and Thomas Mann. Dreams, people, walks, purchases, events, music, status of projects, and daily readings are recorded, rarely with analysis or interpretation.[9] The diary is neither a travelogue of sights and experiences nor a detailed political notebook. Concerned with neither cleverness nor profundity, it grants equal weight to all entries.[10]

As his own law-giver, Schnitzler imposed complete honesty on himself to record insufficiency.[11] Boredom, indifference toward medical studies, and wasting time made him aware that his greatest danger was himself. Self-revelation had a redeeming effect, and became, especially in the last phase of the diary (1918–31), his defense against his ponderous awareness of transience.[12] With his loneliness and fear of dying came a fervent wish for historicity, from which the obvious function of the diary derives, as Nike Wagner states: instead of wishing to live on through his works, Schnitzler's plaguing notion is to survive in life itself.[13]

From the time he started his diary in his late teens, Schnitzler vowed to steer clear of sentimentality, but the honesty he espoused had a stylized veneer, especially in his adolescent stages of identity formation.[14] Borrowing heavily from literary influences such as Goethe and Heine, the young man used old words, as Welzig puts it — even to describe a kiss, which meant more to him in retrospect.[15] Youth is associated with spontaneity and originality, but the first diary entries show Schnitzler's epigonic raid on the literary cache of his social class.[16]

A clear link exists between literary stylization and the allures of snobbery. In his autobiography, Schnitzler writes about standing as a witness in his cousin's wedding in Vienna's *Votivkirche.* The sensation of standing on display in the incense-filled sacristy lost all appeal when he recorded the experience in his diary (*J*, 321). Schnitzler's self-representation becomes more believable to the extent that he sheds the stylization that infused his earliest diary entries, and by 1901, there is scant evidence for

it in the sketches made for the autobiography (*J*, 319). Friedrich Torberg's epilogue to Schnitzler's autobiography expresses amusement that
the immature twenty-five-year-old, winking across the decades at the
fifty-five-year-old, reminds his older self that maturity is not such a certain thing.[17] Torberg delights in the way Schnitzler comments on a passage about complications in love: "Zuviel Psychologie übrigens! Sagen
wir einfach: er war ein Narr, sie war ein kleines Luder, und ich war unge-
schickt" (*J*, 311: Forget the psychology! Let's just say that he was a fool,
she was a little slut, and I was a bumbling fool).

Schnitzler's levity in matters of ritual stemmed from skepticism
whether the concrete occasions for political or religious language could
ever escape the abstractions they constantly invoked.[18] As we will see, his
discomfort with abstractionism is the result of both choice and compulsion. As Heide Tarnowski-Seidel argues, Schnitzler's relief at outgrowing
stylization and snobbery is not matched by a clean triumph over *Schlamperei*. His autobiography hazards that his need for truth developed from
the need to combat slovenliness (*J*, 319). The early diary seems to con-
firm Ernst Mach's premise of an unsalvageable modern ego that consists
of nothing more than sensations without a unifying center — character
traits without a character.[19] Indeed, as a young man Schnitzler comes off
as fragmented due to character traits that offer him little emotional
satisfaction.[20] Even the experience of time becomes suspect. In his urge
to always be elsewhere doing something else, Schnitzler misses the present tense; that is, he appears present only when recording fragmentation.
In other words, Schnitzler is accused of the same crime as his Anatol, but
unlike him derives no satisfaction from frittering away entire days during
his twenties, and, to believe his scathing self-analysis, notes only minimal
improvement of this condition over the decades. He claims to have failed
the task of *Bildung* — liberal education — and fears that nothing will
ever come of him.[21]

This disorientation is not just a stage, Thomé insists, for what seems
either an anthropological norm or a pathological aberration — Schnitzler's
doubt that he will ever know himself or another person meaningfully —
really rests on tenets of nineteenth-century liberalism.[22] Discussing the
notion that the individual path toward knowledge and maturity imitates
the evolution of the human species, Thomé postulates that Schnitzler's
negative experience of the self caused him to doubt his epoch's belief in
progress, as shown in the diary entry of May 9, 1880, where Schnitzler
insists that a lasting improvement of the world order will always remain
a pipe-dream.[23] Thomé attributes Schnitzler's skeptical tone to his failure
to achieve success worthy of liberalism's standard of progress. Is personal

failure necessary, however, to notice the ruptures in untamed optimism? Or is it that he uses himself to disprove the myth of improved world conditions?

The frequent repetition of terms such as "Schlamperei" and "vertrödelt" suggests that Schnitzler was squandering the time necessary for self-actualization. Escaping his father's career plans for him was one thing; escaping the domestic inculcation of liberal values during his migration to full-time writing was another.[24] Johann Schnitzler had encouraged his son's dilettantish attempts at writing, thinking to restrict art to a venting function within the world of duty — or, as Schorske argues, as a way to assimilate into the aristocracy that supplied his patients and acquaintances.[25] A physician's career allowed marveling at art from a safe distance, and indeed Schnitzler's ambivalence about his career did not become critical during two decades of strong economic gains. The eighteen-year-old could afford to consider medicine a chore and view writing as a *Heimat* for which he felt homesick if he neglected it too long.[26] Ignoring the economic arguments against becoming an artist caused a full-blown career crisis in 1885. With nothing but discouragement from his father, Schnitzler experienced the aesthetic realm as genuine and the world of business as usual as vulgar.[27] As the transcript of Schnitzler's attempt to escape from a medical career, the diary becomes a vow never to provide fiction that is purely recreational. His motivation will not be to refresh readers with brief forays into unreality. The bourgeois separation of imagination from substance is as despicable as the memorization of zoological facts in medical school.

Schnitzler recognized long after resolving his career dilemma that it was not predetermined. The conclusion to his autobiography allows for the power of choice in decisions affecting his fate, even when he believes himself affected by chance occurrences. Extending his bachelor years was necessary, he believes, to become what he was destined to become: choosing a career would number him among the chosen ones able to choose (*J*, 316). His ruthless honesty as a writer arrives, Friedrich Torberg asserts, once this individual development is complete.[28]

It is not just his own failure to measure up to liberal idealism that breeds Schnitzler's skepticism. The high standard itself strikes him as flawed, propped up by arbitrary concepts posing as universally valid. Liberalism guaranteed rights and privileges for all, but the diary shows Schnitzler recording his exclusion from promised autonomy. As Thomé writes, Schnitzler's vow at twenty-three to "find himself" came in part because he lacked the comforting pre-modern background of family, corporation, and class by which to measure himself.[29] In its absence, identity had to be formed through exclusion — the qualities of the pre-modern have-nots.[30]

This would appear to raise the thorny issue of free will and determinism. Schnitzler lacked certain aspects of cultural background, some by his own choice and others by compulsion. He excluded himself from the Jewish religious subculture, from political movements, from the collegiality of the medical profession. But the fact that he was excluded from the notion — however discredited — of a liberal German *Kultur-nation* is the overriding issue that excuses his chosen self-exclusions. The question, as one looks forward and backward, is whether Jewish identity must form itself intrinsically by exclusion. According to Thomé, Schnitzler could console himself for failed identity formation, because at least he avoided the temptation of naïve illusions.[31] Whatever the balance of cause and effect, skepticism is clearly a byproduct of being excluded, and Thomé does Schnitzler scholarship a favor by loosening the stigma of amorality so long attached to it. The liberty some enjoy is liberty others register as endangered by the infusion of anti-Semitism. The diary, symbol of the private sphere, thus remains the bastion for criticizing the inconsistencies of the public sphere.

The dynamic of psychological failure and sociological exclusion provides the diary with inexhaustible material. Schnitzler can still write about discontinuity in a format that is finite, dateable and linear. Documenting anything, even inconstancy, sets up an expectation of constancy at least in form. Although Schnitzler's diary suggests that exclusion and shortcomings played a large role in forming his identity, it also reveals his trust in the possibility of social integration through performance and competition. Schnitzler's growing literary production proves that a work succeeds not by fulfilling certain aesthetic principles or containing certain textual characteristics, but because it fulfills the artist and resonates publicly.[32] Art no longer functions to liberate identity from market concerns; rather, art receives its legitimacy from the market. Schnitzler's deepest longing is to have his vanity tickled by outperforming his fellow writers.

The journalistic public sphere delivered the recognition necessary for success, but was marked, as we have seen, by a feuilletonism that softened its credibility.[33] Because of Schnitzler's ruthless honesty toward himself, one can consider his diary incorruptible, Gerhart Baumann argues.[34] Without a doubt, the diary calls the public sphere to account with a pathological elitism. A private man with nothing to hide about his life — a posture that haunts his memory today — Schnitzler refuses to be judged by standards beyond his control that define and delimit public and private, sacred and profane, moral and immoral, political and apolitical. Instead, he shatters reified proprieties by pointing out their interest in suppression and power. The scandals of honor (*Leutnant Gustl*) and sex (*Reigen*), for example, are predictable insofar as the military concept of honor hinges on the concept of shame in the area of sex. Both were supposedly immune from criticism in the Monarchy while remaining binding as restorative trends in the Republic.[35] If Schnitzler offends public taste, it is because he is already the object of public and private insult. Much like his character Professor Bernhardi, in rejecting authorities of any kind, Schnitzler is out for a private justice that appeals to reason.

If the diary entries of the eighties show Schnitzler grappling with an identity of exclusion and difference, the entries during the war (1914–18) reveal that public patriotism forces his private self-confession as German, Austrian, and Jew.[36] The diary represented the private exposure of public hypocrisy and double standards.[37] Here Schnitzler reacted to the monstrosity of war and attributed its causes primarily to insufficient imagination. In its specificity, his private history reads as a response to the hemorrhaging of the public sphere (and especially of the parliament and the newspapers), with its rhetoric, propaganda, patriotism, and forgetfulness. Finding humanism dead on the journalistic battlefield, he protects his own individualism all the more fiercely by recording his impressions for posterity rather than pronouncing his views to a misinterpreting public. Because of his own fragmented ego, the diary is one place Schnitzler refuses to answer the myth of no-fault patriotism on its own terms. Writing about, not fighting about integrity is Schnitzler's way to preserve it. Irene Lindgren has marked the war years as the time the diary changes from serving as a Father Confessor to becoming a loyal and trustworthy conversation partner who helps him achieve a semblance of daily knowledge in the midst of a debilitating societal constellation.[38]

Schnitzler's constant references to his fragmented ego might bring the complaint that preoccupied reflection is a narcissistic hindrance to development. Schnitzler's friend Hugo von Hofmannsthal writes in his diary that life's enormities are surmountable only through constructive action: "Immer nur betrachtet, lähmt es."[39] It sounds convincing to argue that ethics are possible only when another face comes between the diarist and the mirror. But talk of some higher ethical cause is what produced a lifelong uneasiness between Schnitzler and Hofmannsthal. Schnitzler sees no need to leave the private sphere for something weightier that compromised its guarantee, and his own awareness of slippage is suspicious of claims of a restored wholeness never really present in the first place. Rather than viewing the diary as a hobbyist's sentimentalized meaning of life, Schnitzler insists that meaning is to be had from the writing process itself. Meaningful activity consists in writing traces of oneself and knowing when to withhold speech. Refusing epistemological standstill, he doubts whether language actually reflects reality to show an essence, because language cannot help but mediate or interpret reality.

Scholars notice that the diary style during these war years shows more involvement, interpretation, and pathos in a style considerate of a possible future reader, but still free of sentimentality and rhetoric. Through the credibility of a first-hand account, Schnitzler wants to stir the imagination of future readers to aid their memory. In his retreat to a patriotism that is private, not chauvinistic, he becomes aware how important *Heimat* is to him and what value the natural world assumes with war: it is not just nature that is abused, but also the natural element of trust in speech, twisted irreparably into propaganda. Nothing can adequately reflect the shock of the maimed and dismembered — above all, not the adjective "heroic" applied to war.

The same insistence on careful language in the public sphere applies to Schnitzler's contacts on the personal level. His diary becomes a repository for his impressions of the many literati spawned by what Schorske calls a commercialization of literature in Austria's upper middle class.[40] Although he berates them for obliviousness, his image of them is never one-sided or unalterable, and this reflects his own attempts to live with contradiction. Selfish but never presumptuous, sharp but with redeeming sincerity, he finds something closer to truth in the sum of the "on the other hands."[41]

A Bulwark against Melancholy or Its Guarantee?

Schnitzler's novella *Flucht in die Finsternis* (1931), actually completed in 1917, is the subject of Heide Tarnowski-Seidel's *Arthur Schnitzler: Flucht in die Finsternis: Eine produktionsästhetische Untersuchung* (1983). She argues that narcissism is only one of the pathologies revealed in Schnitzler's diaries, assuming one can trust such a dedicated hypochondriac. Entries about fragmentation, manic-depressive states, delusions of grandeur, and an inferiority complex are also frequent. Linking the diary to the production and final form of the novella, Tarnowski-Seidel posits the novella's therapeutic benefits for Schnitzler. Schnitzler is examined within his own "flight into darkness," since the diaries show his instinct of flight prevailing over his instinct to fight. Except for a nod to Mach's empiriocriticism, Tarnowski-Siedel is more intent on taking Schnitzler literally at his word, which entails examining how Schnitzler's diary both reflects and contributes to his narcissistic identity as a whole. In her view, Schnitzler undergoes the same fragmentation in his diary that Robert experiences in the novella, when his character recognizes himself in a mirror which itself has a crack. The subject can neither perceive a totality nor recognize itself as subject, since in the process of observing, it is always already an observer — a non-subject, someone else. Such an existence alongside the self never achieves synchrony.[42]

Tarnowski-Seidel's investigation is important because it features a novella of uncompromising clinical severity. The metaphor of brokenness is appropriate as well, for this chronicle of decline parallels the concern of Schnitzler's diary, especially in the twenties, to track the economic and political devastation of the First Republic. On the personal front, his hearing loss continued, his popular respect declined, his marriage dissolved, and his daughter committed suicide. This is only a sample of the debilitating events and processes in his life, of which most were merely irritating, but one, Lili's suicide, produced pure sadness.[43]

The diary's function for Schnitzler during this time could be compared to Alain Robbe-Grillet's justification of the *nouveau roman* as appropriate for modernity because time no longer matches the development or demise of a novel's characters.[44] According to Elsbeth Dangel, Schnitzler's *Therese* (1928) counts as a modern novel, because the novel starts with the main character's defeat and stays there. Chronicle-style narration prevents the protagonist's unique fate from unfolding in the usual psychological manner. As the events are all external, no glance is provided into her character, which leaves the cycle of banality triumphing over tragedy.[45] Like *Therese,* Schnitzler's diary performs the satirist's function of removing the mask of his own pathologies and those of society. The struggle has meaning, for it is precisely the banal routine that allows him to survive his daughter's suicide.

Welzig attributes to force of habit Schnitzler's ability to keep writing, but only as a habit of survival in which the vita growing in the diary bandages the incisions of reality.[46] Here the liturgy of writing confronts the obligatory rituals occasioned by the cruel life stations of death and divorce. Before the legal divorce ceremony in Vienna, Schnitzler and Olga must undergo a Jewish separation ritual in Munich.[47] Seven years later in Venice, the divorced couple must observe the ritual burial of Lili.[48] A third ritual in the form of Hugo von Hofmannsthal's burial takes Schnitzler to Rodaun, only two days after the suicide of Hofmannsthal's son. More significant than the burial ritual, in Welzig's view, is Schnitzler's choice to remember Hugo through conversations with mutual friends, by re-reading correspondence, and above all by reading his own diary entries about him.[49]

In "Der Anspruch der Toten," the epilogue to the ninth diary volume, Welzig notes that Schnitzler, at home with death and dying, put distance between himself and the details of burial.[50] Rejecting the public death cult of his time, Schnitzler nevertheless builds a cult of his own in remembering the deceased. On the day Lili would have celebrated her twentieth birthday, Schnitzler brings Olga twenty roses.[51] The diary records all anniversaries of Lili's birth and death; for example, he writes in his last year: "Heute vor drei Jahren — Lili!" (Three years ago today — Lili!).[52]

Welzig argues that Schnitzler's obsession with death left him without the strength of the present tense. Far from being banished, the grave remains the prerogative of uncontrollable memory.[53] In the attempt to establish an existence free of commitments, the diary becomes a school of extreme remembrance, and justifies itself by Schnitzler's need for commitment. Schnitzler admits trusting his diary for release from loneliness, as if writing for friends who by reading his entries understood him the best of anyone.[54] Memories haunt the anniversaries of dateable encounters and events all the more because Schnitzler's fear of forgetting dooms him to remember the commitments he has tried to escape.[55]

Ignoring public ritual only enhances Schnitzler's remembrance, especially in the case of his daughter. Noting the amount of commentary from Schnitzler after he had read Lili's diaries, Welzig concludes that although diary entries leave occasional irresolvable differences between the diary persona and the persona known by the diary reader, this is not a problem, as they need not be considered the final authority. As a standard for dealing with intimate diaries, Welzig recommends keeping in mind Schnitzler's observation (January 31, 1929) that Lili was a far more interesting person than her often vacuous diary entries lead a reader to believe.[56] And, whether interesting to German studies or not, the diary functions on the most basic level of language as acclamation and salutation.[57] When Schnitzler in his diary takes stock of 1928 on its final day, he curses the year.

It is worth noting Tarnowski-Seidel's remark that the suicides of Schnitzler's fictional characters enable him to continue living. This is an argument against equating Schnitzler with his characters: because they serve as repositories for his fears, desires, and ambivalence, he can destroy these pathological personas to usher in a satisfying catharsis. Schnitzler claims that his dramas function as death sentences that grant him pardons for real life. Tarnowski-Seidel argues that writing is the source of the conviction that he is not obliged to take his own life, because writing preserves him against a deadly melancholy.[58] Without a doubt, Schnitzler's curse on the year is also a curse on himself.

The act of cursing finds its place among the rhetorical consistencies of *exclamatio, dubatio,* and *conduplicatio* that Konstanze Fliedl has identified for Schnitzler's diary. In the last fifteen years of his life in particular, an exclamation such as "O du mein Österreich!" (There you go again, Austria!) breaks through mere reportage to represent an emotional palette between indignation and resignation.[59] The litany of exclamations shows that the politics of literature in the outgoing monarchy and the new republic have taken the upper hand, and are, writes Fliedl, Schnitzler's briefest form of acknowledging that attacks on the writer are part of the war that anti-Semitic criticism wages on the person (260). With time, Schnitzler even weans himself from the use of "ich" in his diary, in order to express his loss of identity and to assert it in the face of public harassment. The referent is always understood, and the exclamation is the most direct speech of the "I" that is present in helplessness and indignation (261–62). This shift of focus from subject to circumstances is apparent in what Fliedl calls *conduplicatio,* a kind of exclamation in triplicate of global and personal catastrophe: "Krieg, Krieg, Krieg"; "Allein, allein, allein"; "Lili, Lili, Lili!" express Schnitzler's consternation (265). Fliedl makes an intriguing link between Schnitzler's exclamations, which express his reluctance to use language in his diary, and his stories, the domain where the unspoken words of the diary are finally voiced (268).

These rhetorical devices of cursing, exclaiming, and announcing in triplicate are speech acts that respond to events or attempt to control them. As early as his fiftieth year, Schnitzler attempted to fix with legal language the way he himself would be put to rest. A testamentary item from an entry of April 29, 1912 stipulates an avoidance of all ritual accessories and mourning: "Keine Kränze! Keine Parte! . . . Begräbnis letzter Klasse . . . Keine Reden! Vermeidung alles rituellen Beiwerks . . . Keine Trauer tragen nach meinem Tode, absolut keine."[60] Instructions for preserving the diary echoed his belief in its better chances for an afterlife than his own aging body or the fading glory of his plays and novellas, and his belief that it would compete with the works of the greatest.[61] This explains his peculiar interest in knowing for what purpose his diary would best serve German scholars such as Oskar Walzel, Erich Schmidt, Josef Körner, Stefan Hock, Friedrich Kainz, and Herbert Cysarz, all of whom receive a better treatment in its pages than most critics do.[62] Beharriell imagines Schnitzler wishing for a legacy that might justify the kind of daily biography undertaken on Goethe's behalf, based on the similar telegraph-style journal entries of both men.[63]

It is clear that Schnitzler's testamentary provisions reveal more concern for how the diary is treated than for his own burial. He protected the diary the way he treated his daughter, but with comprehensiveness and elitism. In 1918, he stipulated that the volumes of the diaries to the year 1899 not be published for twenty years after his death, the remainder not for forty years.[64] Editing or pricing the diary in any way to make it more visible was not allowed for, regardless of the eventual real cost of converting more than five thousand pages into ten large volumes. The cost of the volumes did not exactly assure the reader of their comprehensibility or value, for the mundane remained juxtaposed with the profound. Schnitzler's insistence appears to counter his wish to survive through his diaries. For whom did he wish to survive? Certainly it was for those who took him seriously.

The precaution Schnitzler took of stowing the diary in a bank safe during the last decade of his life proved warranted. Eric A. Blackall, a British student studying in Vienna at the time, saved the Vienna archival material from the Nazis in 1938. It had been stored since Schnitzler's death in a room of the house his son Heinrich owned, which was accessible only through the garden. The British Embassy affixed a seal to the door preventing the Nazis from entering, despite repeated searches of the rest of the house. Shortly after the Austrian annexation, Blackall took the material to the Cambridge University library. Schnitzler's son Heinrich was already out of the country, and Olga Schnitzler emigrated a few months later, following Heinrich to the United States with the Cambridge portions of the unpublished works that included diaries and letters. Heinrich Schnitzler oversaw this material during his time in the United States (at UCLA) and returned with it to Vienna in 1957.[65] As if to make up for misunderstanding and neglect, as soon as legally possible the Austrian Academy of Sciences began carrying out work on the Schnitzler diary project with support from the Cultural Office of the City of Vienna.[66]

Schnitzler's motivation to keep a diary in the first place — to make himself historical — anticipated the way the diary, as an artifact, made history about him. Not confident his works could rank with the greatest, he nevertheless ensured preservation of his diary. Still, Schnitzler was not writing the diary primarily for publication, but for himself.[67] Given its private scope and unflagging honesty, was Schnitzler, perhaps stereotyped as the clinician of the case study, fully aware of the price of serving himself up as an epochal case study? The contrast is evident posthumously, particularly given Schnitzler's reluctance to grant access to the diary. The familiar question arises: how does one read something meant for posterity but passed off as written only for the moment? Welzig suggests following Martin Walser's suggestion to diary readers not to ask for a description of the event in question, but to ask how the description helps the writer process the event.[68]

To recapitulate: the diary in modernity is not, at its most honest level, about pathos and sentimentality or piety, but, as Manfred Jurgensen maintains, about the Kierkegaardian sickness unto death that shows life in continuous crisis.[69] Schnitzler's diagnostic training serves him well when he is himself the subject under lifelong examination. Roughly stated, in the period covering the years 1879 to his marriage in 1903, the journal was literary in the sense of reflecting the words of others, as in having pre-established categories for describing the experience of "love" literally in quotation marks. Gradually he shed this stylization as he weathered a career crisis and achieved success in primarily short forms of novellas and one-act plays. The diary shows his adherence to liberal values of consistency, industriousness, and justice, but also to competition. With success came an ambivalent advance from privacy to the public sphere and back again, because success demanded his visibility. His diary entries become predictable in format in the decade before the war, a time corresponding to his own maturity and uneasy truce with the impressionism in his character. Only in the war did it appear Schnitzler was writing more for posterity and not for himself alone. Always, though, he intended his personal history to correct, if necessary, the official history of his society. Ideologically, the writing process modeled a logic and fairness in the way it exploded propaganda by refusing ever to allow it the last word. And yet Schnitzler himself also refused to have the last word, for truth was in the becoming.

What Schnitzler considers pathological, his champions consider genius. Baumann, for example, measures Schnitzler's life-long remarkably low self-esteem — evident in his nervousness, disquiet, contradictions, irony, fault-finding, and self-disgust — in terms of a productive unrest. It is not his lack of plans and insights but their perturbing overabundance that damns him to impatience in the realization of imperfection, in what Schnitzler calls an overflowing but not fulfilling existence.[70] As his weaknesses are his strengths, so he is keen to note the weaknesses within others' strengths.[71]

The diary represents Schnitzler's conviction that the measure of character lies in consistency, the opposite of opportunism. Skeptical of transcendent dogma, it serves as an immanent anchor in which the process assumes more significance than the content. Granted, every diary is fictional, but Schnitzler's diary approaches the undistorted mirror surface of one-to-one correspondence. The honesty of reflection is not immediately apparent as fiction, in the sense of writing for didactic, moralistic, self-pleasing or self-aggrandizing purposes, but rather the journal mirror is smooth precisely because Schnitzler is aware of the cracks in the endless series of mirrors involved in knowledge of the Other. Such harsh prosaic restlessness, such hypochondriac urgency in listing pathologies is the function of Schnitzler's diary. It is difficult to know whether the prophetic skepticism would have suffered, had Schnitzler emerged more from the diary to reverse the mere shadow he had become in friendships, as Hofmannsthal complained.[72]

Aspects of Konstanze Fliedl's *Poetik der Erinnerung* (1997)

It would be misrepresentative to end this chapter on memory without hinting at the scope of Fliedl's book. Her achievement bridges the gap between analyzing the findings of research on Schnitzler's memories and contemporary memories of Schnitzler that span the whole range, from populist to critical. The nexus of time and memory is useful for broaching the category of impressionism: Fliedl's analysis extends the ethical thrust of Ernst Offermanns and the capitalism-critical foundation of Manfred Diersch two decades earlier. A few highlights are in order, beginning with Schnitzler's own beginning successes in the figures of Anatol and Gustl. It can be said that neither one experiences continuity, nor desires to do so, and that Anatol represents intentional forgetting, while Gustl's lapses are unintentional. Impressionism discourages recollection in a world understood as contingent and constantly shifting. The ruptures of perception and knowledge at the end of the nineteenth century are both symptom and cause of modernity's crisis of memory. Perhaps the most acute symptom of the crisis, the fear of losing the ability to remember, is a reaction to collective amnesia (PE, 19). Indeed, the individual may find more reason to panic if the collective is seen to encourage memory loss. Fliedl modifies Mach's famous dictum "Das Ich ist unrettbar" (the ego is unsalvageable) to read: "Das Gedächtnis ist unrettbar" (PE, 22: Memory is unsalvageable). At the other extreme, however, is an overabundance of memory, as seen in Max's analysis that his friend Anatol is burdened by unprocessed experiences (PE, 23). Fliedl notices rightly that Schnitzler scholarship has contradicted itself with respect to the impressionist's relationship to time: on the one hand, this white, bourgeois male lives for the moment (PE, 21); on the other hand, he is always seeking to devalue and disperse it. One can have it both ways after all: "Der Impressionist leidet an Amnesie *und* an Hypermnesie" (PE, 24: The impressionist suffers from amnesia *and* from an all-too-acute memory).

Depictions of intentional and unintentional memory loss are the work of an author who is himself in constant struggle against forgetting (PE, 16–17). Schnitzler's concern as a poet is that art should salvage memory (PE, 25), and Fliedl sketches this concern with respect to Freud, art as commodity, and Jewish modes of memory. Freud's life work, of course, is to retrieve memory from regions seeking its repression, in the understanding that nothing in the unconscious is ever ultimately forgotten. Fliedl reviews Schnitzler's willingness to grant certain psychoanalytical interpretations of his texts anchored to dream theory and repression, and his refusal to interpret neuroses as of sexual etiology. As we have seen, Schnitzler's topology of the psyche includes the semi-conscious, a preconscious region the ego can explore voluntarily without the psychoanalytic interlocutor, and which through individual effort can convert repression into memory and self-knowledge. Memory retrieval results less in a state of bliss than in the pain of truthfulness: "Erinnerung kuriert nicht, wie bei Freud, die Schmerzen der Kranken; bei Schnitzler holt Erinnerung die Gesunden aus ihrer Indolenz" (PE, 29: Memory does not cure the pains of the sick, as with Freud, but in Schnitzler's case it purges the healthy of their indolence). Fliedl calls this an ethical view, thus more conservative than Freud's therapeutic position (PE, 30), and attributes it to Schnitzler's experiences as a producer of art.

Schnitzler is writing in a market, Fliedl explains, where art has become a commodity in the fabrication of forgetfulness. This is a vital point. When peddled as wares always about to be replaced by something newer, books scarcely count as memory troves. The book business has turned readers into forgetful consumers (PE, 31). In the view of Horkheimer and Adorno, the culture industry fabricates forgetfulness and scorns memory's lack of market value (PE, 32). The paradox is that Schnitzler, known for his impressionistic sketches, insists on the unity, intensity, and continuity of the artwork. He chose iambic pentameter, a form loaded with "Gedächtnis," for his historical drama *Der Schleier der Beatrice,* risking the misunderstanding he was reviving historicism, when the real motivation was to remind the present of its past (PE, 33).

The fleeting nature of the book-as-commodity resembles the Jewish curse "Nicht gedacht soll deiner werden" (You shall not be remembered), a comparison made by Horkheimer and Adorno and expanded by Fliedl to include the treatment and concerns of Schnitzler the Jew. To be excluded from the memory of one's successors — "Gedächtnistod" —

is, when applied to an author, the death sentence leveled on his works. Fliedl reminds us of the Diaspora, in which memory is clung to as the highest virtue and the sole condition under which individual and collective identity can still be preserved. "Daß nichts vergessen werden darf, war im vielfachem Sinn eine lebenserhaltende Maxime" (PE, 34). Memory became practically an anthropological trademark of Jews, shaped especially during barbaric anti-Semitism. Schnitzler himself, rejecting Jewish religious traditions, is psychologically Jewish, by default a member of an ethnic minority forced to hone its memory in the interest of survival. For that matter, all minorities fine-tune memory as training for survival, according to Fliedl.

Schnitzler's artistic memory counters the amnesia of literature, while his Jewish memory counters the gaps in the dominant collective memory. The outsider has nothing but memory to fall back on, so his identity is threatened by collective forgetfulness in cahoots with power (PE, 35). Clearly, Schnitzler sees memory as the moral duty of the individual, but not something that comes easily, since the mind tolerates a falsified past more than the pain it finds there (PE, 36). "Gedächtnistod" applies to Jewish authors as they are marginalized in the collective memory through active silencing and finally excluded, or conveniently and forcibly forgotten. Considered incapable of a rooted cultural memory among the people with whom he was living as an unwelcome guest, Schnitzler died shortly before the process of exclusion escalated in 1933 with attempts to purge his work from a collective memory that forbade dissent (PE, 40).

I have already used Fliedl's detective-like pursuit of Theodor Reik and Josef Körner as material to round out my discussion of their monographs on Schnitzler. Fliedl shows, for example, how Körner, as a Jewish *Germanist*, disqualifies Schnitzler's reactions to the "Jewish Question" as artistically unacceptable, and how he is trapped a short time later precisely by the very forces of societal repression that informed his concept of art. What I have left untouched thus far is Fliedl's discussion of more comprehensive literary histories such Josef Nadler's (1884–1963) massive *Literaturgeschichte des Deutschen Volkes*,[73] an arrangement of authors according to German tribe, which of course makes a point of excluding Schnitzler from such a constructed cultural memory, and which history then took at its horrible word (PE, 41). When funneled into Aryan tribal categories, Nadler's ancestry (uncontrollable) of the majority is bound to triumph over the memory (controllable) in the Jewish minority. A summary of Fliedl's chapter "Der Fall der Literaturgeschichte" is in order here.

Nadler's 1928 volume "Der deutsche Staat 1814–1914" was the fourth and final volume of his *Literaturgeschichte der deutschen Stämme und Landschaften,* the first three volumes of which appeared in 1912, 1913, and 1918. Fliedl notes that the first sentence of the paragraph on Schnitzler reads: "Zwischen jüdischem und Wiener Wesen ist bei Schnitzler schwer abzurechnen, weil er beides so vollkommen ist" (It is difficult to distinguish between the Viennese and Jewish essence of Schnitzler, so fully he achieves both).[74] In the fourth edition of Nadler's *Literaturgeschichte des Deutschen Volkes* (1941), "vollkommen" has been replaced by "geschickt" (cleverly).[75] Fliedl's point is that tribal, racial, and national arguments had supplanted any claim of humanism in literary science (PE, 494). Having described the route Nadler takes from complaining of being labeled a racial theorist in 1938 to complaining of not being labeled one in 1944, Fliedl notes that the resentment spills over, sounding like a forced apology, in Nadler's 1948 *Literaturgeschichte Österreichs,* which defiantly replaces all references to Schnitzler the word-parsing Jew with references to the dissecting tendencies of Schnitzler the physician.[76] In other words, Nadler is able to take what Victor Klemperer had called a Jewish characteristic and reinstate it for his purposes, without expressly mentioning Schnitzler's Jewishness: "Unter dem Deckmantel der alten Dekadenz-Kritik kann Nadler seine Unterstellungen fortsetzen: das große Blackout hinsichtlich der jüdischen Herkunft des Autors macht er mit Suggestionen wett" (PE, 495). Fliedl calls this a not untypical artificial emptiness of memory which ushers in a new "Sklavensprache der Vergeßlichkeit" (slave-language of forgetfulness) through the things that are left unspoken (PE, 495).

In his *Geschichte der Deutschen Literatur* (1928), Adolf Bartels announces: "Man hat jüdischerseits öfter getan, als ob Schnitzler eine dauernde Größe unserer Literatur sei, aber man täuscht sich da: er ist nur eine Wiener Zeiterscheinung" (Those of Jewish persuasion have suggested Schnitzler is a figure of lasting literary significance, but they're mistaken: he is merely a passing Viennese phenomenon.[77] But Schnitzler is not an author about to disappear any time soon, Fliedl reassures us. Scholarship has become a virtual avalanche, and at the same time Schnitzler's plays have been adapted into readily consumable Viennese folklore, making them as trivial as the originals were suspected to be; impressionism is a stigma attached to Schnitzler's complete works; and the new *fin de siècle* (1999) brings another installment of shrunken collective memory (PE, 41). It is as though human and cyber-memory, interchangeable, are both in danger of being wiped clean. In an endnote, Fliedl explains that in the present crisis of memory, new media technology plays a decisive role: in addition to unheard-of storage capacity for computer memory (making human memory all the more unnecessary), the global consumer industry manufactures forgetfulness on an ongoing basis (PE, 49).

There are few arguments one can pose against Fliedl's estimation of the tyranny of the new. Understandably, her book on memory has given her the authority to become the president of the "Arthur Schnitzler-Gesellschaft," and it is perhaps not so strange that some amount of Internet exposure is necessary to accomplish the society's task of advancing scientific and public debate about a man trivialized by Austrian folklore. The statement reads:

> Die Arthur Schnitzler-Gesellschaft fördert die wissenschaftliche Beschäftigung und öffentliche Auseinandersetzung mit dem Werk dieses politisch wie psychologisch scharfsichtigen österreichischen Autors. Ziel ist es, gegen die österreichische Schnitzler-Folklore das Bild eines streitbaren und hochkontroversiellen Schriftstellers zu halten. Die Aktivitäten der Arthur Schnitzler-Gesellschaft umfassen: Gastvorträge, Podiumsdiskussionen, Symposien, der Arthur Schnitzler-Preis, Ausstellungsprojekte und die gezielte Vermittlung von Kontakten innerhalb der Schnitzler-Forschung.[78]

In this society's attempt to restore Schnitzler's image to one of someone who courted argument and controversy, there is no mention of love, play, and death.

Notes

[1] Werner Welzig, "Zur Herausgabe von Schnitzlers Tagebuch," foreword to vol. 1 (1909–1912), Schnitzler 1981–2000: 9–33, here 32.

[2] Horst Thomé, "Faktizität des Lebens und erfüllte Zeit: Zum Erscheinen von Schnitzlers Tagebüchern," *Orbis Litterarum* 40 (1985): 88–96, here 89.

[3] See esp. Werner Welzig, "Das Tagebuch Arthur Schnitzlers 1879–1931," *Internationales Archiv für Sozialgeschichte der Literatur* 6 (1981): 78–111. An important introduction to the project is Welzig's "Zur Herausgabe von Schnitzlers Tagebuch," mentioned above. Thereafter, Welzig's comments appear as epilogues (for full citations, see the list in my preface).

[4] Welzig, "Tagebuch" (1981), 89.

[5] Welzig, "Tagebuch und Gesellschaftsspiel," epilogue to vol. 3 (1917–1919), 422.

[6] Welzig, "Bicycle-Lektion," epilogue to vol. 5 (1893–1902), 489–502.

[7] Horst Thomé, "Arthur Schnitzlers Tagebuch. Thesen und Forschungsperspektiven," *Internationales Archiv für Sozialgeschichte der Deutschen Literatur* (1993): 176–93, here 177, 180.

[8] Thomé, "Thesen und Forschungsperspektiven" (1993), 179–80.

[9] Thomé, "Thesen und Forschungsperspektiven" (1993), 179.

[10] See Welzig, "Tagebuch" (1981), esp. 91, 94–95, 98.

[11] Welzig, "Tagebuch" (1981), 78–111, here 87.

[12] Welzig, vol. 1, 14.

[13] Nike Wagner, "'Immer alles haben können, immer alles wegwerfen dürfen.' Arthur Schnitzler: Stationen eines einsamen Lebens. *Tagebuch* und *Briefe:* Erste Publikationen aus dem Nachlaß eines Dichters des Fin de siecle in Wien," *Die Zeit,* 8 April 1983, reprinted in Lindken, 490–97, here 493.

[14] Welzig, *Tagebuch* (1981), 78–111, here 83.

[15] Welzig, "Der junge Mann und die alten Wörter," epilogue to vol. 4 (1879–1892), 471–88, here 481–82.

[16] Welzig, vol. 4, 488.

[17] Friedrich Torberg, epilogue to Arthur Schnitzler, *Jugend in Wien: Eine Autobiographie,* ed. Therese Nickl and Heinrich Schnitzler (Vienna: F. Molden, 1968; reprint, with an afterword by Friedrich Torberg, Frankfurt am Main: Fischer, 1981) 324–32, here 328. (Page citations are to the reprint edition.)

[18] The first diary stage (1879–1882) criticizes the sacrament of baptism less in itself than as the opportunistic goal of Jews converting to Catholicism and losing any identity worth respecting. Indeed, he is quick to note the need in others for self-stylization, perhaps hyperaware of what he has already overcome. In Hermann Bahr's case, baptism is pure snobbery requiring public ritual; in Hofmannsthal's case it is both snobbery and the doomed attempt at assimilation. Recording the failed attempts of such assimilation, Schnitzler "saves" himself in private instead of masquerading in public what he believes to be a lie.

[19] See Heide Tarnowski-Seidel, *Arthur Schnitzler: Flucht in die Finsternis: Eine produktionsästhetische Untersuchung* (Munich: Fink, 1983), 28–29.

[20] Thomé, "Thesen und Forschungsperspektiven" (1993), 186–87.

[21] Schnitzler, diary entry of 6 May 1888, quoted in Thomé, "Thesen und Forschungsperspektiven" (1993), 187 n 28.

[22] Thomé, "Thesen und Forschungsperspektiven" (1993), 187.

[23] Quoted in Thomé, "Thesen und Forschungsperspektiven" (1993), 187 n 28.

[24] This is not to say that Schnitzler's perfectionism need derive directly from any source, but it makes sense to consider how the diary reveals and masks various influences on his development. How does the diary reader best sift the information the diary-writing persona chooses to provide?

[25] Carl E. Schorske, *Fin-de-Siècle Vienna: Politics and Culture* (New York: Vintage Books, 1981), 7.

[26] Schnitzler, diary entry of December 15, 1880, quoted in Reinhard Urbach, *Schnitzler-Kommentar zu den erzählenden Schriften und dramatischen Werken* (Munich: Winkler, 1974), 13.

[27] Urbach, *Schnitzler-Kommentar* (1974), 14.

[28] Torberg, epilogue to Arthur Schnitzler, *Jugend in Wien* (1981), 329.

[29] Thomé, "Thesen und Forschungsperspektiven" (1993), 184.

[30] Thomé draws on Thomas Luckmann, "Persönliche Identität, soziale Rolle und Rollendistanz," *Identität,* ed. Odo Marquard and Karlheinz Stierle (Munich: Fink, 1979).

[31] Thomé, "Thesen und Forschungsperspektiven" (1993), 186.

[32] Thomé, "Thesen und Forschungsperspektiven" (1993), 188.

[33] See Schorske, *Fin-de-Siècle Vienna* (1981), 9.

[34] Gerhart Baumann, "Arthur Schnitzler: Die Tagebücher. Vergangene Gegenwart — Gegenwärtige Vergangenheit," *MAL* 10/3–4 (1977): 143–62, here 161.

[35] Urbach, *Schnitzler-Kommentar* (1974), 30.

[36] See Richard Miklin, *Untersuchungen zu Arthur Schnitzlers Tagebuch der Kriegsjahre* 1914–1918 (Vienna: Diss., 1987).

[37] Welzig, "Tagebuch" (1981), 106.

[38] Irene Lindgren, *Arthur Schnitzler im Lichte seiner Briefe und Tagebücher* (Heidelberg: Universitätsverlag C. Winter, 1993), 72–73. We must be careful not to assume that because the diary seems to have held Schnitzler together, it must have been the only thing able to do so.

[39] Quoted in Ralph-Rainer Wuthenow, *Europäische Tagebücher: Eigenart, Formen, Entwicklung* (Darmstadt: Wiss. Buchgesellschaft, 1990), v.

[40] Schorske, *Fin-de-Siècle Vienna* (1981), 8.

[41] Welzig, "Tagebuch" (1981), 153.

[42] Tarnowski-Seidel, *Flucht in die Finsternis,* (1983), 27.

[43] Welzig, "Tagebuch" (1981), 107.

[44] See Elsbeth Dangel, *Wiederholung als Schicksal: Arthur Schnitzlers Roman Therese: Chronik eines Frauenlebens* (Munich: Fink, 1985), 174.

[45] Dangel, *Wiederholung als Schicksal* (1985), 175.

[46] Welzig, "Tagebuch" (1981), 109–10.

[47] Schnitzler, diary entry of 22 June 1921, quoted in Welzig, Tagebuch (1981), 108.

[48] Welzig, "Anspruch der Toten," epilogue, vol. 9 (1927–1930), 504.

[49] Welzig, vol. 9, 504.

[50] Welzig, vol. 9, 501.

[51] Welzig, vol. 9, 505–6.

[52] Schnitzler, diary entry of 26 July 1931.

[53] Welzig, vol. 9, 506. In a bewildering reversal of contemporary piety, well-meaning visitors brought Schnitzler flowers plucked from Lili's grave (507).

[54] Schnitzler, diary entry of 22 August 1918.

[55] Baumann, "Vergangene Gegenwart" (1977), 151.

[56] Welzig, vol. 9, 507–8.

[57] Welzig, vol. 9, 509.

[58] Tarnowski-Seidel, *Flucht in die Finsternis* (1983), 18–20.

[59] Konstanze Fliedl, *Arthur Schnitzler: Poetik der Erinnerung*. (Vienna: Böhlau, 1997), 259.

[60] Quoted in Welzig, vol. 9, 506.

[61] Quoted in Welzig, vol. 1, 15.

[62] Schnitzler, diary entry of 18 December 1929, quoted in Welzig, "Tagebuch" (1981), 93.

[63] Frederick Beharriell, "Arthur Schnitzler's Diaries," *MAL* 19/3–4 (1986): 1–20, here 17.

[64] Beharriell, "Diaries" (1986), 7.

[65] Gerhard Neumann and Jutta Müller, *Der Nachlaß Arthur Schnitzlers* (Munich: Fink, 1969), 14–16.

[66] See for example Welzig, "Nachbemerkung," epilogue to vol. 2 (1913–1916), 429–32, here 432, where Welzig gratefully acknowledges Heinrich Schnitzler's part in preserving the documents and allowing the biography of a society, city, and epoch. Heinrich Schnitzler lived long enough to see completion of the first volume in the diary project.

[67] Baumann, "Vergangene Gegenwart" (1977), 155.

[68] Martin Walser, "Baustein beim Bau der chinesischen Mauer. Über Tagebücher," in Walser, *Wer ist ein Schriftsteller? Aufsätze und Reden* (Frankfurt am Main: Suhrkamp, 1979), 13, quoted in Welzig, vol. 1, 33.

[69] See Manfred Jurgensen, *Das fiktionale Ich: Untersuchungen zum Tagebuch* (Bern: Francke, 1979), 15.

[70] Schnitzler, diary entry of 7 February 1924.

[71] Baumann, "Vergangene Gegenwart" (1977), 152.

[72] "Werden wir nicht ganz allmählich einander zu Schatten, lieber Arthur? Und wie kommt es denn? Woran liegt es denn? Jahre und Jahre lang ist die Aufforderung, einander zu sehen immer von mir, von uns gekommen, immer waren wir die Besuchenden, die Vorschlagenden . . . auf einmal kann man sich fühlen als den, der allein an dem Draht zieht . . ." (Hofmannsthal to Schnitzler, 27 March 1914, quoted in Tarnowski-Seidel, *Flucht in die Finsternis* [1983], 31).

[73] Josef Nadler, *Literaturgeschichte des deutschen Volkes: Dichtung und Schrifttum der deutschen Stämme und Landschaften*, 4th ed. (Berlin: Propyläen, 1938–41).

[74] Josef Nadler, *Literaturgeschichte der deutschen Stämme und Landschaften*, 4 vols. (Regensburg: Josef Habbel, 1912–28), vol. 4: *Der deutsche Staat 1814–1914* (1928), 915–16.

[75] Josef Nadler, *Dichtung und Schrifttum* (1938–41), vol. 4: *Reich (1914–1940)*, 198–99.

[76] Josef Nadler, *Literaturgeschichte Österreichs* (Linz: Österreichischer Verlag für Belletristik und Wissenschaft, 1948), 436, quoted in Fliedl, *Poetik der Erinnerung*, 495.

[77] Adolf Bartels, *Geschichte der Deutschen Literatur*, vol. 3, *Die neueste Zeit* (Leipzig: Haessel, 1923–28), 536.

[78] Statement of the Arthur Schnitzler-Gesellschaft, Vienna: http://www.arthur-schnitzler.at.

Conclusion: *Eyes Wide Shut* and Beyond

ON JULY 16, 1999, THE EVENING OF the debut of Stanley Kubrick's film *Eyes Wide Shut* (based on *Schnitzler's Traumnovelle*), a critic on the "Charlie Rose Show" complained that Tom Cruise had played the physician Bill Harford with a disappointing lack of initiative.[1] Such complaints echo the criticism against Georg von Wergenthin in *Der Weg ins Freie* by contemporaries of Schnitzler armed with theories of proper behavior for novel heroes. For anyone acquainted with *Traumnovelle*, however, the fact that Cruise/Harford is frequently dazzled by what happens to him is a sign he has faithfully rendered the role of a typical Schnitzler anti-hero scarcely a model physician or husband. Kubrick's painstaking deliberateness with Frederic Raphael's screen play ran against the grain of Hollywood's requisite chase scenes and blazing guns to provoke the same response felt by audiences a century earlier, when anti-heroes such as Medardus (*Der junge Medardus*) crossed Schnitzler's stage with nuanced psychology instead of bold, resolute action. If Schnitzler could not count on having the reader of his own time understand his snapshots of the fickle soul, could Kubrick depend on a better viewer at the close of the century? Kubrick (1928–1999) died before he could see the reception of his vision in theaters across the United States.

The uncanny aspect of *Traumnovelle* had been its combination of dream and real world, and Schnitzler had bent the norms of the novella genre without breaking them.[2] As Dorrit Cohn points out, as Schnitzler was beginning the novella in 1907, the story aligned itself with the same dream narratives as might be offered by Beer-Hofmann or Hofmannsthal. By the time it was published in 1926, the expressionist-surrealist generation had fractured the norms of realism so much that a dream-like fictional world was no longer so unheard-of, making Schnitzler's crossing of dream and life appear tame and "almost anachronistically 'Viennese.'"[3] The film is another step removed, translating the story into present-day New York. Kubrick kept news of the film as secret as the exclusive villa society in the film itself. Indeed, one wonders whether secrecy built a false expectation in viewers who were lacking the password for concerns of the *fin de siècle* in the first place. Was a prior understanding of history, Schnitzler in general, or the novella in particular the prerequisite for appreciating the film — or at least how Raphael attempted to do justice or not to the novella? Could surrealism of the twenties be made camera-ready for the nineties without an adequate briefing of viewers beforehand?

Jack Vitek's postmodern reading of the film suggests that Kubrick, a Bronx-born expatriate who lived in London, was "quoting and transforming imperial Viennese Schnitzler" using a grainy film stock that brought out the ambers and golds of Old Vienna to lend a "Klimt-like quality" to contemporary New York.[4] The Jew Kubrick intended to erase Schnitzler's Jewish identity by sending Jewish screenwriter Frederic Raphael a photocopy of the novella with Schnitzler's name excised, and by refusing Raphael's suggestion to give Bill the Jewish-sounding name "Scheuer."[5] Another important ethnic note, as Egon Schwarz notices in his reading, is that like Schnitzler's Romanian seducer at the masked ball, Kubrick's film features a Hungarian seducer at Ziegler's Christmas party: not so much a displacement as an interchangeability of East Europeans who "irradiate the erotic allurement of the exotic but lack the ethical restraints of the West."[6]

Eyes Wide Shut will not be remembered because of its straightforward message that any marital puzzle is solvable with enough communication, but because, as Schwarz states, it shows that Schnitzler's themes of love and death continue their relevance so long as humans are loving and dying. The film has vindicated Schnitzler's view of "the perennial collision of innate erotic desires with the requirements of monogamy and the tenuousness of love."[7] Schwarz believes the film has a harder time conveying mood swings or Bill's semi-conscious, the region that distinguished Schnitzler's work from being attributed solely to Freud.[8] Raphael's 1996 script suggested voiceovers to take us into Bill's thoughts, but this is at best a bumpy translation of the effect. Schwarz concludes: "Such barely conscious thoughts have no equivalent in the police-novel rationality of *Eyes Wide Shut*. There is after all a difference between a puzzle and an enigma."[9]

Another way of expressing this is that Schnitzler's semi-conscious reflects a postmodern blending or transcendence of binary pairs. Vitek's insight is that the mask that Bill neglects to return to the costumier has its equivalent in the slash (/) of the binary "open/shut" that reflects the movie's title: it separates the worlds of waking and sleeping, but also mediates between the binary worlds. "It signifies — in the word of both the novel and the voiceover — the "enigma" that he has become."[10] The voiceover describes Bill's reaction to finding the mask on his pillow: "He thought he must have dropped it in the morning when he packed the costume away, and Alice had found it and placed it on the pillow beside her, as though it signified *his* face, the face of a husband who had become an enigma to her."[11] The mask, a Carnival accessory for anonymous liberties, becomes the catalyst for self-knowledge and responsibility once it is torn off: but the existential moment is necessary to realize what unreflective societal roles one has been playing all along before the Carnival.

Although Kubrick forbade co-stars Cruise and Kidman from reading Schnitzler's novella during the making of *Eyes Wide Shut*, David Hare, author of *Reigen*-based *Blue Room*, made no such prohibition for Kidman when she starred in *Blue Room* during its 1998 London premiere before accompanying it to Broadway. Max Ophüls's *La Ronde* of 1950, the most famous film adaptation of *Reigen*, took liberties with the text, particularly in the figure of an all-seeing ringmaster who incarnates the viewer's desire to know everything; Hare felt that this liberty justified his own liberties with the text, as the author had not envisioned the material ever being performed anyway, and because the sexual daisy chain was a "wonderfully malleable" idea.[12]

Hare preserves some social divisions, outfitting the daisy chain with a prostitute, a cab driver, an au pair, a student, a married woman, a politician, a model, a playwright, an actress, and an aristocrat, but it is clear that taking liberties subtracts from the extremely significant sociohistorical knowledge that Janz and Laermann in particular had underscored in their chapter on *Reigen*. This again poses the question of what interpretation is for when an author's work becomes material for popular plundering. Hare's stage directions require for every sex act a stage blackout, a buzzer, and a screen that flashes the actual sex time. Like *Eyes Wide Shut*, *Blue Room* updates Schnitzler's health issues to AIDS, replacing Alice's marijuana with the model's cocaine. *Blue Room* was scheduled to play at Broadway's Cort Theater from December 13, 1998 to March 7, 1999. Kidman and co-star Iain Glen played all the characters. But were theatergoers interested in how Hare interpreted Schnitzler? No, as Jack Kroll put it: "In turn-of-another-century London and New York, playgoers were queuing up to see Kidman get her kit off, as the British put it."[13]

But *Blue Room* is tame, at least in premise, compared to Suzanne Bachner's *Circle*, a *Reigen*-adaptation that opened in April 2002 at the Kraine Theater in New York's East Village. One reviewer noted that because Bachner was not a physician like Schnitzler, she could produce laughter with impunity, bypassing "the aftertaste and fear" of parts of *Reigen*.[14] The carousel in *Circle* begins with sex between two gay men who meet in a coffee shop, followed in the next scene by one of them convincing a lesbian to carry a child for him and his partner, which leads in the next scene to the surrogate mother's quarreling with her partner. "Eventually . . . we encounter an adventurous couple who come to grief when they discover they are both masochists. One of them gets into a cybersex session with a woman a continent away, who, it turns out, is married to one of the men who met in the coffee shop, and the circle closes." Now with cyberspace and a different continent involved, with sexual "perversions" having become "preferences," any second thoughts are driven out by a pacing as speedy as cyberspace, and sex becomes as casual as following an Internet link out of curiosity, with as few immediate consequences — this is the populist cooptation of Schnitzler.

Without a doubt, New York has served as the Schnitzler magnet in the United States, due, at first glance at least, to its theater life, intellectual milieu, Jewish population, affinity to Viennese cultural life, and general progressiveness. Or is there a deeper reason why New Yorkers (here, representative U.S. citizens) are drawn to adaptations not only of *Traumnovelle* or *Reigen,* but also of *Anatol* and *Liebelei,* and, increasingly, *Das weite Land*? Stephanie Hammer, comparing the fortunes of *Anatol* and *Liebelei* productions in the United States, has shown not only the polarization in the American perceptions of Schnitzler, but also the link between American self-perception and obsession in "our" reception of European art.[15] Anatol, for example, has been interpreted theatrically in roles as *homme fatal,* egotistical playboy, existential neurotic, and sexually ambiguous innocent, leading to the verdict that "a truly definitive theatrical interpretation" is still lacking. No production, no matter how different from the last, has met with a satisfying response across the board (66).

After surveying their production histories, Hammer speculates why *Anatol,* which American theatergoers have judged "as either totally frivolous or deeply depressing," is staged more frequently than *Liebelei,* still considered a crucial entry in the modern repertoire — it is because Americans inscribe the characteristics onto European theater that they have come to expect of it:

> Just as we seek our own reflection — that is to say, the reflection of our concerns and problems — in our own art and theater, so do we usually seek the opposite in European art. It is common knowledge that Europe and its culture have traditionally represented the autocratic, amoral, sensual Other to our democratic essentially puritanical Self; not surprisingly, Americans have always been especially fascinated by those periods and those urban centers which have best represented the easy sensuality and decadence of European society. (Hammer, 68–69)

Hammer furnishes a Sartrean explanation of an Other that is "frightening because it is not like us and is therefore evil and frightening because our overwhelming attraction to it suggests that it is like us after all," postulating that Americans are enthralled by a European Anatol whose "eroticism simultaneously seduces and terrifies" (69–70). This insight is derived from *The Second Sex,* where Simone de Beauvoir links "the virtuous male Self to America and the mysterious, morally disruptive, chaotic female Other to America's perception of Europe."[16] Concerning *Liebelei,* Hammer believes that English-speaking critics have emphasized its tragic, sociocritical aspects at the expense of its hedonistic, erotic tone. Considered terribly serious, it is not Austrian enough to satisfy an American craving for, and fear of, "the artistic presentation of continental degenerateness." That being the case, Schnitzler's play, hugely popular elsewhere in the world, will have to "await the magic of Stoppardization" if it is to win U.S. stage recognition (70).

One hopes that the critical world finds a balance between "involuntary manslaughter" (Kurt Bergel) and veneration of Schnitzler. A few investigations seem to point the way. A look at the monographs on Schnitzler that have been published from 1998–2002, many of them first books by young scholars (revised dissertations, for example), reveals the continuing trend away from the works themselves and either toward Schnitzler the historical figure/epochal exemplar or toward his reception. Examples are Sandra Nuy's investigation *Arthur Schnitzler ferngesehen: Ein Beitrag zur Geschichte des Theaters im Fernsehen der Bundesrepublik Deutschland (1953–1989)* (2000), which is the first complete television history of Schnitzler's dramas; two books on Schnitzler's diaries, the second of which focuses on Schnitzler's Jewishness in diary and letters: Ulrich von Bülow's *"Sicherheit ist nirgends": Das Tagebuch von Arthur Schnitzler* (2000) and Bettina Riedmann's *Ich bin Jude, Österreicher, Deutscher: Judentum in Arthur Schnitzlers Tagebüchern und Briefen* (2002); Bettina Marxer's cultural history of selected correspondence: *Liebesbriefe, und was nun einmal so genannt wird: Korrespondenzen zwischen Arthur Schnitzler, Olga Waissnix und Marie Reinhard: Eine Literatur- und kulturwissenschaftliche Lektüre* (2001); Irene Lindgren's second book on Schnitzler: *"Seh'n Sie, das Berühmtwerden ist doch nicht so leicht!" Arthur Schnitzler über sein literarisches Schaffen* (2002); and Anna Simon, *Schnitzlers Wien* (2002).

Then there are the thematic studies that take the works into close consideration: the first major men's studies project is Jenneke Oosterhoff's *"Die Männer sind infam, solange sie Männer sind": Konstruktionen der Männlichkeit in den Werken Arthur Schnitzlers* (2000); in a short book, Ruth Klüger takes another look at Schnitzler's construction of women in *Schnitzlers Damen, Weiber, Mädeln, Frauen* (2001); Eva Kuttenberg examines a prevalent theme with *The Tropes of Suicide in Arthur Schnitzler's Prose* (2000); Dirk von Boetticher examines the medical dimension in *Meine Werke sind lauter Diagnosen: Über die ärztliche Dimension im Werk Arthur Schnitzlers* (1999); Micke Norbert returns to Freudian language with *Das Eros/Thanatos-Motiv in frühen Erzählungen Arthur Schnitzlers* (2000); Bettina Matthias examines the depiction of death in *Masken des Lebens — Gesichter des Todes: Zum Verhältnis von Tod und Darstellung im erzählerischen Werk Arthur Schnitzlers* (1999); and Guido Montingelli revisits the dramatic works with *Relativität und Subjektivität: Zum dramatischen Werk Arthur Schnitzlers im Kontext des "Pirandellismo"* (1999).

The articles by Schwarz and Vitek on Kubrick's *Eyes Wide Shut* appeared in the first issue of *Modern Austrian Literature* published by the Modern Austrian Literature and Culture Association (MALCA), which succeeded the International Arthur Schnitzler Research Association (IASRA). Editors Geoffrey Howes and Jacqueline Vansant assured their readers that this was no cruel takeover, for MALCA "reflects the expansion of interest in Austrian literature that the Schnitzler association achieved, and encourages fresh and varied perspectives on the field."[17] The issue appearing before the name change was a good portent, having included articles on *Fräulein Else, Das weite Land,* and a condensed version of Sandra Nuy's book, listed above, that examines the filmic narrative of Schnitzler's dramas and their success on German television.

It appears that in terms of volume, depth, and range, Schnitzler criticism is in good hands. This will continue to be the case in Austria, as long as the Arthur Schnitzler-Gesellschaft follows its goal of holding "gegen die österreichische Schnitzler-Folklore das Bild eines streitbaren und hochkontroversiellen Schriftstellers."[18] One can hope the activity of this organization, evident already in a May 2002 conference held at the University of Vienna that attracted the stars of Schnitzler scholarship,[19] will make itself felt well beyond the borders of Austria. And from the perspective of the present, barely into the twenty-first century, I hope that my book has shown a few highlights of the century-long attempt to rescue Schnitzler criticism from the encroaching folkloric obsession with Schnitzler the decadent satyr. Indeed, "rescue" remains the most suitable metaphor, if one recalls Schnitzler's reception during his lifetime.

A brief summary of the territory covered by this book seems an appropriate conclusion. At the beginning of his writing career Schnitzler's efforts were charted by naturalist critics, and by the time he died in 1931, his writings were considered either out of date or inconsistent with the needs of the nation. Many of the charismatic feuilletonists who reviewed debut performances of Schnitzler's plays in Berlin and Vienna employed a critical nonchalance, a free-associating feuilletonism generated in a part by the fierce competition of the newspapers and literary journals. Neither this approach nor the normative approach of critics such as Paul Goldmann fits Otto Brahm's appeal for a criticism befitting the serious issues of modernity. In contrast to Brahm, with his consistent naturalism, Hermann Bahr seemed to rebound from subjective to normative extremes, inventing the concerns of aesthetics as he went along.

Three authors whose work on Schnitzler preceded the official book-burning rituals by the Nazis were Theodor Reik, who psychoanalyzed Schnitzler; Josef Körner, who found Schnitzler's positivism fell short when measured against the metaphysical clarity of expressionism; and Bernhard Blume, who emphasized the role of determinism in Schnitzler's nihilistic universe. All three experienced Nazi hostility. Reik and Blume, like Schnitzler's son and ex-wife, sought refuge in the United States, along with many of the scholars who would become the backbone of the International Arthur Schnitzler Research Association, the body that would shift the locus of Schnitzler scholarship to the United States until well into the sixties. Even in the fifties, as Europe was rebuilding an identity and infrastructure, the United States remained the safe haven for rebuilding the image of Schnitzler on the strength of two initial foci: Schnitzler the psychologist and Schnitzler the ethicist. In the first case, orthodox Freudian interpretations detailing Schnitzler's debt to Freud were supplanted over the decades by research showing Schnitzler's suspicion of any categories that overlooked the *semi-conscious*, a switching yard for converting impulses into conscious thought. In the second case, as soon as it was recognized that Schnitzler was scarcely endorsing the foibles of his impressionists but rather documenting, whether sympathetically or with ironic detachment, their loss of the present tense, research could look beyond character-controllable factors into sociohistorical structures to identify the causes of what Ernst Mach called "das unrettbare Ich."

As scholarship has come to include the prose and recognize an inimitable mastery throughout Schnitzler's works, from *Sterben* to *Therese*, it has also examined the aphorisms and fragments that reveal more of Schnitzler's worldview, unmediated by fiction. A fascination for Schnitzler the man appears to match the unflagging commitment to explore themes in his fiction. The diary was seen to contribute far more than an informational resource. Like the autobiography and correspondence, it has become a viable object of close scrutiny in its own right, especially now in its completed ten-volume *Gestalt* of 8000 pages. One must, however, take the time, as careful stewards such as Werner Welzig and Peter Michael Braunwarth of the Austrian Academy of Sciences have done, to allow the diary to speak for itself over its fifty years; the almost certain result is that one's final impression of Schnitzler will look little like his pre-1900 Anatol. Schnitzler the dialectical *raisonneur*, albeit outfitted with the usual human shortcomings, should at some point usurp Schnitzler the womanizer: if he undresses his characters, it is usually to unmask them.

The diary that assisted Schnitzler in the task of memory he imposed on himself — though he found it lacking in others, especially the press — serves as our handbook for our task of memory as well. Fliedl's observations in particular prompt us to consider who really owns this writer whose universal themes wear local costumes — is Schnitzler's memory best preserved by those closest to his sources of inspiration? It behooves us not to subsume him to his Anatol or Casanova characters, but to consider him a character in a novel that has been appearing in installments for over a century. What he has written about himself in his own fiction, correspondence, diary and autobiography counts as a chapter, but critics must supply the remaining installments. This character has been reprimanded by Bahr, psychoanalyzed by Reik, secretly admired by Freud, silenced by Bartels, resurrected by Weiss, deified by Rey, and defended by Daviau. Diersch has labeled him a bourgeois imperialist; Scheible, Abels, and Gutt have stressed his emancipation; Perlmann has analyzed the dreams of his characters; Janz and Laermann have used his writings as a clear sociohistorical window; Gay has used a diary experience as the leitmotif for his book; Kubrick (though not a critic) has converted his fascination with Vienna's back alleys to London and New York. Criticism of Arthur Schnitzler has its hands full, for the novel that features him is far from complete.

Notes

[1] "Charlie Rose Show," PBS, 16 July 1999.

[2] Dorrit Cohn, "A Triad of Dream Narratives: *Der Tod Georgs, Das Märchen der 672. Nacht, Traumnovelle*," in *Focus on Vienna 1900: Change and Continuity in Literature, Music, Art and Intellectual History,* ed. Erika Nielsen (Munich: Wilhelm Fink Verlag, 1982), 58–71, here 67.

[3] Cohn, "Triad of Dream Narratives" (1982), 69.

[4] Jack Vitek, "Another Squint at Eyes Wide Shut: A Postmodern Reading," *MAL* 34/1–2 (2001): 113–24, here 114, 116.

[5] Vitek, "Another Squint" (2001), 116.

[6] Egon Schwarz, "A Puzzle and An Enigma: Stanley Kubrick's *Eyes Wide Shut* and Arthur Schnitzler's *Traumnovelle*," *MAL* 34/1–2 (2001): 103–11, here 104.

[7] Schwarz, "A Puzzle and an Enigma" (2001), 103.

[8] Schwarz, "A Puzzle and an Enigma" (2001), 110.

[9] Schwarz, "A Puzzle and an Enigma" (2001), 110–11.

[10] Vitek, "Another Squint" (2001), 122.

[11] Stanley Kubrick and Frederic Raphael, *Eyes Wide Shut: A Screenplay*, 1996, 1999. http://godamongdirectors.com/scripts/eyewshu.htm. 20 November 2002.

[12] David Hare, preface to *The Blue Room. Freely adapted from Arthur Schnitzler's* La Ronde (New York: Grove Press, 1998).

[13] Jack Kroll, "Nicole Takes Off," *Newsweek*, 14 December 1998: 68–76, here 68.

[14] D. J. R. Bruckner, "Playing Spin the Bottle (With an Adult Twist)," Review of Suzanne Bachner's *Circle*, *New York Times*, 10 April 2002: sec. E5.

[15] Stephanie Hammer, "Fear and Attraction: *Anatol* and *Liebelei* Productions in the United States," *MAL* 19/3–4 (1986): 63–74, here 63.

[16] See Hammer, 73, n. 19.

[17] Geoffrey Howes and Jacqueline Vansant, "From the Editors," *MAL* 34/1–2 (2001): i.

[18] Statement of the Arthur Schnitzler-Gesellschaft, Vienna: http://www.arthur-schnitzler.at.

[19] The "Arthur Schnitzler Tagung" (14–17 May 2002, Kleiner Festsaal der Universität Wien) featured, among others, scholars I have addressed in detail in this book: Gotthart Wunberg, Hartmut Scheible, Giuseppe Farese, Elsbeth Dangel-Pelloquin, Horst Thomé, Michael Worbs, Alfred Doppler, Norbert Abels, Friedbert Aspetsberger, and Martin Swales.

Works Consulted

Schnitzler, Arthur. 1879. "Grenzen der Kritik." In *Über Kunst und Kritik*. 1993. Frankfurt am Main: Fischer Taschenbuch. Vol. 3 of *Aphorismen und Betrachtungen*. 3 vols. Ed. Robert O. Weiss. A reprint of the original volume of 1967, which was published as vol. 5 of *Gesammelte Werke*.

Schnitzler, Arthur. 1967. *Aphorismen und Betrachtungen*. Ed. Robert O. Weiss. Frankfurt am Main: Fischer.

Schnitzler, Arthur. 1968. *Jugend in Wien: Eine Autobiographie*. Ed. Therese Nickl and Heinrich Schnitzler. Vienna: F. Molden. Reprint, with an afterword by Friedrich Torberg, Frankfurt am Main: Fischer, 1981.

Schnitzler, Arthur. 1975. *Der Briefwechsel Arthur Schnitzler — Otto Brahm*. Ed. and intro. Oskar Seidlin. Tübingen: Max Niemeyer.

Schnitzler, Arthur. 1976. "Über Psychoanalyse." Ed. Reinhard Urbach. *Protokolle: Wiener Halbjahresschrift für Literatur, bildende Kunst und Musik* 2: 277–84.

Schnitzler, Arthur. 1977. *Entworfenes und Verworfenes: Aus dem Nachlaß*. Ed. Reinhard Urbach. Vol. 6 of *Gesammelte Werke*. Frankfurt am Main: Fischer.

Schnitzler, Arthur. 1978. *The Letters of Arthur Schnitzler to Hermann Bahr*. Ed., intro., and annotated by Donald Daviau. Chapel Hill: U of North Carolina P.

Schnitzler, Arthur. 1977–78. *Gesammelte Werke in Einzelausgaben: Das erzählerische Werk* (7 vols.) and *Das dramatische Werk* (8 vols.). Frankfurt am Main: Fischer Taschenbuch Verlag. Based on Fischer Verlag's *Gesammelte Werke: Das erzählerische Werk* (2 vols., 1961) and *Das dramatische Werk* (2 vols., 1962).

Schnitzler, Arthur. 1981–2000. *Tagebuch 1879–1931*. Ed. Kommission für literarische Gebrauchsformen der Österreichischen Akademie der Wissenschaften. 10 vols. Vienna: Verlag der Österreichischen Akademie der Wissenschaften.

Schnitzler, Arthur. 1993. *Über Kunst und Kritik*. Vol. 3 of *Aphorismen und Betrachtungen*. 3 vols. Ed. Robert O. Weiss. Frankfurt am Main: Fischer Taschenbuch. A reprint of the original volume of 1967, which was published as vol. 5 of Gesammelte Werke.

Bahr, Hermann. 1893. Das junge Österreich. Deutsche Zeitung, 20 September 1893 (1–2); 27 Sept. (1–3); 7 Oct. (1–3), morning ed. Abridged and reprinted in Wunberg, 1981: 287–309.

Bahr, Hermann. 1894. "Die Décadence." In Bahr, Hermann. *Studien zur Kritik der Moderne*. Frankfurt am Main: Rütten & Loening. 26–32. Reprinted in Wunberg, 1981: 225–32.

Kerr, Alfred. 1896a. "Arthur Schnitzler." Review of *Anatol* and *Liebelei*, by Arthur Schnitzler. *Neue Deutsche Rundschau* 7/3 (March 1896): 287–92.

Altenberg, Peter. 1899. Review of *Die Gefährti*,. by Arthur Schnitzler. *Extrapost*, 6 March 1899, 5. Reprinted in Werba, 1974: 177.

Bahr, Hermann. 1899. *Das Wiener Theater* (1892–1898). Berlin: Fischer.

Goldmann, Paul. 1900. Review of *Der Schleier der Beatrice*, by Arthur Schnitzler. In Goldmann, 1905. *Aus dem dramatischen Irrgarten: Polemische Aufsätze über Berliner Theateraufführungen*. Frankfurt am Main: Literarische Anstalt Rütten & Loening.

Goldmann, Paul. 1902. Feuilleton. Berliner Theater. *Lebendige Stunden* von Arthur Schnitzler. *Neue Freie Presse*, 22 January 1902, 1–4.

Goldmann, Paul. 1903. *Die neue Richtung: Polemische Aufsätze über Berliner Theateraufführungen*. Vienna: C. W. Stern.

Bahr, Hermann. 1904. Review of *Der Puppenspieler*, by Arthur Schnitzler. Carl-Theater, 12 December 1904. In Bahr, 1907: 440–49.

Kerr, Alfred. 1904. Review of *Der einsame Weg*, by Arthur Schnitzler. *Neue Rundschau* 15/4 (April 1904): 504–8.

Goldmann, Paul. 1905. *Aus dem dramatischen Irrgarten: Polemische Aufsätze über Berliner Theateraufführungen*. Frankfurt am Main: Literarische Anstalt Rütten & Loening.

Bahr, Hermann. 1906. Review of *Zwischenspiel*, by Arthur Schnitzler. In Bahr, 1907: 91–92.

Goldmann, Paul. 1906. Review of *Der Ruf des Lebens*, by Arthur Schnitzler. In Goldmann, 1908: 164–73.

Kerr, Alfred. 1906. "Oedipus und der Ruf des Lebens." *Neue Rundschau* 17/5 (May 1906): 492–98.

Polgar, Alfred. 1906. "Der Wiener Feuilleton." Reprinted in Weinzierl, ed., 1980: 33–37.

Bahr, Hermann. 1907. *Glossen zum Wiener Theater, 1903–1906*. Berlin: Fischer.

Goldmann, Paul. 1908. *Vom Rückgang der deutschen Bühne: Polemische Aufsätze über Berliner Theateraufführungen*. Frankfurt am Main: Literarische Anstalt Rütten & Loening.

Reik, Theodor. 1913. *Arthur Schnitzler als Psycholog*. Minden: Bruns.

Brahm, Otto. 1915. *Über Drama und Theater*. Vol. 1: *Kritische Schriften*. Ed. Paul Schlenther. Berlin: Fischer.

Körner, Josef. 1916–17. "Arthur Schnitzler und Siegmund Freud." Review of *Arthur Schnitzler als Psycholog*, by Theodor Reik. *Das literarische Echo*. 19 (October): col. 802–5.

Körner, Josef. 1921. *Arthur Schnitzler: Gestalten und Probleme*. Zürich: Almathea.

Körner, Josef. 1923. "Review of *Arthur Schnitzler: Der Dichter und sein Werk. Eine Studie*," by Richard Specht. *Preussische Jahrbücher* 194: 202–5.

Körner, Josef. 1927. "Arthur Schnitzlers Spätwerk." *Preussische Jahrbücher* 208: 53–83; 153–63.

Liptzin, Sol. 1932. *Arthur Schnitzler*. New York: Prentice Hall.

Blume, Bernhard. 1936. *Das nihilistische Weltbild Arthur Schnitzlers*. Stuttgart: Buchdruckerei Knöller.

Newmark, Maxim. 1938. *Otto Brahm: The Man and the Critic*. Menasha, WI: George Banta Publ. Co.

Auernheimer, Raoul. 1948. *Das Wirtshaus zur verlorenen Zeit: Erlebnisse und Bekenntnisse*. Vienna: Ullstein Verlag.

Beharriell, Frederick J. 1951. "Arthur Schnitzler's Range of Theme." *Monatshefte* 43/7: 301–11.

Oswald, Victor A. Jr., and Veronica Pinter Mindess. 1951. "Schnitzler's *Fräulein Else* and the Psychoanalytic Theory of Neuroses." *Germanic Review* 26/4: 279–88.

Beharriell, Frederick J. 1953. "Schnitzler's Anticipation of Freud's Dream Theory." *Monatshefte* 45/2: 81–89.

Freud, Sigmund. 1955. "Briefe an Arthur Schnitzler." Ed. Heinrich Schnitzler. *Die Neue Rundschau* 66: 95–106.

Blume, Berhard. 20 October 1956. "Arthur Schnitzler." In *Aufsätze aus dem Stuttgarter Neuen Tageblatt und der Stuttgarter Zeitung 1933–1966* (Stuttgart: n.p.), 23–26.

Weiss, Robert O. 1958. "A Study of the Psychiatric Elements in Schnitzler's *Flucht in die Finsternis*." *Germanic Review* 33/4: 251–75.

Paupié, Kurt. 1960. *Handbuch der österreichischen Pressegeschichte 1848–1959*. Vol 1: *Wien*. Vienna: Wilhelm Braumüller.

Beharriell, Frederick J. 1962. "Freud's Double: Arthur Schnitzler." *Journal of the American Psychoanalytic Association* 10/4: 722–33.

Lawson, Richard H. 1962. "A Reinterpretation of Schnitzler's *Leutnant Gustl*." *Journal of the International Arthur Schnitzler Research Association* 2/1: 4–19.

Rey, William. H. 1962. "Das Wagnis des Guten in Schnitzlers *Traumnovelle*." *German Quarterly* 35/3 (May 1962): 254–64.

Schnitzler, Olga. 1962. *Spiegelbild der Freundschaft*. Salzburg: Residenz Verlag.

Bergel, Kurt. 1963. Introduction to *Studies in Arthur Schnitzler*. Ed. Herbert W. Reichert and Herman Salinger. Chapel Hill: U of North Carolina P.

Reichert, Herbert W. 1963. "Arthur Schnitzler and Modern Ethics." *Journal of the International Arthur Schnitzler Research Association* 2/1: 21–24.

Reik, Theodor. 1963. *The Need to be Loved*. Toronto: Ambassador Books.

Weiss, Robert O. 1963. "Arthur Schnitzler's Literary and Philosophical Development." *Journal of the International Arthur Schnitzler Research Association:* 2/1: 4–20.

Allen, Richard. 1964. "Arthur Schnitzler's Works and Their Reception: An Annotated Bibliography." Diss., U of Michigan.

Geissler, Rolf. 1964. *Dekadenz und Heroismus: Zeitroman und völkisch-nationalsozialistische Literaturkritik*. Stuttgart: Deutsche Verlags-Anstalt.

Hofmannsthal, Hugo von. 1964. *Hugo von Hofmannsthal — Arthur Schnitzler: Briefwechsel*. Ed. Therese Nickl and Heinrich Schnitzler. Frankfurt am Main: Fischer.

Offermanns, Ernst. 1964. "Materialien zum Verständnis der Texte." *Anatol.* Berlin: Walter de Gruyter & Co., 165–80.

Rey, William H. 1964. "Beiträge zur amerikanischen Schnitzlerforschung." *German Quarterly* 37/3: 282–89.

Schlawe, Fritz. 1965. *Literarische Zeitschriften 1885–1910*. Stuttgart: Metzler.

Allen, Richard. 1966. *An Annotated Arthur Schnitzler Bibliography: Editions and Criticism in German, French, and English 1879–1965*. Chapel Hill: U of North Carolina P.

Derré, Françoise. 1966. *L'oeuvre d'Arthur Schnitzler: Imagerie viennoise et problèmes humains*. Paris: M. Didier.

Foltin, Lore. 1966. "The Meaning of Death in Schnitzler's Work." In *Studies in Arthur Schnitzler: Centennial Commemorative Volume*. Ed. Herbert W. Reichert and Hermann Salinger. New York: AMS Press.

Hamann, Richard, and Jost Hermand. 1966. *Deutsche Kunst und Kultur von der Gründerzeit bis zum Expressionismus*. Vol. 3: *Impressionismus*. 2nd ed. Berlin: Akademie-Verlag.

Grunberger, Richard. 1967. "Jews in Austrian Journalism." In *The Jews of Austria: Essays on their Life, History, and Destruction*. Ed. Josef Fraenkel. London: Vallentine, 83–95.

Horkheimer, Max. 1968. "Geschichte und Psychologie." Vol. 1 of *Kritische Theorie: Eine Dokumentation*. Ed. Alfred Schmidt. Frankfurt am Main: Fischer.

Politzer, Heinz. 1968. "Diagnose und Dichtung: Zum Werk Arthur Schnitzlers." In *Das Schweigen der Sirenen: Studien zur deutschen und österreichischen Literatur*. Stuttgart: Metzler, 110–41.

Rey, William. 1968. *Arthur Schnitzler: Die späte Prosa als Gipfel seines Schaffens*. Berlin: E. Schmidt.

Weiss, Robert O. 1968. "The Psychoses in the Works of Arthur Schnitzler." *German Quarterly* 41/3: 377–400.

Bareikis, Robert. 1969. "Arthur Schnitzler's *Fräulein Else*: A Freudian Novella?" *Literature and Psychology* 19/1: 19–32.

Neumann, Gerhard, and Jutta Müller. 1969. *Der Nachlaß Arthur Schnitzlers: Verzeichnis des im Schnitzler-Archiv der Universität Freiburg i. Br. befindlichen Materials*. Munich: Fink.

Hausner, Henry. 1970. "Die Beziehungen zwischen Arthur Schnitzler und Sigmund Freud." *MAL* 3/2: 48–61.

Kesting, Marianne. 1970. *Entdeckung und Destruktion: Zur Strukturumwandlung der Künste*. Munich: Fink.

Lukács, Georg. 1970. *Writer & Critic, and other Essays*. New York: Grosset & Dunlap.

Nickl, Therese, and Heinrich Schnitzler, eds. 1970. *Arthur Schnitzler — Olga Waissnix: Liebe, die starb vor der Zeit: ein Briefwechsel*. Vienna: Molden.

Scheible, Hartmut. 1970. "Diskretion und Verdrängung. Zu Schnitzlers Autobiographie." *Frankfurter Hefte* 25: 129–34.

Zweig, Stefan. 1970. *Die Welt von gestern: Erinnerungen eines Europäers*. Frankfurt am Main: Fischer. Reprint of Stockholm: Bermann Fischer, 1946.

Farese, Giuseppe. 1971. "Arthur Schnitzler alla luce della critica recente" (1966–1970), *Studi Germanici* 9/1–2 1971: 234–68.

Swales, Martin. 1971. *Arthur Schnitzler: A Critical Study*. Oxford: Clarendon Press.

Johnston, William. 1972. *The Austrian Mind: An Intellectual and Social History 1848–1938*. Berkeley: U of California P.

Kilian, Klaus. 1972. *Die Komödien Arthur Schnitzlers: Sozialer Rollenzwang und kritische Ethik*. Düsseldorf: Bertelsmann Universitätsverlag.

Aspetsberger, Friedbert. 1973. "Arthur Schnitzler's *Der Weg ins Freie*." *Sprachkunst* 4/1–2: 65–80.

Beharriell, Frederick J. 1973. Review of *Arthur Schnitzler: A Critical Study*, by Martin Swales. *Journal of English and Germanic Philology* 72: 424–28.

Diersch, Manfred. 1973. *Empiriokritizismus und Impressionismus: Über Beziehungen zwischen Philosophie, Ästhetik und Literatur um 1900 in Wien*. Berlin: Rütten & Loening.

Krotkoff, Hertha. 1973. "Zur geheimen Gesellschaft in Arthur Schnitzlers *Traumnovelle.*" *German Quarterly* 46: 202–9.

Offermanns, Ernst L. 1973. *Arthur Schnitzler: Das Komödienwerk als Kritik des Impressionismus.* Munich: Fink.

Segar, Kenneth. 1973. "Determinism and Character: Arthur Schnitzler's *Traumnovelle.*" *Oxford German Studies* 8: 114–27.

Fritzsche, Albert. 1974. *Dekadenz im Werk Arthur Schnitzlers.* Bern: Herbert Lang.

Urbach, Reinhard. 1974. *Schnitzler-Kommentar zu den erzählenden Schriften und dramatischen Werken.* Munich: Winkler.

Urban, Bernd. 1974. "Arthur Schnitzler und Sigmund Freud: Aus den Anfängen des Doppelgängers. Zur Differenzierung dichterischer Intuition und Umgehung der frühen Hysterieforschung." *Germanisch Romanisch Monatsschrift* 24/2: 193–223.

Werba, Robert. 1974. "Ein Außenseiter der Theaterkritik: Peter Altenberg und das Wiener Theaterjahr 1898/99." *Maske und Kothurn* 20/2: 163–90.

Seidlin, Oskar. 1975. Introduction to *Der Briefwechsel Arthur Schnitzler — Otto Brahm.* Ed. Oskar Seidlin. Tübingen: Max Niemeyer Verlag.

Swales, Martin. 1975. "Nürnbergers Novel: A Study of Arthur Schnitzler's *Der Weg ins Freie.*" *Modern Language Review* 70/3: 567–75.

Urban, Bernd. 1975. "Vier unveröffentlichte Briefe Arthur Schnitzlers an den Psychoanalytiker Theodor Reik." *MAL* 8/3–4: 236–47.

Scheible, Hartmut. 1976. *Arthur Schnitzler in Selbstzeugnissen und Bilddokumenten.* Reinbek bei Hamburg: Rowohlt.

Seidler, Herbert. 1976. "Die Forschung zu Arthur Schnitzler seit 1945." *Zeitschrift für Deutsche Philologie* 95: 567–95.

Baumann, Gerhart. 1977. "Arthur Schnitzler: Die Tagebücher. Vergangene Gegenwart — Gegenwärtige Vergangenheit." *MAL* 10/3–4: 143–62

Janz, Rolf-Peter, and Klaus Laermann. 1977. *Arthur Schnitzler: Zur Diagnose des Wiener Bürgertums im Fin de siècle.* Stuttgart: Metzler.

Nehring, Wolfgang. 1977. "Schnitzler, Freud's Alter Ego?" *MAL* 10/3–4: 179–94.

Scheible, Hartmut. 1977. *Arthur Schnitzler und die Aufklärung.* Munich: Fink.

Urbach, Reinhard. 1977. "Heinrich Schnitzler — 75 Jahre." *MAL* 10/3–4: 1–18.

Bailey, L. H. 1978. "Ferdinand Kürnberger, Friedrich Schlögl, and the Feuilleton in Gründerzeit Vienna." *Austrian Life and Literature 1780–1938.* Ed. Peter Branscombe. Edinburgh: Scottish Academic Press, 59–71.

Berlin, Jeffrey B. 1978. *An Annotated Arthur Schnitzler Bibliography 1965–1977. With an Essay on the Meaning of the "Schnitzler-Renaissance."* Munich: Wilhelm Fink.

Daviau, Donald. 1978. Introduction to *The Letters of Arthur Schnitzler to Hermann Bahr.* By Arthur Schnitzler. Chapel Hill: U of North Carolina P.

Gutt, Barbara. 1978. *Emanzipation bei Arthur Schnitzler.* Berlin: Volker Spiess.

Jurgensen, Manfred. 1979. *Das fiktionale Ich: Untersuchungen zum Tagebuch.* Bern: Francke.

Luckmann, Thomas. 1979. "Persönliche Identität, soziale Rolle und Rollendistanz." *Identität.* Ed. Odo Marquard and Karlheinz Stierle. Munich: Fink.

Vogel, Margot Elfving. 1979. *Schnitzler in Schweden: Zur Rezeption seiner Werke.* Stockholm: Almquist & Wiksell.

Walser, Martin. 1979. *Wer ist ein Schriftsteller? Aufsätze und Reden.* Frankfurt am Main: Suhrkamp.

Fish, Stanley. 1980. *Is There a Text in This Class? The Authority of Interpretive Communities.* Cambridge, MA: Harvard UP.

Arens, Detlev. 1981. *Untersuchungen zu Arthur Schnitzlers Roman* Der Weg ins Freie. Frankfurt am Main: Lang.

DeLay, Brigitte. 1981. Review of *Emanzipation bei Arthur Schnitzler,* by Barbara Gutt. *MAL* 14/1–2: 141–43.

Doppler, Alfred. 1981. "Der Wandel der Darstellungsperspektive in den Dichtungen Arthur Schnitzlers. Mann und Frau als sozialpsychologisches Problem." In Scheible, 1981: 41–59.

Jennings, Lee B. 1981. "Schnitzler's *Traumnovelle* — Meat or Poison?" *Seminar* 17/1: 73–82.

Klein, Dennis B. 1981. *Jewish Origins of the Psychoanalytic Movement.* Chicago: U of Chicago P.

Möhrmann, Renate. 1981. "Schnitzlers Frauen und Mädchen. Zwischen Sachlichkeit und Sentiment." In Scheible, 1981: 93–107.

Scheible, Hartmut, ed. 1981. *Arthur Schnitzler in neuer Sicht.* Munich: Fink.

Schorske, Carl E. 1981. *Fin-de-Siècle Vienna: Politics and Culture.* New York: Vintage Books.

Schwarz, Egon. 1981. "Arthur Schnitzler und die Aristokratie." In Scheible, 1981: 54–70.

Wagner, Renate. 1981. *Arthur Schnitzler: Eine Biographie.* Vienna: Fritz Molden.

Welzig, Werner. 1981. "Das Tagebuch Arthur Schnitzlers 1879–1931." *Internationales Archiv für Sozialgeschichte der Literatur* 6: 78–111.

Welzig, Werner. 1981. "Zur Herausgabe von Schnitzlers Tagebuch." Foreword to vol. 1 (1909–1912) of Schnitzler, 1981–2000: 9–33.

Welzig, Werner. 1981. "Nachbemerkung." Epilogue to vol. 2 (1913–1916) of Schnitzler, 1981–2000: 429–32.

Welzig, Werner. 1981. "Tagebuch und Gesellschaftsspiel." Epilogue to vol. 3 (1917–1919) of Schnitzler, 1981–2000: 419–27.

Welzig, Werner. 1981. "Der junge Mann und die alten Wörter." Epilogue to vol. 4 (1879–1892) of Schnitzler, 1981–2000: 471–88.

Welzig, Werner. 1981. "Bicycle-Lektion." Epilogue to vol. 5 (1893–1902) of Schnitzler, 1981–2000: 489–502.

Welzig, Werner. 1981. "Preisgeschichten." Epilogue to vol. 6 (1903–1908) of Schnitzler, 1981–2000: 471–90.

Welzig, Werner. 1981. "Glossar einer Ehescheidung." Epilogue to vol. 7 (1920–1922) of Schnitzler, 1981–2000: 489–98.

Welzig, Werner. 1981. "Der Traum: Ein Text." Epilogue to vol. 8 (1923–1926) of Schnitzler, 1981–2000: 487–96.

Welzig, Werner. 1981. "Der Anspruch der Toten." Epilogue to vol. 9 (1927–1930) of Schnitzler, 1981–2000: 499–509.

Wolff, Lutz-W. 1981. "'Bürger der Endzeit.' Schnitzler in sozialistischer Sicht." In Scheible, 1981: 330–59.

Wunberg, Gotthart, ed. 1981. *Die Wiener Moderne: Literatur, Kunst und Musik zwischen 1890 und 1910.* Stuttgart: Reclam.

Abels, Norbert. 1982. *Sicherheit ist nirgends. Judentum und Aufklärung bei Arthur Schnitzler.* Königstein: Athenäum.

Cohn, Dorrit. 1982. "A Triad of Dream Narratives: *Der Tod Georgs, Das Märchen der 672. Nacht, Traumnovelle.*" In *Focus on Vienna 1900: Change and Continuity in Literature, Music, Art and Intellectual History.* Ed. Erika Nielsen. Munich: Fink, 58–71.

Daviau, Donald. 1982. "Arthur Schnitzler im Spiegel der Kritik: Fünfzig Jahre nach seinem Tod." *Text & Kontext* 10/2: 411–26.

Hacker, Friedrich. 1982. "Im falschen Leben gibt es kein richtiges." *Literatur und Kritik* 163–64: 36–44.

Heresch, Elisabeth. 1982. *Schnitzler und Rußland: Aufnahme, Wirkung, Kritik.* Vienna: W. Braumüller.

Lindken, Hans-Ulrich. 1982. "Zur Ätiologie und Semiotik des Wahns in Schnitzlers *Flucht in die Finsternis.*" *Text und Kontext* 10/2: 344–54.

Schwarz, Egon. 1982. "Milieu oder Mythos? Wien in den Werken Arthur Schnitzlers." *Literatur und Kritik* 163–64 (April-May): 22–35.

Swales, Martin. 1982. "Schnitzler als Realist." *Literatur und Kritik* 161/162 (Feb.–Mar.): 52–61.

Lebensaft, Elizabeth. 1983. "Schnitzler aus tschechischer Sicht. Zur Rezeption in der CSSR." *MAL* 16/1: 17–22.

Tarnowski-Seidel, Heide. 1983. *Arthur Schnitzler: Flucht in die Finsternis: Eine produktionsästhetische Untersuchung.* Munich: Fink.

Wagner, Renate. 1983. *Frauen um Arthur Schnitzler.* Frankfurt am Main: Fischer.

Lindken, Hans-Ulrich. 1984. *Arthur Schnitzler: Aspekte und Akzente: Materialien zu Leben und Werk.* Frankfurt am Main: Peter Lang.

Thomé, Horst. 1984. "Kernlosigkeit und Pose. Zur Rekonstruktion von Schnitzlers Psychologie." *Text & Kontext* 20: 62–87.

Dangel, Elsbeth. 1985. *Wiederholung als Schicksal: Arthur Schnitzlers Roman Therese. Chronik eines Frauenlebens.* Munich: Fink.

Farese, Giuseppe, ed. 1985. *Akten des Internationalen Symposiums "Arthur Schnitzler und seine Zeit."* Bern: Lang.

Miller, Norbert. 1985. "Das Bild des Juden in der österreichischen Erzählliteratur des Fin de siècle. Zu einer Motivparallele in Ferdinand von Saars 'Seligmann Hirsch' und Arthur Schnitzlers Roman *Der Weg ins Freie. Juden und Judentum in der Literatur.*" Ed. Herbert Strauss and Christhard Hoffmann. Munich: Deutscher Taschenbuch, 172–210.

Müller-Seidel, Walter. 1985. "Moderne Literatur und Medizin. Zum literarischen Werk Arthur Schnitzlers." In Farese, 1985: 60–92.

Rieckmann, Jens. 1985. *Aufbruch in die Moderne: Die Anfänge des Jungen Wien. Österreichische Literatur und Kritik im Fin de Siècle.* Tübingen: Athenäum.

Schwarz, Egon. 1985. "Arthur Schnitzler und das Judentum." *Im Zeichen Hiobs: Jüdische Schriftsteller und deutsche Literatur im 20. Jahrhundert.* Ed. Gunter Grimm and Hans-Peter Bayerdörfer. Königstein: Athenäum, 67–83.

Sebald, W. G. 1985. "Das Schrecknis der Liebe: Überlegungen zu Schnitzlers *Traumnovelle.*" *Merkur* 39/2 (February 1985): 120–31.

Thomé, Horst. 1985. "Faktizität des Lebens und erfüllte Zeit: Zum Erscheinen von Schnitzlers Tagebüchern." *Orbis Litterarum* 40: 88–96.

Beharriell, Frederick. 1986. "Arthur Schnitzler's Diaries." *MAL* 19/3–4: 1–20.

Bergel, Kurt. 1986. "The Recent Reception of Arthur Schnitzler's *Das weite Land* on Two American Stages." *MAL* 19/3–4: 91–96.

Derré, Françoise. 1986. "Schnitzler in Frankreich." *MAL* 19/1: 27–48.

Hammer, Stephanie. 1986. "Fear and Attraction: *Anatol* and *Liebelei* Productions in the United States." *MAL* 19/3–4: 63–74.

Jaron, Norbert, Renate Möhrmann, and Hedwig Müller. 1986. *Berlin — Theater der Jahrhundertwende: Bühnengeschichte der Reichshauptstadt im Spiegel der Kritik (1889–1914)*. Tübingen: Max Niemeyer.

Nehring, Wolfgang. 1986. "Zwischen Identifikation und Distanz. Zur Darstellung der jüdischen Charaktere in Arthur Schnitzlers *Der Weg ins Freie*." *Kontroversen, alte und neue: Akten des VII. Internationalen Germanisten-Kongresses (Göttingen 1985)*. Ed. Albrecht Schöne. Vol. 5: *Auseinandersetzungen um jiddische Sprache und Literatur: Jüdische Komponenten in der deutschen Literatur*. Tübingen: M. Niemeyer, 162–70.

Stoppard, Tom. 1986. *Dalliance: Undiscovered Country*. Adapted from Arthur Schnitzler. London and Boston: Faber and Faber.

Weber, Eugen. 1986. *France, Fin de Siècle*. Cambridge, MA: Belknap Press of Harvard UP.

Calinescu, Matei. 1987. *Five Faces of Modernity: Modernism, Avant-Garde, Decadence, Kitsch, Postmodernism*. 2nd ed. Durham, NC: Duke UP.

Miklin, Richard. 1987. *Untersuchungen zu Arthur Schnitzlers Tagebuch der Kriegsjahre 1914–1918*. Diss., U. of Vienna.

Perlmann, Michaela. 1987a. *Arthur Schnitzler*. Stuttgart: Metzler.

Perlmann, Michaela. 1987b. *Der Traum in der literarischen Moderne: Untersuchungen zum Werk Arthur Schnitzlers*. Munich: Fink.

Weinhold, Ulrike. 1987. "Arthur Schnitzler und der weibliche Diskurs. Zur Problematik des Frauenbilds der Jahrhundertwende." *Jahrbuch für Internationale Germanistik* 19/1: 110–45.

Berman, Russell. 1988. "From Empire to Dictatorship, 1870–1933." Trans. Simon Srebrny. In Hohendahl, 1988a: 277–357.

Hohendahl, Peter Uwe, ed. 1988a. *A History of German Literary Criticism, 1730–1980*. Lincoln and London: U of Nebraska P, 1988.

Hohendahl, Peter Uwe. 1988b. "The Epoch of Liberalism, 1820–1870." Trans. Jeffrey S. Librett. In Hohendahl, 1988a: 179–276.

Jauß, Hans Robert. 1988. "Literaturgeschichte als Provokation der Literaturwissenschaft." *Rezeptionsästhetik: Theorie und Praxis*. Ed. Rainer Warning. 3rd ed. Munich: Fink, 126–62.

Thomé, Horst. 1988. "Sozialgeschichtliche Perspektiven der neueren Schnitzler-Forschung." *Internationales Archiv für Sozialgeschichte der Deutschen Literatur* 13: 158–87.

Worbs, Michael. 1988. *Nervenkunst: Literatur und Psychoanalyse im Wien der Jahrhundertwende*. Frankfurt am Main: Athenäum. Reprint, Frankfurt: Europäische Verlagsanstalt, 1983.

Roelofs, Hans. 1989. *Man weiss eigentlich wenig von einander: Arthur Schnitzler und die Niederlande 1895–1940*. Amsterdam and Atlanta: Rodopi.

Willi, Andrea. 1989. *Arthur Schnitzlers Roman* Der Weg ins Freie: *Eine Untersuchung zur Tageskritik und ihren zeitgenössischen Bezugen.* Heidelberg: Carl Winter Universitätsverlag.

Knoben-Wauben, Marianne. 1990. "Ambivalente Konstruktion der Weiblichkeit: Das Bild der Frau aus der Sicht des Wissenschaftlers Sigmund Freud und des Dichters Arthur Schnitzlers." *Grenzgänge: Literatur und Kultur im Kontext.* Ed. Guillaume Van Gemert and Hans Ester. Amsterdam: Rodopi, 279–96.

Luprecht, Mark. 1990. *What People Call Pessimism: Sigmund Freud, Arthur Schnitzler and Nineteenth-Century Controversy at the University of Vienna Medical School.* Riverside, CA: Ariadne Press.

Thompson, Bruce. 1990. *Schnitzler's Vienna: Image of a Society.* London and New York: Routledge.

Butzko, Ellen. 1991. *Arthur Schnitzler und die zeitgenössische Theaterkritik.* Frankfurt am Main: Peter Lang.

Berman, Russell A. 1992. Introduction to *The Road into the Open.* By Arthur Schnitzler. Trans. Roger Byers. Berkeley, CA: U of California P.

Daviau, Donald. 1992. "The Reception of Arthur Schnitzler in the United States." *The Fortunes of German Writers in America: Studies in Literary Reception.* Ed. Wolfgang Elfe and Jim Hardin. Columbia: U of South Carolina P, 145–65.

Leitch, Vincent. 1992. *Cultural Criticism, Literary Theory, Poststructuralism.* New York: Columbia UP.

Rossbacher, Karlheinz. 1992. *Literatur und Liberalismus: Zur Kultur der Ringstraßenzeit in Wien.* Vienna: J&V.

Lindgren, Irene. 1993. *Arthur Schnitzler im Lichte seiner Briefe und Tagebücher.* Heidelberg: Carl Winter Universitätsverlag.

Pfoser, Albert, Kristina Pfoser-Schewig, and Gerhard Renner. 1993. *Schnitzler's* Reigen: *Zehn Dialoge und ihre Skandalgeschichte: Analysen und Dokumente.* Frankfurt am Main: Fischer Taschenbuch Verlag.

Thomé, Horst. 1993. "Arthur Schnitzlers Tagebuch. Thesen und Forschungsperspektiven." *Internationales Archiv für Sozialgeschichte der Deutschen Literatur* 18: 176–93.

Macksey, Richard. 1994. Foreword to *The Johns Hopkins Guide to Literary Theory & Criticism.* Ed. Michael Groden and Martin Kreiswirth. Baltimore: Johns Hopkins UP.

Weinzierl, Ulrich. 1994. *Arthur Schnitzler: Lieben, Träumen, Sterben.* Frankfurt am Main: Fischer.

Freud, Sigmund. 1995. "The Uncanny." Trans. Alix Strachey. *Psychological Writings and Letters.* Ed. Sander L. Gilman. New York: Continuum, 120–53.

Ozawa, Yukio. 1995. *Japanisches bei Arthur Schnitzler: Japanische Einflüsse auf Schnitzler und die Rezeption Schnitzlers in Japan.* Bern: Lang.

Scheible, Hartmut. 1996. *Liebe und Liberalismus.* Bielefeld: Aisthesis.

Wisely, Andrew. 1996. *Arthur Schnitzler and the Discourse of Honor and Dueling.* New York: Peter Lang.

Fliedl, Konstanze. 1997. *Arthur Schnitzler: Poetik der Erinnerung.* Vienna: Böhlau.

Müller-Seidel, Walter. 1997. *Arztbilder im Wandel: Zum literarischen Werk Arthur Schnitzlers.* Munich: Verlag der Bayerischen Akademie der Wissenschaften.

Weinberger, C. J. 1997. *Arthur Schnitzler's Late Plays: A Critical Study.* New York: Peter Lang.

Hare, David. 1998. *The Blue Room: A Play in Ten Intimate Acts. Freely Adapted from Arthur Schnitzler's* La Ronde. New York: Grove Press.

Kroll, Jack. 1998. "Nicole Takes Off." *Newsweek* (14 December 1998): 68–76.

Sprengel, Peter, and Gregor Streim. 1998. *Berliner und Wiener Moderne: Vermittlungen und Abgrenzungen in Literatur, Theater, Publizistik.* Vienna: Böhlau.

Charlie Rose Show. PBS. 16 July 1999.

Edelstein, David. 1999. "The Naked and the Dead: *Eyes Wide Shut* is a Fearfully Distant Orgy." *Slate Magazine* (16 July 1999). http://slate.msn.com/default.aspx?id=32113 accessed 3 December 2002.

Eyes Wide Shut. 1999. Dir. Stanley Kubrick. Screenplay by Frederic Raphael. Perf. Nicole Kidman and Tom Cruise. Warner Brothers.

Johnson, Diane. 1999. "Stanley Kubrick (1928–1999)." *New York Review of Books* (22 April 1999): 28.

Farese, Giuseppe. 1999. *Arthur Schnitzler: Ein Leben in Wien.* Trans. Karin Krieger. Munich: Beck.

Gay, Peter. 2001. *Schnitzler's Century: The Making of Middle-Class Culture 1815–1914.* New York: Norton.

Howes, Geoffrey, and Jacqueline Vansant. 2001. From the Editors. *MAL* 34/1–2: i.

Schwarz, Egon. 2001. "A Puzzle and An Enigma: Stanley Kubrick's *Eyes Wide Shut* and Arthur Schnitzler's *Traumnovelle.*" *MAL* 34/1–2: 103–11.

Smith, Dinitia. 2001. "Dissecting the Era of Virgins and Satyrs." Review of *Schnitzler's Century: The Making of Middle-Class Culture 1815–1914.* By Peter Gay. *New York Times,* 10 November 2001: A13, A17.

Vitek, Jack. 2001. "Another Squint at *Eyes Wide Shut:* A Postmodern Reading." *MAL* 34/1–2: 113–24.

Arthur Schnitzler-Gesellschaft, Vienna. 2002: http://www.arthur-schnitzler.at.

Bruckner, D. J. R. (10 April 2002). "Playing Spin the Bottle (With an Adult Twist)." Review of *Circle*. By Suzanne Bachner. *New York Times:* E5.

Kubrick, Stanley, and Frederic Raphael. 2002. *Eyes Wide Shut: A Screenplay,* 1996, 1999. 3 December 2003 http://godamongdirectors.com/scripts/eyeswshu.htm.

Reich-Ranicki, Marcel. 2002. "Auch das Grausame kann diskret sein." In *Sieben Wegbereiter: Schriftsteller des zwanzigsten Jahrhunderts.* Stuttgart and Munich: Deutsche Verlags-Anstalt. Reprinted from *Frankfurter Allgemeine Zeitung* (4 February 1984).

Index